101 Reasons to Avoid RITALIN Like the PLAGUE

Including 1 Great Reason Why It's Almost ALWAYS Unnecessary

101 Reasons to Avoid RITALIN Like the Including PLAGUE

1 Great Reason Why it's Almost ALWAYS Unnecessary

by HOWARD GLASSER, MA

Executive Director
The Children's Success Foundation

101 Reasons to Avoid Ritalin Like The Plague
including 1 Great Reason Why It's Almost Always Unnecessary

For information contact: Nurtured Heart Publications
4165 West Ironwood Hill Drive
Tucson, Arizona 85745
Email: adhddoc@theriver.com

For information about bulk purchasing discounts of this book or other Transforming the Difficult Child books, videos, or DVDs, please contact Fulfillment Services at 800-311-3132. For orders within the book industry, contact Brigham Distributing at 435-723-6611.

Cover photograph by Alice Rose Glasser.
Book design by Richard Diffenderfer.
Copy editing by Chris Howell and Mahesh Grossman.
Printed by Vaughan Printing, Nashville, TN.

Library of Congress Card Catalog Number: Pending

ISBN 0-9670507-6-6

Printed in the United States

First Printing: May 2005

This book is dedicated to my inspiration,
Alice Rose Glasser

Grimmy Inc. Reprinted with permission of King Features Syndicate.

Table of Contents

Foreword iii

Introduction 1

The 101 Reasons

Section One:
Damaging Psychological Side Effects 9

Section Two:
Damaging Physical Side Effects 40

Section Three:
Damage to the Relationship Between Parent and Child 55

Section Four:
Use and Abuse of Stimulant Drugs 66

Section Five:
Questionable Research: No Physical Basis for ADHD 76

Section Six:
Ritalin and Other Stimulants Don't Help A Child Heal 95

Section Seven:
The Dangers of Polypharmacy 111

Section Eight:
**The Conspiracy to Drug America's Children
into Submission: Doctors and Drug Companies** 122

Section Nine:
The Conspiracy, Continued: Teachers and Schools 140

Section Ten:
The Conspiracy, Part III: the Government 150

Section Eleven:
Reason 101: Why Ritalin is Almost Always Unnecessary 155

Epilogue:
Ten Days on Ritalin 175

Epilogue:
An Alternative Medicine Perspective 189

Epilogue:
Arrested Development and the Loss of Social Capital 193

Note to Readers 199

Bibliography/Recommended Reading 200

About Howard Glasser 201

Support The Children's Success Foundation 202

Foreword

by S. DuBose Ravenel, M.D., F.A.A.P.

P RIMARY CARE PHYSICIANS AND PSYCHOLOGISTS are faced with a flood of children who are being referred for ADD/ADHD evaluations. Some of these children have problems with their attention level or ability to focus; others are referred because of impulsive behaviors; and a few have a combination of these "symptoms."

My busy pediatric practice is no exception. Beneath the pressure to diagnose and medicate increasing numbers of children, I have found myself thinking that something has to give. Virtually all relevant professional organizations and individuals considered to be experts in the diagnosis and management of ADD/ADHD stress that behavioral methods should be tried prior to resorting to medications.

In reality, unfortunately, this is rarely done, or only token efforts are made in a half-hearted manner before medication is prescribed.

Drug advocates would say that this is because ADHD and ADD simply do not respond to behavioral therapy—that we are dealing with a disorder that can only really be treated with medication. The true reason that behavioral therapies don't work more often is that the usual methods of behavioral management are completely inadequate in dealing with highly inattentive and/or impulsive children.

At one point, even I had lost hope of finding a behavioral therapy that really worked for ADD/ADHD. The definitive study to date of the diagnosis and management of ADD/ADHD, the MTA study, included a behavioral approach that was so intensive (and expensive financially and logistically but questionably effective) as to be impractical for widespread application—and yet even this rigorous attempt to manage these children without medication was found to add virtually no improvement in the core behaviors defining ADD/ADHD.

And so it was with great skepticism that a few years ago I first learned of alternative behavioral approaches that promised to provide an effective way to manage these children without relying on drugs.

Beginning only hesitantly and tentatively with select families who were highly motivated to avoid medicating their children, I found that it is possible, in fact, to put in place powerful behavioral approaches that lead to resolution of the ADD/ADHD behaviors within weeks. First, I used the

Caregivers Skills Program described by Dr. David B. Stein in his books for parents. I subsequently tried an approach incorporating principles outlined by psychologist and best-selling author John Rosemond. With these approaches, I have seen first-hand that it is indeed possible to give families the needed tools to adopt new parenting practices that can, in many cases, lead quickly to substantial correction of the behaviors defining ADD/ADHD. These gains have been documented to remain at follow-up a year or so later. It is important to understand that these are children who completely fulfill the existing DSM criteria for ADD or ADHD and/or Oppositional Defiant Disorder (ODD).

After reading about Howie Glasser's approach *(Transforming the Difficult Child: the Nurtured Heart Approach, 1998)* for highly misbehaving and inattentive children, I attended one of his workshops and got to know him personally. I discovered yet another fellow professional who shares my own passion for helping parents and their inattentive/misbehaving children to deal with these behaviors and habits in a corrective manner, without having to rely on a diagnosis of "disease" or "disorder" and giving them powerful psychotropic drugs. In reading about Howie's experience and studying data compiled during his work in Tucson with his **Nurtured Heart Approach,** it has become clear to me that he has found an excellent way to put in place a powerful application of life-changing parental and educational strategies.

The Nurtured Heart Approach is about implementing a powerful system of encouraging, training, and correcting the child in a manner that can lead quickly to lasting change. Best of all, these children internalize the idea that they are "special," not diseased or disordered, and learn ways to assume accountability and responsibility for their behavior. These children learn that they can behave and think adaptively without depending upon a daily pill. In the course of this wonderful process, their creativity is celebrated rather than subdued.

The precepts behind **The Nurtured Heart Approach** are sound and represent a novel and intensive way to "capture" the child into behaving well, literally creating success where failure has been the child's template and experience—to the point of his internalizing this in his inner core beliefs about who he is. This approach transforms the child in a positive way instead of reinforcing in the child's heart that he is in some manner defective and incapable of learning self-control.

Howie's writing is encouraging and moving in its tenderness and transparent belief in the child's potential. His belief is based not only in his own deep faith in the value and beauty of each child, but also in some compelling data collected during the implementation of **The Nurtured Heart Approach** in Tucson. In Howie's reports of outcomes among 211 children referred in 1998—and 160 of whom were not on stimulant medication before they were referred—only eight required subsequent referral for psychiatric medication, and only four were eventually prescribed medication. The overall rate of utilization of medication was less than 3% of the entire group. These were children with behavioral symptoms mostly categorized as indicative of ADHD or ODD, with problems of aggression, compliance, impulsivity, distractibility, and a preponderance of school-related issues.

Even more remarkable is the experience of a school in Tucson, where the principal embraced *The Nurtured Heart Approach*. A two-hour training session was held for teachers, and another two-hour session for parents to explain the school's approach. Over the following five years, this population of children—70 percent of whom received either free or reduced cost lunch, and where prior to adoption of *The Nurtured Heart Approach*, there were 30 suspensions in one year—had no suspensions; had no referrals for evaluation of ADD/ADHD behaviors; and had observable increases in academic performance.

If you are a professional who works with children, I urge you to consider carefully what Howie has to say in this volume. You may be, as I was initially, skeptical that a nurturing approach for these problem children can be effective. You may further view Howie's message regarding the reliance on stimulant (or other) psychotropic drugs as extreme or one-sided. It is, in fact, not a balanced picture of these drugs, but reflects his passion for knowing that many of these children can be helped without drugs. He seeks to counter the overwhelming influence of the misleading information that comes from pharmaceutical companies—the information to which most people are exposed when they seek help for a difficult child. The drug companies have given themselves plenty of good press; Howie's job here is to give us the other side of the story, and he does so passionately, but not carelessly.

Many of the 101 reasons Howie gives not to put your child on drugs are compelling and insightful observations or questions that cannot be satisfactorily answered by medical science. We simply do not know the long-term—over years, or over a lifetime—psychological or physical consequences of reliance on psychotropic drugs to enable children to function day-to-day. Many of his insights struck me as profound, particularly where he points out that "...any drug that takes away or distances you from feelings without resolving the reasons beneath them will hamper personal growth." Equally profound is the question he raises about whether so-called "co-morbid" (co-existing) conditions such as anxiety and depression may in fact represent the internalization of the child's view of himself as biologically abnormal...or even an effect of the medications used to treat the "disorder."

It is intuitive, and should be undeniable, that an effective approach to managing problem children's behavioral issues without powerful drugs is preferable to years or even decades of relying on drugs. We owe it to our children at least to try an approach that cannot harm, and in many cases, can assist them to attain self-control and responsibility. After all, in a worst-case scenario, an unsatisfactory response can within a few weeks or months allow one to turn to medication, knowing that a serious attempt has been made to accomplish what is universally recommended but seldom attempted.

S. DuBose Ravenel, M.D., F.A.A.P.
Cornerstone Pediatrics
High Point, North Carolina
January 2005

Dr. Ravenel is a pediatrician who has been in private practice since 1970. Educated at Duke University and Johns Hopkins University, Dr. Ravenel is a well-known expert on the risks of corporal punishment, a subject about which he has been interviewed in appearances on NBC, CBS, ABC, and CNN, has appeared on radio programs and published extensively. He is also an expert on ADD/ADHD and alternatives to Ritalin.

Dr. Ravenel regularly publishes articles and letters in medical journals, including Pediatrics *and the* Journal of the American Medical Association. *He has been listed in* The Best Doctors In America® *four times.*

Introduction

Settling for Ritalin says we prefer to locate problems in our children's brains rather than in their lives.

—Lawrence Diller[1]

We are the first adults to handle the generation gap through the wholesale drugging of children.

—Peter Breggin, M.D.[2]

What we have after years of soaring use of psychotropic drugs is a crisis in mental health, an epidemic of mental illness among children. Instead of seeing better mental health with ever more medicating, we see a worsening of mental health.

—Robert Whitaker[3]

Revolution Redux

Let's imagine ourselves back to the days when the United States of America did not yet exist, when it was just a set of colonies owned by Great Britain. Between 1765 and 1775, the colonies became increasingly resistant to all of the laws passed and taxes levied by the British government. The colonists were working hard to establish themselves in their new home, and they didn't like seeing the higher-ups across the sea profiting so much from their labor. There was much discontent and protest up until the war broke out in 1775. And we all know how this story ends: with victory and the establishment of the United States of America in 1783.

Now, let's rewrite history. Imagine that instead of rallying together and protesting their unjust treatment, the colonists believed that they themselves were the problem. Imagine that the British government and its agents had convinced them that they were suffering from an anger disorder and that they should just take some medicine to help them feel better. The Revolutionary War might never have happened.

Let's try to imagine any other major social problem this way. Equal rights for African-Americans? We could have given them some drugs to help them accept their lot in life instead of feeling so *angry* about it. Anger is just so

1

unhealthy. Drugs would have helped them feel better and enjoy their lives. What about women who protested inequality and insisted upon their rights to vote, to work, to be treated as first-class citizens instead of the property of their husbands? If we'd given all of those protesters medications to soothe their frustrations, maybe they would have accepted their lot, too.

I'm sure you see where I'm going with this. Children who don't fit into the educational system or modern, busy lifestyles often act out, behaving in ways that make the adults around them uncomfortable. Their behavior inconveniences adults and other children. But this kind of behavior may really be more of a cue regarding vital information to help us eventually find a higher order solution. We may be forcing children into school systems and lives that don't make sense to them. Their instincts tell them that this isn't the way things are supposed to be. And instead of hearing their message and having it motivate us to move forward, we tell them they have a brain disease that causes them to feel and act the way they do. Then, we effectively force them to take drugs that keep them quiet.

Half a Century of Drugging Intense Children

By the middle of the 1950s, stimulant drugs—a class of drugs that today includes methylphenidate (now sold as Ritalin, Concerta, Methylin, and Metadate CD), methamphetamines (Desoxyn and Gradumet) and amphetamines (including Dexedrine and Adderall)—had been approved for the treatment of behavior problems in children. The first Congressional hearings held due to concern about the widespread use of these drugs occurred in the 1970s. At that time, between 100,000 and 200,000 American children were taking stimulants to control their behavior.

In the year 1952, the first edition of the Diagnostic Statistical Manual (DSM)—the "bible" of psychiatric diagnoses—was published. It contained only three diagnosable psychological disorders that affected children. By 1980, the DSM contained more than ten times this number of pediatric diagnoses. And increasing numbers of children were being given a growing list of psychiatric drugs, with stimulants near the top of the list.

In 1995, the International Narcotics Control Board—an agency of the World Health Organization—reported that "10 to 12 percent of all boys between the ages of six and 14 in the United States have been diagnosed as having attention deficit disorder and are being treated with methylphenidate." No other nation was using even close to this amount of this drug or others in its class (Adderall, Concerta, Metadate, Dexedrine).

Today, the United States uses 90 percent of the world's Ritalin.[4] In recent years, its use has even shot up in an age group for which this drug has not been approved by the FDA: children between two and four years of age.

2

Between 1990 and 1995, production of Ritalin rose sixfold to keep up with demand, which continues to increase. Some parts of the U.S. are using more than others. A recent study of schools in an area of Virginia found that 20 percent of white fifth-grade boys were on Ritalin. According to researcher John Breeding, seven million American children were taking stimulants in the year 2000—40 times the number that were taking them in 1970. Over-prescription of Ritalin is recognized by the American Academy of Child/Adolescent Psychiatry; by the American Psychiatric Association; by the American Academy of Pediatrics; and even by Novartis, the makers of this medication.

The Image Game: Meds in the Media

In recent years, the competition between the makers of Ritalin—a shorter-acting drug that is effective only for three to four hours—and those who manufacture Concerta and Metadate CD, longer-acting stimulants, has led to a flurry of direct-to-consumer marketing on television and in print. The increased abundance of drugs used to treat attention deficit hyperactivity disorder (ADHD) has served to dramatically increase the amount of advertising for these drugs as their makers try to demonstrate that their product is the best choice, and that parents should ask doctors for it by name. (On more than one occasion, drug makers have been subjected to disciplinary action by the Drug Enforcement Agency or the Food and Drug Administration for making claims that are not supported by research.)

This enormous presence of psychiatric drugs in the media often makes consumers believe that they are benign, and perhaps even necessary—just like most of the other things seen advertised in their newspapers and on TV.

The use of other psychiatric medications in children has also increased dramatically. Between 1995 and 1996, for example, use of the antidepressant Prozac rose an astonishing 400 times in children aged six to 12.

If we're using this much medication to control our children's behavior, our children must really be out of line, and the drugs must be exceedingly effective and safe. This is what most parents believe when they make the decision to medicate their child.

With such minimal risk and pronounced benefits, why *shouldn't* we use drugs to help our kids behave?

After all, virtually everyone knows an adult who uses some kind of psychoactive drug. Antidepressants, anti-anxiety drugs, even stimulants (for "adult ADD") are used by millions of adults to cope with daily life. Children shouldn't have to struggle through without these drugs if they're so helpful and safe...right?

A Dangerous Diagnosis

The catch is that psychoactive drugs are not as helpful or as safe as we have been led to believe. They are dangerous—both physically and psychologically. Psychiatric medicine, pharmaceutical companies, consumer 'advocacy' groups, school systems, and even the arm of the government charged with regulating medicine have all conspired to paint a portrait of these medications that fails to reflect the reality of their risks and benefits.

That picture, when viewed clearly, is nothing less than terrifying—particularly in light of the scale on which these medications are being used. In the pages of this book, you will find out everything you need to know about the risks of Ritalin and other stimulant drugs. You will also find out a fact that is little-known by the general public, but that no psychiatrist can deny based on the scientific research: *no physical cause for ADHD symptoms has been discovered.* Despite all of the rhetoric that refers to ADHD as a biological disorder caused by an imbalance in neurotransmitters or other 'problems' with brain function, there is no solid evidence that this is the case. If you find this hard to believe, keep reading.

And, as you'll see, these drugs do not help the child perform better in school, interact with peers more easily, be less at risk for future drug abuse or feel more self-esteem, despite some misleading research that has been touted by the medical community and by advocacy groups for years. All they do is create an illusion that the child has more control. They put a pharmacological leash on a child whose behavior is disruptive or unmotivated. This might help maintain order in a classroom or in the home, but *it doesn't help the child*...and there is almost always ultimately a big price to pay.

There are many eloquent critics of Ritalin and other psychotropic drugs. Peter Breggin, M.D., Lawrence Diller, M.D., Dr. Mary Ann Block, Ty Colbert, Ph.D., Fred Baughman, M.D., David Stein, Ph.D., and others make compelling arguments against the use of stimulant drugs in children under any but the direst of circumstances. Surely, these experts—physicians, psychotherapists, and other scientists—say it every way it needs to be said: *Stimulant drugs are not the solution; they are, indeed, an important part of the problem.*

Why do I feel compelled to add my voice to those who warn against the overuse of Ritalin?

I have created an approach, *The Nurtured Heart Approach*, that has been used with dramatic success by parents, teachers, therapists, and school systems to help 'ADHD kids' thrive without taking drugs to control their behavior. The great news I have to report is that not only are medications not necessary for the vast majority of children—but the same intensity that people consider to be the *enemy*, the disturbing undercurrent of the syndrome construed as attention deficit hyperactivity disorder, can indeed be fully transformed to be a wonderful propelling force for a child's success. And when this occurs we now have the best child on the block.

My Perspective as Counselor and 'Patient'

I've seen it firsthand thousands of times. I've seen the "symptoms" both in others and in myself. If the diagnosis had existed when I was a kid, I would have been handed Ritalin prescriptions left and right. My own intensity and distractibility frightened me and it frightened others. It stood in my way for a long time. By the grace of God and by sheer luck and determination, I have overcome the problems and made the most of my intensity. However, I know the secret—which is that, for every one of me that stumbles through to the other side, 99 others do not quite make it beyond lives of disrepair, despair and lack of fulfillment...and only rarely to loving their intensity. Without a method that propels transformation, these children are set up to fail and medications actually make the situation worse.

This motivated me to be passionate in my desire to help children labeled ADHD or ADD to overcome their obstacles and thrive. And the solution is actually easy. As I will explain when I talk about *The Nurtured Heart Approach*, normal parenting and teaching methods systematically backfire with intense and sensitive children. And the harder conventional techniques are tried, the worse the situation gets, despite the best of intentions. The culprits aren't the children, the parents or the teachers. The culprits are the methods we have at our disposal.

If I didn't have a non-drug solution, I wouldn't be bashing the medications. I would probably be recommending them, just as the vast majority of practitioners in related fields of psychology, medicine and education do. However, there is an alternative, and it works. In the final chapter of this book, I will describe *The Nurtured Heart Approach* in enough detail to get things going in a powerful way. Readers who wish to find out more can refer to my earlier book, *Transforming the Difficult Child* (written with fellow therapist Jennifer Easley, M.A.).

One aspect of the problem with which I feel intimately familiar is the many psychological side effects of both the ADHD diagnosis and the drugs used to 'treat' it. Physical side effects are much easier to characterize and tabulate. You can see some of the physical side effects of these drugs simply by looking at the package insert or in the *Physician's Desk Reference*. Infinitely more can be easily found on the Internet. But *psychological* side effects—those that involve the emotional health of a child, today and in years to come—are more difficult to pinpoint.

The psychological side effects are just as prevalent and much more insidious. In my opinion, they cause more damage than physical side effects and damage that is harder to repair. Physical side effects are typically dealt with by adding other meds, a practice that is extremely common (and risky, as you'll see in Section Seven), or by stopping medication altogether. Psychological side effects tend to persist, sometimes for a lifetime.

Over many years of working with intense children—children who have been stamped with labels of ADHD or conduct disorder or bipolar disorder or the many other psychiatric diagnoses that are now used to explain disagreeable behavior—I have developed *The Nurtured Heart Approach*, an approach that has been used to bring these kids into success instead of failure, without medication. It is, as my friend and colleague Dennis Embry, Ph.D., describes it, an "industrial-strength intervention" that really works to bring troubled children into their best, most loved and loving selves. Along with presenting the growing evidence to avoid Ritalin *like the plague,* it will be my great honor to share with you this wonderful way of bringing children to their greatness and inner wealth.

—Howard Glasser

NOTES

1. Lawrence Diller, M.D., by permission

2. Peter Breggin, M.D., "Kids are suffering legal drug abuse," *Boston Globe*, 9-26-99

3. Robert Whitaker, *Mad in America: Bad Science, Bad Medicine, and the Enduring Mistreatment of the Mentally Ill*, Perseus Publishing, MA, 2002, p. 187

4. www.pbs.org/wgbh/pages/frontline/medicating/backlash/un.html

The 101 Reasons

Section One
Damaging Psychological Side Effects

I T IS RELATIVELY EASY TO FIND INFORMATION about the physical side effects of stimulant drugs. Quite a few are listed in the package insert, and anyone who wishes to know what they might be can find them there or in the *Physician's Desk Reference* (PDR), the drug "bible" used by physicians when they need drug information. On the Internet, a search for Ritalin side effects will bring up more information than any one person can read in a sitting.

The *emotional* and *psychological* side effects are less easy to pinpoint in scientific studies and have been conspicuously avoided as topics of research. However, they are far greater and far more extensive than any family is ever told. There are emotional and psychological side effects during the time the child uses Ritalin or related medications, and they worsen the longer the child is medicated.

Then, once the meds are stopped, other unexpected emotional and psychological "fallout" is the rule rather than the exception. It's new territory, because these are relatively new drugs, and the first generation of millions of children who have been taking them for years are now becoming adults. The full scope of the real psychological and emotional impact for children who spend their formative years taking stimulant drugs to control their intensity has yet to be seen.

1 **By inferring that something is biologically wrong with a child's brain that needs medication to fix it, we are forever changing that child's view of himself and the view his parents have of him.**

Through extremely effective "destigmatization" campaigns, drug companies have joined forces with government to help promote people's willingness to acknowledge that they have a brain disorder that has definitive physical causes. We are encouraged to face the "fact" that we are "mentally ill" with "brain diseases" so that we can avail ourselves of "effective treatments." In most cases, the effective treatments being referred to involve the use of some sort of psychotropic drug, and less and less often involve counseling or other non-drug approaches, which are costly and time-consuming in comparison with the meds.

Some parents feel relieved at being told their child has a brain disease. They no longer feel as though the problems are caused by their own mistakes or by some other mysterious dynamic, and they no longer feel guilty about seeking help from doctors to control the child. These same parents might believe that telling an out-of-control child that he isn't responsible for his own bad behavior is helpful rather than hurtful. "It isn't your fault, honey," the parent might say. "You have a disease. There's something out of balance in your brain, and you need medicine to help balance it out again." It is astounding that leaders in the field are currently encouraging parents in this situation to explain matters to their challenging child in this way.

This approach certainly simplifies things. The drug becomes the supposed magic bullet that fixes the problem. All of the complexities, complications and the evasive and mystifying components of the "illusion" we call ADHD become easy to grasp, even for a very young child. But the truth is that when we tell ourselves or our children that ADHD symptoms are caused by a biochemical imbalance, we are *lying,* just as the doctors and promotional materials have done to us. It's not a malicious kind of lying, but it's a lie all the same.

The reality is that it's cruel, demoralizing, and unfair to tell a child that something is wrong with his brain that can only be fixed with a drug. From that point on, he will see himself as sick or different, and that will alter his entire self-image—the way in which he values himself and the ways in which he relates to the world.

2 Ritalin sends this message to the child: "Your intensity is a problem. This huge part of your personality has no value. In fact it's the enemy. You cannot handle your own intensity, nor can your parents or teachers, so we need to make it disappear with a pill."

Children feel fear when they sense that adults do not know how to handle them. They learn healthy power by experiencing healthy power in the adults in their life. When adults put a child on stimulant medication, they are in essence giving up on handling that child in any other way. I believe that this contributes to the ongoing, pervasive anxiety that I have often seen in ADHD kids who are taking medications.

The use of medication to help a child deal with his intensity also sends a clear message that intensity is undesirable. Would you miss your intensity if you woke up tomorrow morning and it was gone? That driving force, that lust for life, the passion that motivates you at your deepest level? Without this intensity, you would likely have trouble engaging the gears of your life force. When you are divorced from your life force, fulfilling your dreams becomes a chore rather than a pleasure.

Giving a child medication drives a wedge between the child and his life force. Medications rain on the child's ability to fully see the possibilities of life and to tap into her ability to make it happen. The real irony is that strongly intense children have something special to offer the world—something that is enmeshed with that intensity. If we can support them in handling and putting to use their intensity, rather than stifling it or denigrating it, we can help their greatness emerge.

And what of the growing number of children who are diagnosed with "primarily distractible" ADD—that which does not involve hyperactivity, but is more about daydreaming or not being able to stay "on task"? Is that distractibility, that day dreaminess, an intrinsic part of that child, something that may not jive well with the expectations of schools but that is its own kind of gift? I believe that the answer to this question is an emphatic "yes." Daydreaming and distractibility are often signs of a highly imaginative and creative mind. Attempting to drug these characteristics out of a child and telling them that they have a diagnosable and pathological disorder is every bit as harmful as doing so with a behaviorally challenging child's intensity. It turns out that these children, when exposed to *The Nurtured Heart Approach,* are equally great candidates to have their own brand of intensity emerge in a positive way.

3 **The child labeled ADHD comes to be afraid of his or her own aliveness, life force, intensity. Once this has happened, the child has to struggle to rediscover it, and may never do so.**

When I was in my 20s, someone innocently said to me, "Oh, you're really intense!" It scared the heck out of me that somebody had seen this. At that moment I recognized that I had always felt that my intensity should be kept secret, that it was overwhelming to others, that it made people uncomfortable. I realized I had been imbued with the belief that it was bad, and because of that, it terrified me to a depth beyond my ability to adequately describe in words.

It took me a long time to appreciate my own intensity as a great thing. It's my aliveness, an important part of who I am. Through a lot of reflection and study and through my work with intense kids, I've come to recognize that it's possible to be *married* to your intensity in a wonderful way. Intense people can embrace their intensity as a source of energy and drive.

Thom Hartmann, in his book *ADD: A Different Perception*, writes:

ADD is neither a deficit nor a disorder. It is...an inherited set of skills, abilities and personality tendencies which would enable a hunter or warrior on lookout to be eminently successful—and would condemn a farmer or an accountant to certain disaster.[1]

And way back in 1890, William James wrote in his *Principles of Psychology:*

There is a normal type of character...in which impulses seem to discharge so promptly into movements that inhibitions get no time to arise. These are 'dare-devil' and 'mercurial' temperaments, overflowing with animation, and fizzling with talk...(p. 800)

What we're seeing with the ADHD "epidemic"—and, really, the epidemic of psychiatric diagnosis and drugging in both children and adults—is actually an epidemic of misguided people trying to stuff square pegs into round holes. We're taking the higher level of intensity that is born into some people or acquired through other life circumstances, that is a valuable survival trait—one that engenders creativity, ingenuity, fearlessness, aliveness, and entrepreneurship—and we're pathologizing it. In many cases, this is only because these kids find it hard to sit still and behave in the average classroom setting!

Once we have squashed a "hunter-warrior" child into the mold of the less adventuresome, less energetic (but no less valuable) "farmer or accountant," he will forever believe that his natural self is not of value. He will lead a diminished life, distrusting, fighting and fearing his true nature. He will believe that his intensity, life force, and aliveness are symptoms of a disease and lose the magic of the inner sense of who he really is. It's impossible to manifest our greatness if we are divorced from our life force. ADHD medications drive a giant wedge between a child and his intensity. This dooms a child to a loss of self beyond what I believe any doctor has ever described to a family as he hands them the child's prescription.

 Children who take Ritalin become drug-reliant, thinking that pills are the way to fix problems.

When you don't believe in yourself, you can't really engage the gears of greatness. There's always the voice in your head that tells you that the bottom might drop out, that you can't hack it, that you'll crumble under pressure.

The whole modern medical model supports the notion that pills are the way to fix problems. Instead of finding ways to support the body in its innate, instinctive movement toward balance, and instead of promoting better immune function and digestive function and alertness with pure food, clean water, a healthy emotional life, and adequate rest, we burn the candle at both ends, live on junk food, and deprive ourselves of sleep and outlets for emotional issues. When we get sick, we can usually deal with it by swallowing one or more medications.

The biomedical model of psychiatric illness works on the same premise: rather than addressing lifestyles, school systems, or relationships that cause enormous stress and unhappiness, we swallow one or more medications. Problem behaviors or feelings might seem to improve when we do this—but only as long as we continue to swallow the drugs.

When we tell a child that we can fix her behavior problem with a pill, we're not doing her any favors. I'll let the words of a good friend and colleague, Stephen Crippen, M.A., speak for themselves:

In grad school a few years ago...one of my professors said that in her view, when a child takes a med, it's like taking a "message in a pill," and the message is: "I'm broken. I can't be strong enough to handle things. Something's wrong INSIDE of me."

[The professor's] solution was to forget the meds and instead help the child and the family focus on strengths, on solutions they've already tried, on successes they've already experienced but not celebrated...The mental picture of the pill carrying a message into the child has never left me.

I think you're right, Howie, that on meds, kids feel that their true self doesn't belong here—it doesn't belong in the classroom, or in the home. It's like they're aliens from another planet, and instead of wearing gas masks to adapt their inadequate selves to our atmosphere, they have to take pills to adapt.

It reminds me of a child client of mine who brightened and listened attentively when we began listing all the rules he's following that other people also have to follow! You're not from Mars, an alien who has to take an Earth pill to thrive here. No, you and I and your mom and your teacher—we're all the same, we all succeed when we follow rules, we're all getting stronger and learning and growing, we're all "challenging" to others in different ways, and we're all going to start noticing each other's successes more often.

A child who thinks answers come in pill form is more likely to deal with pain or conflict through drug addiction or other addictive behaviors. (This is further developed in Section Four.) A child in this situation is also more likely to feel incapable when they forget their medication or when it's unavailable, and to feel "excused" when the medication effects wear off or do not seem to work as well on a given day.

To the degree that a child comes to believe in medications, to the same degree she comes to doubt herself. She can never really know for sure if she can take credit for something done well or if the drug gets the credit. Was it the drug that produced the success or failure or was it really me? The pervasive doubt brings with it a pervasive free-floating anxiety as to whether one can really make it through the day without the perceived support of medication. An underlying love/hate relationship with the drug contributes to what can often manifest as an ongoing and distracting angst.

5

Persona non grata: An ADHD child can easily wind up feeling "personally unacceptable or unwelcome."

One example of this is that an ADHD diagnosis can interfere with a child's future eligibility for military service. If your child continues to be treated for ADHD in adolescence (age 12 or older), or is first diagnosed and treated during those years, the military probably won't be an option for him.

Here's what can be found on this topic at www.help4adhd.org:

Enlistees must also meet the "Physical Standards for Appointment, Enlistment, or Induction" (Department of Defense...) These standards use the ICD (International Classification of Disease) codes to identify those conditions that could result in a separation from duty or a medical waiver...For individuals with AD/HD, the applicable section of the DOD directive is, "E1.28. Personality, Conduct, and Behavioral Disorders." In part, this section states the following:

"The causes for rejection for appointment, enlistment, or induction are a history of such disorders resulting in any or all of the below:...

E1.28.2. Personality (301), Conduct (312), or Behavior (313) Disorders. Where it is evident by history, interview, or psychological testing that the degree of immaturity, instability, personality inadequacy, impulsiveness, or dependency will seriously interfere with adjustment in the Armed Forces as demonstrated by repeated inability to maintain reasonable adjustment in school, with employers and fellow workers, and other social groups...

*E1.298.4. Specific Academic Skills Defects. Chronic history of academic skills (314) or perceptual defects (315), secondary to organic or functional mental disorders that interfere with work or school after age 12. **Current use of medication to improve or maintain academic skills.**"* [emphasis added]

With the information highway growing in breadth and width every day, it is not inconceivable that employers will continue to have greater access to medical information, despite legal restrictions. It is not inconceivable that employment, college entrance, scholarship eligibility and such will be tainted by access to these kinds of records, which can easily become public information and contribute to a double edged sword of loss for the child on the ADHD/medication track.

One edge of the sword involves falling off the cliff of worthiness of opportunity as alluded to in the examples above and the child coming to anticipate that as the case. The other edge of the sword is a parallel universe that I feel develops as a result of the use of medications—the feeling of actually wanting to *disappear* or blend into the woodwork. It is not unusual for children on medications like Ritalin to have a tainted inner sense of worthiness of opportunity. The child can come to feel that people can see through to his lack of confidence and he can preemptively take himself out of the ballgame. The inner feeling is *why bother.*

6 Persona non grata: "Unanchored on troubled seas."

I was contemplating the fact that children diagnosed as ADHD and taking medications can be excluded from other important life opportunities, and I realized that they can become "persona non grata" in other ways. One such way is that a child diagnosed with ADHD can have trouble finding affordable health insurance in adulthood if ADHD is viewed as a chronic illness.

A young adult who has been covered by his parents' health insurance and who is newly attempting to get his own private insurance may be in for some unpleasant surprises in the form of outright denial or inflated rates. Unfortunately, even the admission that one has had any type of counseling or psychotherapy can have a similar effect on eligibility for affordable health insurance.

In today's climate of diagnosis and medication, consulting with a mental health professional will almost always get you a diagnosis, and that diagnosis will follow you for the rest of your days, possibly interfering with your hopes and dreams at every turn. If you can, try to avoid doing this to your child. You can get her the help she needs without having her stigmatized with a diagnosis—one that many experts feel is not even a real illness as much as it is a set of behaviors that has been grouped and labeled to create a market for a drug.

As I was wondering where in this volume to include the reason above and whether this really should be construed as a psychological side effect, I took a break to continue reading a book by Arundhati Roy entitled *The God of Small Things.* The very next paragraph provided the explanation I needed to consider:

"We are prisoners of war...Our dreams have been doctored. We belong nowhere. We sail unanchored on troubled seas. We may never be allowed ashore. Our sorrows will never be sad enough. Our joys never happy enough... Our dreams never big enough...Our lives never important enough to matter."

The author is referring to an entirely different situation...life for "outcasts" in India, but it also served as a perfect description of how so many children diagnosed as ADHD and taking medications can come to feel adrift in life itself. The message essentially to them is that they can't handle themselves, nor can anyone else. Once on medication, the child comes to feel further incongruence every day. In my opinion, the child senses deep inside that there is a better answer than medication. Despite the medication, they still feel less than fulfilled in terms of personal and relational success. The greater intensity these children have sets them up for greater dreams of life, but once medications come into the picture the dreams get rained upon. The child's feeling is that no one is any longer fighting for his true dream: expressing the gift of their individuality...who they really are. To the child, it seems like the important people in his life instead dream that he will transform into the conventional picture of what a child is *supposed* to be like. This, of course, has a negative impact on the child's ability to fight for his own dream of life.

Combined with how the medication itself muddies one's life force and makes it harder to experience one's real joys and other vital emotions, it becomes easier to see how the experience of being on a medication such as Ritalin leads to a child feeling utterly unanchored. Our dreams provide our compass and ultimately our direction, and to the extent that our dreams are rendered unavailable, the beauty of life and life's fulfillment become equally unavailable.

7 Children on Ritalin come to believe in the medication rather than in their own inner strength. This interrupts the natural trajectory of personal and spiritual growth.

Medications like Ritalin continually raise the question: is this me, or is this my medication? It's easy to see how this could interfere with one's personal and spiritual growth. When you can't distinguish your own emotions and instincts from the effects of a medicine, you can't rely upon those inner signals to help you navigate your life path.

Personal growth is a spiraling process. Instead of noticing issues, dealing with them, and then evolving and emerging at a higher level, people on psychoactive medications interrupt the spiral altogether. A more apt metaphorical description might be that the person keeps going around and around in circles rather than moving up in a spiral. The meds defuse the inner strength we need to struggle on to the next level. This is true not only of Ritalin and other stimulant drugs, but also of the wildly popular antidepressant and anti-anxiety drugs like Prozac, Effexor, Celexa, and Zoloft. Any drug that takes away or distances you from feelings without resolving the reasons beneath them will hamper personal growth. In effect, you lose the bearings of your inner compass. When you can't fully identify or trust your feelings and instincts, you are, to that extent, removed from your sense of guidance, which hampers your spiritual growth.

And when you don't believe in yourself, you're already more likely to become "stuck"—unwilling to move through difficult issues and take the risks that are necessary to move on to the next level.

When we can collaborate with this spiritual journey, when we congruently join forces between our inner world and outer world and trust enough to follow our own unique path, we move toward deeper levels of self-realization, joy and fulfillment in increasingly encompassing aspects of life. When we have to look outside ourselves for answers and rely more on the outer vestiges for signals on what to do and how to conduct ourselves, our path becomes a much more slippery slope. When a child has taken Ritalin for a significant portion of her life, her ability to reach deep inside for answers is compromised. You can strive for personal and spiritual growth by attending religious services all day long and reading every self-help book, but still, to the extent that you doubt yourself and look outside for answers, these kinds of strides will remain elusive.

 Ritalin takes the child out of the loop of helping herself, of learning healthy ways of exercising self-control.

In his book *ADHD and the Nature of Self Control* (The Guilford Press, 1996), Russell Barkley, Ph.D., states that "Acting without much forethought and responding on impulse to events that occur around them, their emotional reactions to these events often readily apparent, are typical characteristics of young children." Children seek and expect immediate gratification. They have little restraint. In other words, they lack self-control. One of our jobs as parents is to slowly but surely help to inculcate the self-regulation, organization, and goal-orientation that enables children to put off immediate gratification for the sake of a controlled, predictable, and organized life.

From my point of view, in the beginning there is no self-control at all. If there were, we wouldn't have a diaper industry. Hopefully control evolves in a way that's commensurate with the neediness, sensitivities and intensities of the child. Every child has moments, as we all do, where whatever is going on inside us overwhelms our current capacity to exercise control. For some challenged children, moments of being overwhelmed are more predominant. It's not at all like they don't have any control. They may actually have more control than the average child. It's just that they may have an abundance of inner forces (intensity, sensitivities, neediness) propelling them, both more often and to an extent that exceeds their current ability to exercise control.

According to Dr. Barkley and many others, a child whose inability to control her impulsivity or focus her attention to an extent that exceeds that of "normal" children has a brain dysfunction called ADHD. Dr. Barkley and his co-conspirators believe that it is frequently necessary to use drugs to exert control over the uncontrollable child.

This risks setting that child up for failure in many important aspects of her life.

In contrast, the much more optimal and simple outcome is helping a child to rise to the occasion, evolving her ability to use control and subsequently getting to enjoy that aspect of mastery for a lifetime. With the right strategies, such as *The Nurtured Heart Approach,* this is actually very easy to achieve. And was it really a brain disorder if the child is thriving in this regard within a month of when the wheels were falling off?

The first problem with Barkley's commonly held notion is that what is "normal" is not well-defined. There is no absolute threshold at which we can say that a child is abnormal. It's a subjective diagnosis, made in many different ways by practitioners coming from many different backgrounds. This is why the rate of ADHD diagnosis and Ritalin usage varies so dramatically from place to place. It isn't something in the water. It isn't reasonable to believe that more children with brain dysfunction are being sent to school in certain school districts. And it isn't—as Dr. Barkley might suggest—that ADHD is *underdiagnosed* in any place where the rate of Ritalin use is low.

Self-control, too, is not an absolute term. Virtually every person could, theoretically, exert a bit more self-control in various circumstances, and by doing so could have a better organized and more healthful existence. If we could resist that extra scoop of ice cream, or that one drink too many, or self-destructive habits like smoking or nail-biting...if we could be more disciplined at putting off life's pleasures until we fulfilled our responsibilities...we, too, could very possibly have more of what we are looking for in life. Those of us who have problems with anger or depression could prevent outbursts or relapses if we had better self-control. Where do we draw the line and say that a person needs drugs to accomplish this? Again, it's a subjective assessment. One psychiatrist might prescribe meds, while another might not. There's no biological test that shows us where that line is.

The second problem with Barkley's theory is that giving a child drugs does not teach her self-control. It only subdues her behavior. The day the child is taken off medications is the day the problems resume. What are the implications of controlling a child with drugs during the years when she most needs to be learning how to control herself...when the window of opportunity is most available? It's impossible to say, since no research has answered this question. Currently, we're conducting an uncontrolled experiment on millions of children who will reach adulthood without having learned self-control. One could argue that even if these kids do have a more difficult time with self-control than others, it doesn't make creating a false sense of control through the use of medications any less problematic.

Real self-control can be taught to the vast majority of children. We can "hijack" children who appear to lack self-control into a new portfolio of success by enabling them to see the control they are already using and enjoy their victories over their impulses. We can bring them to see the power they are using to make good decisions and to use good judgment, thoughtfulness and consideration...all relevant factors to eventually having the child come to see and believe that *he* indeed has control over his impulses—that his actions and decisions make a big difference in the quality of his life. What I'll explain in sufficient detail in the last reason is that these children also desperately need us to not accidentally reward poor choices and times when they lack control. Normal approaches to parenting and teaching reward negativity all too often by way of all the conversation and energy that transpires when the problems are happening. Children who are challenging can easily form an impression that they are loved <u>more</u> when things are going wrong. In contrast, the energy and conversation have to happen when the problems aren't happening. When problems happen, parents and teachers need a simple and unceremonious way of delivering a consequence for breaking a rule that allows for clarity and completion so we can get that child right back to successes. All the lessons that have impact for these children are really learned through successes, not the harshness of punishments.

Children accused of being ADHD need a greater amount of indirect guidance in learning self-control than the average child. If they're controlled with meds, adults won't see that need in the same imminent way.

When medication is used to exert control, there is less frustration and the parent is typically much less motivated to learn and implement alternative methods to help the child. Largely because of the "improvement" they perceive via meds, complacency rules. They are much less likely to go the extra mile and much more likely to remain out of the loop in terms of finding what works best for their child. And to the extent that this occurs, the child will remain unable to discover the beauty of his own intensity and how to manage it internally. The child will be none the wiser in knowing what works best for him and will remain oblivious to the joy and satisfaction gained in conjuring up his wherewithal to meet his own needs, in handling his impulses and in bringing out the best in himself.

9

Eventually, Ritalin will be made a part of judicial system excuses: "My Ritalin wore off...I couldn't help it."

At what point can we hold a person responsible for his actions when he is mentally ill? If a defendant was truly not in control of his actions when he committed the crime, what he needs is not jail time, but mental health treatment that will improve his self-control and make him a functioning member of society. In some instances, medication is a necessary part of that treatment. If a person who is being treated with psychotropic medication forgets to take it, and then proceeds to commit a crime, is that person to be held accountable? What about the teenager whose Ritalin is wearing off and ends up causing an accident while driving his car?

It isn't uncommon for a child on Ritalin to become extremely hyperactive or distractible when his medication wears off. Doctors who prescribe the drug have long been experimenting with ways to prevent this rebound, which is a common problem for kids who take Ritalin. Extended-release forms of the drug help, but then there's the issue of the drug causing insomnia if its action extends too late into the evening.

Once we start denying responsibility for our actions because of conditions for which there is no hard evidence of a biological basis, we start down a slippery slope. The only evidence that leads to a diagnosis of ADHD is observed behavior—the same observed behavior that could be construed as criminal if it were to harm others. How can we say that a person has a disease that caused him to commit a crime, even while saying that the criminal behavior constitutes the disease? It doesn't make sense.

And by the way, being on medication doesn't stop a child from continuing to commit criminal acts. If you ever want a really rude awakening, go to a juvenile detention center and interview almost any child there. Invariably they have been on prescribed stimulant medications and moved on to street drugs, winding up incarcerated because of criminal activity.

10

Social relations on Ritalin become fear-based for many children. Their previous difficulties relating to others may become worse as they lose touch with their emotions and appear robotic or sad to their peers.

Think back to a time when you had one too many cups of coffee. Really remember how it feels, if you can. You're trembling and nervous, you're jumpy, you're talking too fast and giggling or lashing out grumpily for no reason. Some people find that they can't focus at all when they are over-caffeinated; others find they become overly focused, able only to focus on one thing at a time—sort of like a child on Ritalin. It's that singular focus that sometimes gets you through but at the price of great inner discomfort.

How do you cope? You white-knuckle it through the hours it might take for you to come down from your caffeine high. You try to avoid having important conversations or performing demanding tasks, thinking: "I don't want anyone to think this is what I'm really like!" You just want to get through the day.

This is comparable to the way many children describe feeling when they are on Ritalin: "like a ghost," "not like myself," "numb."

If children have trouble being social before they go on the drugs because of unpredictable and inappropriate behavior in school, they don't have less trouble being social while on the drugs. They lose their mooring. They become overly focused and zombie-like. An adult who looks at the child sees him focusing (perhaps with great relief), but the child is having a horrible time. And when you're having a horrible time, you don't really feel like socializing. To other people, you look robotic and sad, and they aren't inclined to approach you.

Childhood and adolescence are prime times for learning how to properly relate to peers. When we force children to take stimulant drugs during these important formative years, we rob them of the opportunity to experience first-hand the ups and downs of making and maintaining friendships based on a truer sense of self. On the other hand, the ability to make healthy friendships is part of the benefit of *The Nurtured Heart Approach*. The child emerges with a new inner wealth of enhanced ways of experiencing himself and a new inner strength that is based on success. This makes it infinitely easier to make friendships based on something positive instead of insecurities and other negative factors.

11

Children on Ritalin seem to have a pervasive sense of sadness or failure while on the medication. Rats exposed to Ritalin as juveniles showed greater increases in "learned-helplessness" behavior and acted "clinically depressed."

At the University of Texas, researcher William Carlezon did a series of experiments where juvenile rats were exposed to Ritalin over an extended period of time. (The Ritalin dosage the rats received was comparatively equivalent to what an ADHD child would receive.) After observing the rats' behavior over time and administering tests to measure reward-seeking behavior, Dr. Carlezon concluded that "rats exposed to Ritalin as juveniles showed larger increases in learned-helplessness behavior during adulthood, suggesting a tendency towards depression." When exposed to methylphenidate in their youth, these rats became less responsive to stimuli that should have been rewarding, and their reactions to stress became more intense. They were less likely to use cocaine when it was offered (and rats *love* cocaine), but they acted clinically depressed.

Learned helplessness was first described in the 1960s by psychologist Martin Seligman. He did a series of experiments with dogs, confining them and subjecting them to harmless but unpleasant electrical shocks. After the dogs had been shocked and restrained for a while, he put them into a cage from which they could easily escape. When the dogs were shocked again, they didn't even try to get away. They had learned that they were helpless, that they had no control. Learned helplessness is a significant part of depression. When we feel we have no control, when we feel trapped, depression is a typical response.

Learned helplessness and depression certainly make dogs and rats (and children) more manageable. They don't try to escape, they don't resist directives. They don't generally argue, or hit, or complain, and they can function well in a boring environment. But at what cost? We're not talking about improving the child's life. We're talking about a pharmacological variation of learned helplessness. In the words of Peter Breggin, M.D., Ritalin makes "good caged rats."

Rats on Ritalin display behaviors that are meaningless, compulsive, repetitive, and inflexible. They chew, posture, pace, and rear up for no apparent reason. Children on Ritalin and other stimulant drugs have been found to become subdued, passive, and extremely compliant. Their emotions become flattened. They lose initiative and cease to demonstrate interest or aversion. They lose their curiosity and don't show surprise or pleasure. Sense of humor, novelty-seeking behavior, and exploration dwindle. Like the rats on Ritalin, children on stimulant drugs become subject to obsessive-compulsive, repetitive, meaningless behaviors.

Kids feed off of the energy given to them by adults. ADHD kids seem to require more of that energy, and they're willing to get into trouble in order to bring that energy out of the adults in their lives. You can look at this energy as currency, a sort of money that is desperately wanted by intense kids. Intense kids get attention by breaking rules. Adults tell them over and over not to break the rules, but the energy that comes from the adults' reactions to rule-breaking is far greater than the energy that comes from their reactions to the child being successful.

It's like saying to the child, "Don't break the rules," but every time she does, we slip her a hundred bucks. Energetically we pass out those hundred dollar bills left and right through warnings, reprimands, lectures and other emotional responses. It's confusing. We tell them not to break the rules but we demonstrate that we in effect *love* them more when they do. The kid can't figure out how to get what she needs without misbehaving. Confusion begets depression. It's textbook learned helplessness. We have to give that energy to the child when he *isn't breaking the rules and is doing the right things*, and withhold it when he does misbehave. This is the essence of *The Nurtured Heart Approach* described at the end of this book.

12 The child who is given Ritalin may wind up confused about who he really is.

Stimulant medications give children a sense of being and feeling "not like themselves." They feel conflicted, often in a deep and existential way. We all want to find our deepest, truest self, and we all feel off-center when we sense we are operating on a level that is in contradiction with a more meaningful inner level.

The use of medications may shift a child's underlying faith in himself and in others. Dr. Breggin states that "a person's ultimate faith can be determined in terms of where he or she turns when feeling frightened, self-doubting, depressed, anxious, hopeless, or shaken to the core." Does the use of medication reduce the likelihood that a child will turn to his loved ones, toward inner guidance or to spiritual-seeking when in crisis? Does it instead direct that child toward answers in a pill bottle, faith in chemistry, and trust in biological psychiatry, medical-sounding diagnoses, and drugs?

Is he the person he is when on the drug, or the one who has to be given the drug to "help" him to "behave?" His inner dialogue becomes confused; he loses track of his authentic self, making it that much harder to feel his feelings and trust his instincts.

The child may come to fear life without Ritalin. The child's sense is that it's not *him* doing the desirable things, like being focused or more cooperative; instead, it's the drug. "How will I disappoint others if I don't take these pills?" he might ask himself. He becomes fearful about how he will be able to cope without the drugs.

13 There's a love/hate dichotomy in the child's drug-induced ability to please others, and a sense of failure because the drugs are responsible for any positive shifts in behavior.

There is a pervasive sense of sadness in most children on stimulants. It is almost impossible for the child to put his finger on that feeling or to adequately express it. In my own conversations with these kids, I have found that there is commonly a sense of being in a perpetually dark room without a flashlight. There is an emptiness, a sense of failure about life in general—despite the lower incidence of their past "problems" and greater approval from important people like parents and teachers. There is a sense that the medication is responsible for the positive changes. When someone approves of the child's "improved behavior" while on stimulants, the child resents that the "non-me" on meds is being applauded instead of the "real me" that the meds bury.

The child on medications feels himself robotically going through the motions, but is devoid of the essential, heart-centered aspect of aliveness, the wellspring of purpose that motivates direction and activates accomplishment. It's all the more subconsciously maddening for the intense child who instinctually senses the greater loss of momentum.

14 The child whose behavior is being controlled by stimulants is no less vulnerable to negative attention from peers.

The child often feels a sense of social isolation when taking medications. She may feel somewhat like a social outcast, particularly if other children know that she is on drugs to control her behavior—a fact that's hard to hide when she has to go to the nurse's office every day for her daily dose. Add to this the possible mood swings of children whose meds wear off during the school day, and you have a situation where the child is at greater risk of being singled out and ridiculed by peers. It is not unusual for the child on ADHD medications to harbor anger and resentment for these reasons as well for the growing frustration connected with loss of self.

On the other hand, some marginal children in a classroom might see the ADHD kid on Ritalin receiving special attention from adults, and might see how getting a pill for their "behavior problems" makes that child more attractive to important adults like teachers and other school staff. Those children might decide that the answer to their problems is in those pills, too.

In addition, even when the stimulant medications appear to be working optimally, the child is still none the wiser about how to best get along, how to use better judgment, how to be more thoughtful and considerate—and still none the richer in terms of personal, first-hand experiences of social success. The pill itself has not created social improvement. Take the pill away, and the child is still essentially where she was on day one.

Opinion leaders who insist that children who are not medicated for ADHD symptoms will face catastrophe in both social and academic arenas are not looking at the facts: research has not reliably demonstrated that drugs help kids in either of these areas!

15

If a child does in fact have "co-morbid conditions" (i.e., co-existing) such as clinical depression or bipolar disorder, Ritalin can make them worse. But in many cases, the drugs or the ADHD diagnosis are the cause of these so-called co-morbid conditions.

It's reported in the research that 24 to 30 percent of people with ADHD could also be diagnosed with clinical depression. Other conditions that psychiatry claims are commonly found in people with ADHD: bipolar disorder, anxiety, learning disability, conduct disorder, and oppositional defiant disorder. Recurrent depressive episodes are more common in adults with ADHD than in those without ADHD.

This comes as little surprise to those who are critical of the widespread over-diagnosis of ADHD. Depression is one of the side effects of medications used to treat the symptoms that are construed as ADHD. Aside from this, having the kinds of difficulties that end up bringing about an ADHD diagnosis can make a child or an adult feel like a misfit—someone who just can't seem to fit in or live harmoniously with others, no matter how hard he tries. This can lead to depression. In addition, for reasons discussed at the end of this book when I describe *The Nurtured Heart Approach,* you'll come to see how utterly confusing life is for challenging children in relation to normal parenting and teaching approaches. If the only change that transpires as a result of professional intervention is the introduction of medications and not a change to a more extraordinary approach to help the child feel successful, the continued use of conventional methods will perpetuate depression as well. Ongoing confusion will breed depression in anyone. Then, psychiatry claims that in order to treat the ADHD, one also must treat the so-called "co-morbid condition" of depression.

Rapidly shifting moods—often leading to a diagnosis of bipolar disorder—can also be a product of a square peg trying to fit into the round hole of modern life. According to psychiatrists Glenn Byrnes, M.D., Ph.D., and Carol Watkins, M.D., "Some say that rapid mood shifts and frequent irritability are characteristics of AD/HD. Others diagnose a rapid cycling mood disorder."[2] Believe it or not, experts estimate that between 22 and 90 percent of people who suffer from bipolar disorder also suffer from ADHD.

Some say that *oppositional defiant disorder* exists in nearly half of kids with ADHD. This disorder is characterized by "stubbornness, outbursts of temper, and acts of defiance." It's easy to see how this "disorder" could very well be confused with ADHD or be part and parcel of ADHD in many children. Keep in mind that these diagnostic categories have been created by psychiatrists, virtually plucked out of thin air in an attempt to explain, treat, and in most cases, medicate undesirable or disruptive behaviors.

I cannot emphasize enough that the diagnosis of any psychiatric disorder is highly subjective. When treatment with Ritalin pushes other problems to the forefront, such as depression or mood swings, the medication itself rarely takes the blame in the eyes of the medical community. Even more seldom does the diagnosis of a nonexistent "biological condition" take the blame. Instead, it is assumed that the person needs an additional diagnosis and additional drugs! It's a real life Alice in Wonderland scenario.

Millions of people are being medicated with multiple drugs because they have been led to believe that there is something wrong with their brains, when in reality there is nothing wrong with their brains *until they start taking psychotropic medications.*

As soon as your medical team begins to say things like, "Oh, we may have initially misdiagnosed your son...we believe he really has bipolar disorder," or "Your little girl has oppositional defiant disorder along with her ADHD, and if we don't treat both, neither disorder will improve," you're on a slippery slope. Next thing you know, the doctors are rationalizing and re-hypothesizing about their new diagnosis and trying medication upon medication. *This is a highly predictable pattern that is more a function of the side effects from the meds than of any real disorder.* In other words, it's well-intentioned doctors on a wild goose chase, refusing to depart from the limitations of the medical model that sees side effects as only treatable by additional medications and additional diagnosis to justify the reactive stance.

An example from an ADHD discussion board:

My son is nine. He was put on ADHD meds. We started noticing depression and mania and they are now saying he might be bipolar. The doctor wants to put him on a mood stabilizer. I have him on no meds right now, but I have to get things under control with him by the time school starts in a couple of months and I'm tempted to try what is being recommended even though it frightens me to go down this road.

Another posting responds:

My son is nine too, and he was diagnosed with ADHD at six. Ritalin slowed him down and improved his impulse control, but he soon fell into depression, anxiety, paranoia and increased aggression. His appetite was almost nonexistent and he wasn't sleeping well. We then tried Concerta. The afternoon symptoms continued. Then Strattera, which helped with impulse control and he began eating and sleeping better, but he was still anxious, depressed, and aggressive.

We were then referred to a psychiatrist, who prescribed Risperdal [an anti-psychotic] in addition to the Strattera. It worked to some extent because we ended up with maybe only one in five days where the aggressiveness arose instead of daily, and he was able to snap out of it quickly—often on his own. The psychiatrist called this use of Risperdal "off-label." We were told to watch him for tardive dyskinesia, though. [irreversible muscular changes that resemble symptoms of Parkinson's disease] *The doctor checks his neck and spine with each visit and we have to watch for tics. The problem is that he is still anxious, depressed and just not himself and I can't stop myself from feeling that the doctors will continue to change his diagnosis and medications as he gets older.*

As a result of these types of shifting diagnoses and prescriptions, your child may develop new and complex psychological (and possibly physical) side effects. Even if the new medication combinations and diagnoses seem to bring about improvements, your child will still be confused about his self-image and his need for potent chemicals just to get through the days. Eventually, even a medication combination that works well may cease to do so, as the child's brain chemistry changes to try to overcome the effects of the drugs. The human body is miraculous and often makes a remarkable adaptation to foreign substances. So there will eventually be more adjustment of the medications. For the very few children with bona fide mental illness, this is necessary and beneficial—but not for the vast majority of the millions who are currently being medicated for the symptoms considered to be ADHD.

16 Adults are Increasingly using "adult ADHD" as an excuse for poor performance in work, relationships, and school.

Because ADHD has been defined as a disease, it is not legal to discriminate against someone whose performance is affected by it. In other words, a person who blames ADHD for their difficulties can't be fired or flunked out of school unless the employer or school wants to risk being sued. This has been wittily called "affirmative action for wealthy white people."

Children and adolescents who take Ritalin for ADHD end up using their "disease" to excuse poor performance in school and in the workplace. There has recently been a dramatic increase in the number of college-bound kids requesting extra time for standardized tests such as the SAT, LCAT, and MCAT because of ADHD. An Ivy League professor states that many students come to him "waving doctor's letters and pills" to get extra time to complete assignments. And with the recent surge in adults who are being diagnosed as ADD or ADHD, it is becoming more common for some to make excuses for poor performance or absences, knowing that they have the safety net of discrimination laws to protect them.

17

Children who are given drugs for ADHD do not get the help they need to deal with social and school problems.

Learning disability is a common finding in children who are diagnosed with ADHD. All too often, a child who is having trouble in school will get a quickie ADHD diagnosis and a prescription for Ritalin, and everyone will think the problem has been solved—when what the child really needs is help with problems relevant to learning, organizational skills or simply feeling successful.

A child who has difficulty in social situations may act out because of anger, fear, or shame. A child who suffers from crippling shyness may have difficulty focusing because she's afraid of social interaction. Neither of these children will get the help they really need if we pump them full of drugs. When learning disability or social problems are misdiagnosed and treated as ADHD or ADD, children continue to not get the right kinds of needed interventions and guidance pertinent to academic and social success.

Because the ADHD diagnosis is applied so often to such a wide spectrum of issues, children with visual or sensory problems may be diagnosed as having ADHD while their real condition goes undiagnosed and untreated. As an example, here's one story I found on an Internet discussion board:

My twelve-year-old son has always sort of had his head in the clouds, daydreaming all the time. His teacher told me he didn't pay attention and couldn't follow directions, and was passive-resistive. His math skills weren't up to par. She suggested I have him evaluated for ADD. The pediatric neurologist we saw said that my son had ADD symptoms, and that he'd benefit from medication, based only on the teacher's answers on a set of questions—even though I told him that every day he'd come straight home from school and after snack he'd work straight through to completion on his homework. When I resisted the drugs and said I'd rather see an educational therapist first, the doctor was surprised, and said that most parents march into his office demanding a prescription for their child.

Thank goodness we chose the route we did, because the educational therapist found that my son had a non-verbal learning disability. His verbal skills tested fine, but when faced with a series of instructions, he can't formulate a picture in his mind based on those instructions. If the teacher says, "We're going to write a paper. Center the title, and put your name and the date in the upper right hand corner. The paper will be three paragraphs long, with each paragraph indented and double spaces between each para-graph. Let's begin." The other kids are putting together a picture of what the paper will look like, but my son can't do this. All he hears is a long string of words. When the teacher tells him to begin, he doesn't know how to start. We also took him to an ophthalmologist, where we found that if he were taking a driver's test, he'd be considered legally blind. He got glasses, which he's probably needed since kindergarten.

I returned to the pediatrician and told her about my son's results. I was surprised to find that drugs are routinely recommended before thorough testing to discover the child's true problems. She said that usually, drugs are tried first, and if there isn't a significant improvement, then they look for a learning disability! It's so scary to think that we might have ended up giving him drugs that would mask his LD. With some research, I have found that non-verbal learning disabilities are often misdiagnosed as ADD, and that the misdiagnosis is often not discovered until the child bottoms out in middle school. My son is one of the lucky ones whose problems were discovered early, who got the help they really need.

18

ADHD symptoms are a child's ways of letting adults know that she needs a different kind of relationship, parenting, teaching and/or support than normal approaches can provide. Giving drugs to shut down that message is like killing the messenger.

Many parents hope that medications will solve their child's problems, and they are often initially relieved by an illusion of improvement. It's not unusual for a parent in this situation to lose their motivation to find additional methods to create further change. When the child's problematic symptoms appear to dissipate with the medications, parents can hang their hats entirely on that hook. This symptom "improvement" serves as apparent proof that, yes, my child *does* have ADHD, a brain disease for which he requires medication.

The parents then are none the wiser on how to best parent the child; they are none the wiser about what works best; and they are still in a compromised position before the meds kick in or after they wear off. And they, too, can find themselves fearful about taking their child off medications, despite obvious side effects, because they know they'd automatically be back to square one—ill-equipped to handle the problems, and not wanting to re-experience the behaviors that existed prior to medication.

Anecdotal experiences bear this out: as soon as a child is taken off medications, she is often back to square one behaviorally...unless the parents and teachers have in the meantime learned and applied an approach that works!

19

Of the children who have committed violent crimes injuring or killing classmates or relatives, most are believed to have been taking at least one psychoactive drug to control their behavior.

One of the Columbine shooters took Ritalin. The 13-year-old who shot and killed classmates in Jonesboro, Arkansas, was also on a stimulant medication. And Thomas "TJ" Solomon, who shot six classmates in Conyers, Georgia, was said to have taken Ritalin "on and off" for a few years before his crimes. In addition:

- On May 25, 1997, 18-year-old Jeremy Strohmeyer raped and murdered a seven-year-old girl in Las Vegas, Nevada. Strohmeyer had been diagnosed with ADD and prescribed Dexedrine immediately prior to the killing.

- In 1998, Kipland Kinkel, a 15-year-old from Springfield, Oregon, murdered his parents and then proceeded to his high school where he killed two students and wounded 22 others. Kinkel had been prescribed both Prozac and Ritalin.

- On October 1, 1997, in Pearl, Mississippi, Luke Woodham stabbed his 50-year-old mother to death. He then went to high school and shot nine people, killing two teenage girls and wounding seven others. Published reports say that he was on Prozac.

- April 16, 1999: 15-year-old Shawn Cooper of Notus, Idaho, brought a 12-gauge shotgun to school and began firing, injuring one student and holding the school hostage for about 20 minutes. Cooper had been taking Ritalin when he made the choice to fire that shotgun.

- Rod Mathews, a 14-year-old who had taken Ritalin since the third grade, beat a classmate to death with a bat.

- James Wilson, a 19-year-old who had been on psychiatric drugs for five years, took a .22 caliber revolver into an elementary school in Breenwood, South Carolina, killing two girls and wounding seven other children and two teachers.

- On December 1, 1997, 14-year-old Michael Carneal opened fire on students at a high school prayer meeting in West Paducah, Kentucky. Three teens were killed; another five were wounded, and one of them was paralyzed. Reportedly, Carneal was on Ritalin.

- In Huntsville, Alabama, in February 1998, a young man who was taking Ritalin chopped up his parents with an ax, murdered one sibling, and almost murdered another.

- On March 24, 1998, in Jonesboro, Arkansas, 11-year-old Andrew Golden and 14-year-old Mitchell Johnson shot 15 people. They killed four students and one teacher and wounded 10 others. Some reports suggest that the boys were on Ritalin.[3]

Although no causal relationship has been established between the use of stimulants and gun violence or other aggressive behavior, it is hard to entirely dismiss the possible link. These children were obviously troubled, and it's impossible to know if their acts of aggression were precipitated or amplified by the prescribed medications.

Although anyone trying to establish a causative link between Ritalin and a child's violence in a court of law might have a difficult time making their case, the situation is different with the selective serotonin reuptake inhibitors (SSRIs) like Prozac, Luvox, and Zoloft. Recent research suggests strongly that these drugs can push troubled kids over the edge into violent behaviors—against themselves and others. Columbine shooter Eric Harris was on Zoloft, then on Luvox. Kip Kinkel, the shooter in Springfield, Oregon, who killed two and injured 22, was on Prozac (and Ritalin).

In the United Kingdom, all of the SSRIs except Prozac have been banned for pediatric populations because of the evidence that these meds can bring out violence against self (suicide) and against others. Similar research is going on in the U.S., and parents and teachers are being warned to watch kids on SSRIs very carefully to ensure that the drugs aren't moving them in the direction of violence. Ritalin is often a gateway drug that leads to the prescription of SSRIs (see Section Seven, The Dangers of Polypharmacy, for more on this).

Opponents of psychotropic drugging of children use school shootings as an argument against the drugs, but their argument is weak. Of the millions who take Ritalin or other psychopharmaceuticals, only a handful ever bring a gun to school and commit acts of violence. When we turn to the school shooter argument for fuel against wholesale drugging of kids, we're treading on thin ice, and it can hurt our credibility; however, I can personally state with a high level of confidence that medications can put children in a compromised position in terms of their ability to exercise good judgment and they can put children over the edge in terms of overwhelming inner stimulation. I can also say with certainty that medications do not help a child with tendencies toward aggression gain any ability to better manage their strong feelings or exercise healthy control over their impulses or intensities. **Medications are not the answer to any degree for children needing desperately to learn important life lessons.**

20 Children on Ritalin report being cut off from their feelings.

Feelings are our guide, our barometer, and can be a source of joy. It's hard enough to stay in touch with them *without* being given drugs that suppress them.

Children often refuse to take Ritalin, pretending to swallow it and "cheeking" the tablet instead. They say that it deadens them, controls them, makes them feel like babies; others can't explain why, but know they do not want to take it.

According to the biological psychiatry model, psychiatric drugs are supposed to help disturbed or depressed patients respond better to psychotherapy. By reining them in from the emotional extremes to which their "illness" makes them vulnerable, they can more calmly communicate with the therapist.

Here's what Peter Breggin, M.D., and his coauthor David R. Cohen, Ph.D., have to say about this theory:

The authors' experience is very different. We have found that psychiatric drugs suppress feelings and estrange people from themselves. This makes it more difficult to explore, identify, and channel emotions. Weaning off psychiatric drugs can improve your ability to benefit from any personal or educational relationship, including therapy. (Breggin and Cohen, *Your Drug May Be Your Problem,* p. 25)

Being out of touch with emotions is dangerous. When you can feel your feelings and tolerate the intensity and possible discomfort, feelings ultimately provide information which can then be interpreted and used to move through life. You can ask for what you need and want when you are able to download that vital information as a result of feeling your feelings. You can make better choices when making important decisions. When one is detached from feelings, this becomes an almost impossible task. The numbness that comes from suppressing and ignoring our feelings leads us into escapist types of behaviors such as overeating and drug and alcohol abuse. These may give us temporary relief, but we continue to feel divided, conflicted, stressed, and out of integrity.

Being cut off from our feelings is significantly connected with depression. Not surprisingly, depression is a common side effect with Ritalin and other stimulants.

21 Instinct, creativity, and spontaneity suffer in children who take stimulants.

According to an e-mail I received from Kathy Kolbe, world-renowned expert on instincts, "drugging kids simply so that they will conform to standardized classroom behaviors is child abuse."

Instinct is an innate, inborn pattern of behavior that exists in most animals. Instinctive reactions to events or environments come from long-ingrained drives toward self-preservation and the satisfaction of basic biological needs. Most animals operate primarily on the level of instinct, and it's virtually impossible to get them to do anything else. Humans, of course, are another story.

When we act on instinct, we act without conscious intention. While conscious intention is all well and good, humans have a bad habit of over-thinking, over-analyzing, or talking themselves out of doing what their instincts are screaming at them to do. Instincts may not fall into lockstep with the civilized ways of modern life, but they do have value. Many of us strive to better hear what our instincts are telling us when we have to make an important decision. Psychotropic drugs add another layer of confusion. Is it the drugs talking, or our instincts, or our thinking, reasoning mind?

More loosely, we can refer to our instincts as an important source of creativity and spontaneity. If so, the drugs cheat kids of these life-enhancing qualities, too.

Here's an excerpt from an e-mail Kathy Kolbe sent me:

I am considered the leading expert on human instincts, and have worked with many families whose children have been on Ritalin, or in which parents have been advised to give Ritalin. Doctors recommended we put our own two children on the drug.

Any doctor who prescribes drugs for a child without an awareness of the potential implications to the conative part of the mind (from which we act according to our instincts) is irresponsible. Instinct-driven actions give every individual a pattern of behavior that is dependable because it is intrinsic. Mind-altering drugs can take a child out of their natural zones, disrupting the personal rhythm of their actions and denying them their unique abilities.

Teachers tend to see their own ways of acting—their "modus operandi," or MO—as the acceptable or normal way to behave. Over 20 percent of students have natural ways of taking action that are quite contrary to this stereotype of normalcy. These kids could excel if given a chance to perform using their own MO, rather than having to work against their own grain most of the time in the classroom setting. Rather than changing the classroom to make it work for all kids, the drug-them-into-submission approach tries to change the child's natural way of operating so that they fit into the very limiting classroom "box."

Think of it as similar to the mind control that might be used on prisoners of war. If the purpose is to get kids to submit to the rule of authority, act out less aggressively when confined to a mental "box," and do what they are told to do, then Ritalin is your answer. If you want to nurture your child's innate strengths and encourage him to find ways to self-manage his natural drives, then Ritalin is as much the enemy as anyone who puts a gun to your child's head.

Those who believe that there is one right way to think and take action have put a "disabled" label on those who do not conform to that way. Children who mimic the status quo MO are rewarded with good grades and praise. Parents often become desperate to push their child into conforming and become willing to try anything to make that happen.

It's wonderful that we have drugs to help highly dysfunctional children to cope with the world around them. It is criminal that those drugs are being recommended to push children who are not all that dysfunctional into conformity—to stifle their attempts to use their God-given abilities to fight their way out of a "box" that isn't right for them.

22 It's hard not to draw parallels between the use of highly toxic neuroleptics and antipsychotics for people with schizophrenia and the widespread drugging of difficult children.

Robert Whitaker's groundbreaking work *Mad in America* describes the "enduring mistreatment of the mentally ill." He traces the history of the treatment of schizophrenia from the 1700s through the 1930s. Over this time period, mentally ill people were subjected to "treatments" that today sound more like torture. Patients were placed in asylums and subjected to such horrors as induced coma (created by giving high doses of insulin), drowning and resuscitation, lobotomy, electroconvulsive therapy, restraint in chairs that spun violently, or immersion in bathtubs full of water for days on end.

All of these so-called "treatments" were designed to inflict fear, nausea, and pain on the patients, whose out-of-control behavior was often subdued once the doctors were finished with them. Having feared for their lives and been more physically miserable than they could ever imagine, these patients tried their best to behave so that they would not have to go through more of the same. The doctors charged with their care cited the patients' less trouble-some behavior as evidence that their "treatments" were working.

In the worst cases—those whose brains had been surgically altered with prefrontal lobotomy—the mentally ill became "vegetables," unable to do anything beside sleep, eat, and watch television. As recently as the mid-20th century, this was considered to be a highly scientific and miraculous treatment for insanity. An article in the *New York Times* dated June 7, 1937, stated that severing nerve fibers in the prefrontal cortex of the brain could successfully treat "tension, apprehension, anxiety, depression, insomnia, suicidal ideas, delusions, hallucinations, crying spells, melancholia, obsessions, panic states, disorientation, psychalgesia [pain of psychic origin], nervous indigestion and hysterical paralysis." Portuguese neurologist Egaz Moniz, the man who created prefrontal lobotomy, won a Nobel Prize for his efforts.

Since the 1930s, powerful neuroleptic drugs have been the standard therapy for people with schizophrenia. These drugs affect the function of neurotransmitters in ways that effectively subdue even the most psychotic patient, but they can cause serious and permanent side effects, including a form of Parkinson's disease. Their effects on patients have been widely referred to as "chemical lobotomy." It's hard to keep patients on these drugs. Many prefer the terrors of mental illness to the deadened, zombie-like state into which neuroleptics push them.

What does the treatment of schizophrenia—a serious mental illness that is characterized by near-total breaks from reality, hallucinations, delusions, paranoia, and bizarre behaviors that are definitely not socially acceptable—have to do with the treatment of ADHD? Both diseases are considered to be "biopsychiatric," but a biological basis has not been ascertained for either. The diagnostic criteria for both are much more subjective than we are led to believe. When a drug alters the behavior of a person with schizophrenia or ADHD in ways that make the person fit in more readily, the medical community uses this as evidence that the disorder stems from a "broken brain" that can be repaired—at least temporarily—with drugs. In *Mad in America*, Whitaker writes:

Once neuroleptics were deemed "antischizophrenic," the presumed medical model at work was straightforward. There was a diagnosable disorder, called schizophrenia, that could be successfully treated with a medication specific to it. That precise correlation of diagnosis and medication even spoke of medicine at its best. An artful diagnosis begat a singularly appropriate treatment. Regardless of the merits of the drugs, it was a model that could be valid only if American psychiatry could reliably diagnose this disorder. But by the 1970s, it became evident that psychiatry had no such skill and that schizophrenia was a term being loosely applied to people with widely disparate emotional problems. It was also a label applied much more quickly to poor people and African-Americans. (p.165)

He goes on to say that "in one experiment, 69 percent of American psychiatrists shown a video of a socially inept, moody thirty-year-old bachelor diagnosed him as schizophrenic, whereas only 2 percent of the British psychiatrists did." Whitaker also reports that in 1982, an analysis of case records at Manhattan State Hospital found that 80 percent of those who had been diagnosed as schizophrenic had "never exhibited the symptoms necessary to support such a diagnosis."

In yet another chilling illustration of the subjective nature of a diagnosis that could devastate a person's life, Stanford University professor David Rosenham and seven other people went to 12 different mental hospitals for evaluation. They complained of hearing vague voices saying words such as "thud," "empty," or "hollow." Their behavior was calm and they reported no other symptoms. Other aspects of their lives were truthfully described. Based on these evaluations, every one of these so-called "patients" was admitted to the mental hospital. All but one was diagnosed with schizophrenia.[4]

For a few moments in history, humane treatments were attempted with schizophrenic patients. The Quakers were pioneers of such humane treatment. They created hospitals run by caring laypeople rather than physicians, and they created a highly structured, interesting, and comfortable environment for the distressed people entrusted to their care. With humane treatment, more people recovered from this supposedly incurable disease—and were able to return to society as functioning people—than with any other kind of treatment.

What does this tell us about the right way to "treat" difficult children?

23 At the point of giving a child drugs, we blur the line between the behaviors that come from the child's intensity and the behaviors that come from unpredictable responses to psychoactive medications.

Too many children end up being put on medication after medication when one doesn't seem to do the job. The process by which physicians make the choice of which drug to try next is, to say the least, unscientific—switching not only drugs, but also diagnoses to try to medicate the child into submission.

Early in my career, I attended numerous medication monitoring sessions. Although the doctors were trying hard to help the child, it was perfectly clear that the tweaking of dosages or addition of new meds was—even for the brightest doctors—little more than a subjective guessing game, not an objective or scientific endeavor. The dosages and additions were, at best, well-intended hunches.

Take, for instance, the story of a boy named Danny, as described to me in an e-mail from his mother, Brenda. (Comments from me are in brackets.)

My six-year-old son Danny was originally put on Zoloft because of anxiety symptoms. He would get very panicky with a racing heartbeat when I would leave him for even short periods of time. One day, he heard on the news about a teenage girl who got beat up by her peers in a hazing incident. He obsessively worried for weeks about that girl and whether that could happen here. Finally, I took him to see a psychiatrist, who prescribed Zoloft.

Danny had an immediate response to Zoloft. His pupils were as big as his eyes and he didn't eat or sleep for two days. I must say his behavior and mood were improved, however. I called the doctor, who said to just reduce the dose, but he was not better. Then, the psychiatrist decided to try Adderall, conveniently changing his diagnosis from anxiety to ADHD. (I had mentioned Danny's difficulty focusing in class.)

On the Adderall, Danny cried for three straight days. My husband and I decided to stop all the meds. Danny started having more problems with hitting and kicking. He never did this behavior outside the home—he had been voted nicest kid at school recently—but at home, he was getting out of control. We went back to the doctor again, and he was put on Gabitril [an anti-seizure medication]. *For the first few days, it was heaven. Then, he got even more whiny and difficult to control, and he was having scary night sweats.*

We talked to the doctor again and he wanted to increase the meds. I think we tried that too, but continued to be alarmed by the overall side effects [most common: confusion, dizziness, impaired concentration/speech/language, nervousness, sedation, sleepiness, abdominal pain]. *So, the doctor suggested Depakote* [another anti-convulsant, sometimes used to treat bipolar disorder; has a long list of potentially life-threatening side effects]. *He felt Danny had a mood disorder. Keep in mind that all of these appointments were 15 minutes long or by e-mail.*

The doctor said that we couldn't give Danny any other SSRI because of his reaction to the Zoloft and that the Depakote might cause him to get a mild tremor and we would have to change meds if he did. Since I am a therapist, I drew the line there. I knew Danny wasn't bipolar—not even close. He obviously had sensitivity to medication.

I decided at that point I would not give my son any more drugs. I wrote to your web site and got advice and the rest is history.

Brenda later wrote to me that they still have occasional issues, but these issues are handled better now that they have an approach that truly fits their son's dynamics. This, in the end, is the sign of a family that has healed. Uniformly "good" and docile behavior is not.

Also, it is fairly common for human beings to adapt to foreign substances. What has worked for a month or two may one day not continue to be effective. Early studies on animals found that the calming effects of low-dose stimulants wore off within 16 weeks.

In the experimental process where a doctor attempts to find the *right* medication, the child becomes an *it,* a real life victim of a system that isn't working, as do the parents, hoping and praying for a solution, feeling all too reliant on misguided expert opinions.

24 The so-called "therapeutic" effect of stimulant drugs is really the creation of obsessive-compulsive behaviors.

One of the creepiest aspects of these medications is the obsessive-compulsive behaviors they often elicit in children. The child can become *perseverative,* compulsively persisting with meaningless activities. Kids on stimulants often become mentally rigid, their thinking becomes inflexible, and their focus may become overly narrow. Studies have shown that behaviors such as these occur to some degree in nearly one-half of all children treated with stimulant medications.

To parents and teachers who have been dealing with a difficult child for years and are at their wit's end, this kind of behavior may be a welcome respite. Instead of having to watch little Joseph like a hawk 24 hours a day, and instead of having to shout and plead and punish and argue at every turn, the parent can suddenly leave him to play with his Legos and not hear a peep for hours on end. Instead of having to repeatedly discipline little Jenny in class and deal with her disruptive behaviors, the teacher can reliably expect her to sit bent over her worksheet without looking up for long periods of time.

In his book *Talking Back to Ritalin,* Peter Breggin, M.D., discusses a study by Borcherding and colleagues that examined obsessive-compulsive behaviors in children on Ritalin and Dexedrine.[5] Slightly over half of the 45 children in the study displayed such behaviors. One six-year-old on Dexedrine spent 36 hours straight playing with Legos and puzzles, without stopping to eat or sleep. An eight-year-old on Dexedrine became "frantically goal-oriented" and isolated. Two children compulsively buttoned and folded dirty laundry. Several children had perseverative (repetitious, extended) speech and excessive detail orientation. Others over-erased, clenched and pressed down too hard on pencils and crayons, were unable to stop activities at school or home, and compulsively cleaned, organized, or lined things up. And one 11-year-old raked leaves for seven hours, then stood under the tree and waited for more leaves to fall so that he could rake them individually.

The question is: can we justify drugging children so that we can take a load off ourselves and our children's teachers? Not when we know the facts about how harmful these drugs can be. While some of these behaviors might sound less than horrifying to a beleaguered parent (particularly the ones involving household chores!), in my opinion they reflect a child's pained and uncomfortable inner status and are caused by the drugs used to treat the children's so-called "disorder." Perseverative behaviors are not a reflection of a child manifesting inner health. If a drug to treat ADHD causes OCD (obsessive-compulsive disorder), we are not doing the child a service by prescribing a stimulant medication.

NOTES

1. Excerpt from www.insiderreports.com/storypage

2. ncpamd.com/ADDComorbidity.htm

3. Mary Ann Block, "Violence and psychiataric drugs," at www.block-center.com/pages/pages_news.asp#4

4. Lauren Slater, *Opening Skinner's Box: Great Psychological Experiments of the 20th Century*, WW Norton and Co., New York, 1964

5. BV Borcherding, et al, "Motor/vocal tics and compulsive behaviors on stimulant drugs: Is there a common vulnerability?" *Psychiatric Research*, 33:83-94

Section Two
Damaging
Physical Side Effects

THE PHYSICAL SIDE EFFECTS OF RITALIN use are far worse than most families are ever told. Some information is usually shared about physical side effects, but parents whose children suffer serious side effects often report that they weren't given the full story before they filled their child's prescription. In many instances, side effects of the drugs are attributed to the child's "illness." Some children end up being given progressively higher doses of stimulants, or stronger and more dangerous drugs are added to counter these seemingly new manifestations of their "disease"—potentially condemning them to a lifelong regimen of psychotropic drugs along with the almost equally damaging stigma of mental illness.

Physicians who prescribe Ritalin and drugs like it are rarely well-apprised about the possibly damaging effects of these medications. In much of the promotional material that can be found about ADHD drugs, journalists and physicians claim that "we don't really know *how* these medicines calm hyperactive children and help them focus; we only know that they WORK."

To the contrary, we *do* know how they work, but telling someone that you are causing a neurotransmitter imbalance in a child's brain to drug him into submission—just doesn't sound like good medicine.

The manufacturers and distributors of ADHD drugs have conspired with physicians, patient advocacy groups like Children and Adults with ADD (CHADD), and even with schools to convince parents that these side effects are not really anything they need to concern themselves with.

Drugs are designed to target, as specifically as possible, a single physiological variable. A perfectly designed ADHD drug would do nothing but rein in the child's unacceptable behaviors, preserving his creativity and intensity; but the drugs we have don't work so specifically. They alter many aspects of the child's biochemistry, and the results are side effects.

Drug side effects are like an overflowing teacup: the cup itself is the "disease state" that is being treated, and we want to fill it to the brim without it overflowing. As you will see, drugs that alter the function of the central nervous system have far-reaching effects throughout the body—lots of tea overflowing onto the tablecloth. The cleanup not only gets dicey but the tablecloth inevitably shows the wear and tear of toxicity and staining.

Stimulant drugs appear to cause permanent physical changes in some people. As with any drug that alters the neurotransmitter systems that conduct the delicate business of the nervous system, there is real potential for permanent changes in levels of these neurotransmitters.

This section only touches upon a few of the possible side effects of stimulant drugs.

Excerpts from *Precautions, Warnings, Drug Interactions, and Adverse Effects: Ritalin Package Insert* (from the FDA posted Ritalin drug insert at www.fda.gov/cder/foi/label/2002/18029slr032lbl)

Contraindications

Marked anxiety, tension, and agitation are contraindications to Ritalin, since the drug may aggravate these symptoms....

Warnings

Ritalin should not be used in children under 6 years, since safety and efficacy in this age group have not been established.... Although a causal relationship has not been established, suppression of growth (i.e., weight gain and/or height) has been reported with the long-term use of stimulants in children. Therefore, patients requiring long-term therapy should be carefully monitored. Ritalin should not be used for severe depression of either exogenous or endogenous origin. Clinical experience suggests that in psychotic children, administration of Ritalin may exacerbate symptoms of behavior disturbance and thought disorder. Ritalin should not be used for the prevention or treatment of normal fatigue states. There is some clinical evidence that Ritalin may lower the convulsive threshold in patients with prior history of seizures, with prior EEG abnormalities in absence of seizures and, very rarely, in absence of history of seizures and no prior EEG evidence of seizures. Safe concomitant use of anticonvulsants and Ritalin has not been established. In the presence of seizures, the drug should be discontinued. Use cautiously in patients with hypertension. Blood pressure should be monitored at appropriate intervals in all patients taking Ritalin, especially those with hypertension....

Usage in Pregnancy

Adequate animal reproduction studies to establish safe use of Ritalin during pregnancy have not been conducted.... Therefore, until more information is available, Ritalin should not be prescribed for women of childbearing age unless, in the opinion of the physician, the potential benefits outweigh the possible risks.

(continued next page)

Excerpts from *Precautions, Warnings, Drug Interactions, and Adverse Effects: Ritalin Package Insert.*

(continued from previous page)

Drug Dependence

Ritalin should be given cautiously to emotionally unstable patients, such as those with a history of drug dependence or alcoholism, because such patients may increase dosage on their own initiative. Chronically abusive use can lead to marked tolerance and psychic dependence with varying degrees of abnormal behavior. Frank psychotic episodes can occur, especially with parental abuse. Careful supervision is required during drug withdrawal, since severe depression as well as the effects of chronic overactivity can be unmasked. Long-term follow-up may be required because of the patient's basic personality disturbances.

Precautions

Patients with an element of agitation may react adversely; discontinue therapy if necessary. Periodic CBC, differential, and platelet counts are advised during prolonged therapy. Drug treatment is not indicated in all cases of this behavioral syndrome and should be considered only in light of the complete history and evaluation of the child. The decision to prescribe Ritalin should depend on the physician's assessment of the chronicity and severity of the child's symptoms and their appropriateness for his/her age. Prescription should not depend solely on the presence of one or more of the behavioral characteristics. When these symptoms are associated with acute stress reactions, treatment with Ritalin is usually not indicated. Long-term effects of Ritalin in children have not been well established….

Adverse Reactions

Nervousness and insomnia are the most common adverse reactions but are usually controlled by reducing dosage and omitting the drug in the afternoon or evening. Other reactions include hypersensitivity…; anorexia; nausea; dizziness; palpitations; headache; dyskinesia; drowsiness; blood pressure and pulse changes…; angina; cardiac arrhythmia; abdominal pain; weight loss during prolonged therapy…. In children, loss of appetite, abdominal pain, weight loss during prolonged therapy, insomnia, and tachycardia may occur more frequently; however, any of the other adverse reactions listed above may also occur….

25

High doses of stimulant drugs are known to cause high blood pressure, irregular heart rhythms, and damage to the nervous and cardiovascular systems. More than 100 children on Ritalin have died. Some of these deaths were directly attributed to heart damage done by long-term prescribed stimulant use.

In an article entitled "Effects of methylphenidate (Ritalin) on mammalian myocardial ultrastructure," Theodore A. Henderson, Ph.D., and W. Vernon Fischer, Ph.D., reported on a study of lab mice injected with methylphenidate (Ritalin) in which it caused heart lesions to form. These lesions were significant and persistent, even months after the Ritalin exposure stopped.[1]

What does this mean for the millions of children who take stimulants for years and years? Are we setting ourselves up for an epidemic of stimulant-induced heart disease a few decades from now? It seems within the realm of possibility.

Between the years 1990 and 2000, 569 children were reported hospitalized—38 with life-threatening problems—because of health concerns related to stimulant side effects. In that time, 186 deaths related to Ritalin use were reported to the FDA Medwatch program. (Medwatch is a voluntary reporting program, and it is estimated that only 10 to 20 percent of adverse drug events are reported.)

On March 21, 2000, Matthew Smith died suddenly while skateboarding at his home.[2]

He was 14 at the time and had been on Ritalin since he was seven. The cause of death? According to Oakland, Michigan, chief medical examiner Ljubisa Dracovic, a forensic pathologist, it was long-term use of Ritalin. During an autopsy, Dr. Dracovic found clear signs of small vessel damage that had cut off blood supply to Matthew's heart. The normal weight of a grown man's heart is about 350 grams; Matthew's heart was significantly enlarged, weighing 402 grams. There was no test aside from an EKG that could have detected this damage, and EKGs are not recommended for children on stimulant drugs. Since his reporting of Matthew's case to the FDA, Dr. Dracovic has received hundreds of communications from parents who are concerned about their children's chest pains, heart palpitations, and irregular heartbeats while on Ritalin. The rise in blood glucose and blood pressure that usually occurs with Ritalin therapy could increase risk of deadly atherosclerotic heart disease in children and young adults.

The potential for cardiac damage with Ritalin should come as little surprise, considering what is known about the effects of other stimulants—including cocaine and the now-banned weight-loss drug fenfluramine, which is chemically similar to Ritalin—on the heart.

It is well-known in medicine that stimulants cause hypertension, irregular heartbeat (which can be dangerous, even fatal), and extremely rapid heartbeat. The heart is not the only organ damaged by these drugs, either; Cyclert (pemoline), another stimulant prescribed for ADHD, has been linked with 13 cases of liver failure that either caused death or required transplant surgery.

Here's what I am fighting for in writing this book: the truth. When was the last time a parent showed up at their child's psychiatric evaluation and was told the full version of the truth when handed a prescription for a stimulant medication: "Oh, by the way, Ritalin is a Class II narcotic, chemically equivalent to cocaine AND, by the way, occasionally children die merely from taking their prescribed dosage AND, by the way, your child, by virtue of taking this medication, will have twice the risk of future drug abuse . . . and if they do go down that road, they will start typically at a point beyond the normal entry level of abuse . . . AND by the way, your child will have an almost 50% chance of developing symptoms of Obsessive-Compulsive Disorder within the first year of taking this medication." That's what I'm fighting for...the truth, so that parents can make well-informed decisions instead of being railroaded by a combination of frustration, pressure and misinformation.

26 Stimulants may also kill or cause permanent damage by affecting the brain in dangerous ways.

Other studies have shown that Ritalin causes brain atrophy, and there is significant evidence that stimulants cause permanent changes in brain chemistry. Studies of monkeys given amphetamines show that these drugs, when used long-term, cause damage to cerebral (brain) blood vessels, neuron (brain cell) death, and microhemorrhages (leakage of blood from tiny blood vessels in the brain). Stimulant drugs change behavior by increasing the presence of neurotransmitters—including dopamine, serotonin, and norepinephrine—in the spaces between brain cells. This does not correct an imbalance, but creates one. If a child isn't "biochemically imbalanced" before using Ritalin, she *will* be—starting the day she swallows the first pill.

In his book *Talking Back to Ritalin*, Dr. Breggin discusses research that shows a lasting loss of dopamine and serotonin receptors in the brain in response to stimulant therapy. This loss of receptor activity is the brain's effort to re-balance itself as it is thrown out of whack with neurotransmitter-altering drugs. In the end, this receptor loss could explain drug tolerance and could cause lifelong dulling of neurotransmitter activity—especially if the drug is started when the child is very young.

Another tragic story is that of 12-year-old Stephanie Hall as recounted in the CBS program *"Hard Copy."* She had been taking Ritalin during the school year since the first grade. Throughout the years, she had suffered from chronic headaches, nausea, and stomachaches, none of which she experienced on weekends or in the summers when she did not use Ritalin. Stephanie also exhibited poor coordination, mood swings, disconnectedness, and bizarre behavior. For example, at age seven she bolted from an after-school day care, ran across a five-lane highway full of traffic, shouted that she was "ten-and-a-half now," bought a newspaper, and brought it several blocks to where her grandmother worked before snapping out of what seemed to be full-blown psychosis. *None* of these symptoms existed before Stephanie took Ritalin.

She hallucinated that she saw blue and red angels with four wings and exhibited signs of Tourette's syndrome, cursing uncharacteristically at classmates. Her parents believed that increasing her medication was the only way to control her, and her dosage was doubled in the days before her death. She died in her sleep. (Both Stephanie's and Matthew's stories are on the web site www.ritalindeath.com.)

The side effects Stephanie experienced point to the very real possibility that long-term Ritalin use causes damage to the brain. Some experts have put forth the theory that Stephanie—whose cause of death was listed as "natural causes"—may have suffered from Ritalin-induced encephalopathy (brain dysfunction).

For every child who dies from being medicated for ADHD or other "disorders," how many more suffer less-than-fatal—but still significant—damage or toxicity to their bodies? What impact will that damage have later in their lives? Will these children be more vulnerable to heart disease later on? We don't know—and as long as we don't know, we have no business forcing these medications on children.

It is my belief that parents deserve to be told about the possible side effect of death prior to being given a prescription. If I were a parent in this situation, I would want to know nothing less than the whole truth. In the dozens of medication evaluations that I have attended, despite well-intentioned doctors trying to do their level best, never has a parent been told anything close. At most they are informed that there may be issues related to weight loss and possible problems with rebound effect and sleep, but no red alerts to any potential problems that are more drastic.

27

Ritalin can cause loss of appetite, weight loss, and stunting of growth in children.

Up to 22 percent of kids on Ritalin lose weight. With childhood obesity on the rise, there are those who might not consider the loss of appetite and weight to be an *adverse* effect. But some children lose significant amounts of weight—enough to dramatically alter their appearance. On message boards on the Internet, many parents plead for advice on how to get their children to eat while on stimulant drugs. One desperate mother wrote that her 12-year-old son's weight had fallen from 73 pounds to 57 pounds in a year's time. When she told her son's psychiatrist that she wanted to discontinue the Concerta (long-acting methylphenidate) her son had been taking, the doctor told her he would rather add a medication to encourage his appetite. (The boy was also taking drugs to treat a seizure disorder and obsessive-compulsive disorder.)

It's hard enough as it is to get children to eat healthy foods, and when a child never really gets hungry, parents may not be able to get him to eat the foods that will best promote better mood, focus, and behavior naturally. Junk food and other highly processed foods have actually been targeted as a major factor in ADHD. Suppressing a child's appetite with stimulants may make it impossible for parents to "clean up" the child's diet.

Stimulant medications also significantly reduce a child's interest in drinking water. Water intake is so utterly vital to healthy functioning and the body's normal ongoing detoxification. This reduced water intake, combined with the extreme inherent toxicity of substances such as stimulant medications, puts children at further risk.

Stimulant-induced appetite loss may end up affecting adult height. Ritalin and other stimulant drugs prescribed for ADHD inhibit the production of growth hormone, a hormone that promotes the building of bone and muscle. This occurs because an overabundance of the neurotransmitter dopamine causes a suppression of growth hormone in the pituitary gland. So-called pituitary dwarfism is caused by a lack of growth hormone.

Not only does Ritalin interfere with growth hormone's effects on height, but it also slows the growth of organs, including the brain. Some studies show that the size of the head is reduced in animals given long-term Ritalin, and other evidence from animal studies demonstrates that the thyroid gland, pituitary gland, adrenal gland, and testicles reduce in size with methylphenidate administration.

Children on Ritalin may grow almost a half-inch per year more slowly than their non-drugged counterparts. Proponents of Ritalin point out that research shows a rebound in growth after the drug is stopped. This has been demonstrated in several studies, but this doesn't mean that the drug isn't causing harm to the child. No one knows the long-term consequences of slowing down, then speeding up, a child's growth. The later the drug is stopped, the less likely the child's growth will undergo a rebound. Many children continue to take stimulant drugs into adolescence, and they may well end up significantly shorter than they would have been otherwise.

Here's what a child interviewed on PBS's *"Merrow Report"* said regarding Ritalin use and his appetite:

Like if they're going to give me my Ritalin, I'm going out for dinner or something, I'll tell them not to give it to me or something, just let me eat, I can be fine, and then my mom like brings it up when we're out at dinner, oh you need your Ritalin you're so active and I'm like, no, I want to eat. It's just messed up. I hate, I hate taking Ritalin.

28 Brain shrinkage may be another adverse effect of Ritalin.

Dr. Breggin writes in an Internet article entitled "Suppressing the Passion of Children":

There is reason to be concerned about brain tissue shrinkage as a result of long-term Ritalin therapy, similar to that associated with neuroleptic treatment. A 1986 study by Henry Nasrallah and his colleagues of "Cortical Atrophy in Young Adults with a History of Hyperactivity," published in Psychiatric Research,[3] *found the brain pathology in more than half of twenty-four young adults. Since all of the patients had been treated with psychostimulants, "cortical atrophy may be a long-term adverse effect of this treatment" (p. 245). One study is suggestive rather than conclusive, but there remains a cause for concern.*[4]

Dr. Nasrallah's study looked at 24 young adults with history of hyperactivity and Ritalin use. He used CT scans to evaluate brain size, and compared the results with 27 age-matched control subjects who had never been diagnosed with ADHD or given stimulant drugs. The hyperactive subjects had significantly greater frequency of cortical atrophy, or shrinkage of the frontal area of the brain where complex thought takes place.

Many of those who wish to support the biological basis of the ADHD "disorder" shouted that this was the proof they had been waiting for—that ADHD brains are *different* from "normal" brains—when in truth, the study did not demonstrate that the brains of the non-stimulant-using subjects with ADHD were abnormal in any way.

29 Disfiguring tics that may or may not go away can be another byproduct of Ritalin use.

Here's the story of one acquaintance of mine. It's one of many hundreds of similar stories from parents who gave their kids Ritalin without having had the risks fully disclosed to them and before learning of alternatives like *The Nurtured Heart Approach*:

My stepson was a real handful as a kid. Even at only five years of age, he was the cause of much eye-rolling, head-shaking, and barely controlled fury on the part of teachers and parents. He would impulsively hit and push other children. The slightest setback would cause him to burst into hysterical tears. He always seemed to be wound so tight, and the smallest thing could set him off. He would always have to get really close to others—he seemed to have no sense of physical boundary or "personal space." Getting in other people's space somehow seemed to soothe him, but it drove us crazy, and started a lot of hitting and kicking fights between he and his younger brother. All the kids at school were scared of him. He couldn't make friends. It was terrible.

By the time he was six, his teacher was telling his mom that she would have to either put him on Ritalin or have him placed in a special education classroom. She hated to do it but capitulated. No one gave her any other options that could work as fast as they had to in order to keep her son out of special education. She gave him half the dose they recommended and didn't give it at all on weekends or vacations. She told him it was a "behavior pill," never told him there was anything wrong with him, just tried to cast it in as positive a light as possible. It did calm him down and he was able to stay in a normal class, which was good because on all fronts he was very bright.

Then, the tics started. First, there were these strange guttural sounds in his throat. They were annoying and we asked him what he was doing and if he could stop. (Of course, no one told us he might start having tics because of Ritalin.) He tried to stop but couldn't, poor guy—as if he didn't already have enough to worry about! Then, he started doing this thing where he'd open his mouth reeeeeally wide and bug his eyes out. That was especially charming during meals. From there, he became a mess of tics. Some were audible, some just physical, but they were very obvious.

He'd work so hard to control them while in school, and then once home he'd "release" them and he'd tic like mad until he fell asleep at night. I remember putting a baby monitor in the kids' room so I could hear my daughter at night and hearing him just laying there in bed having tics for a full half-hour before falling asleep.

*His mom stopped giving him Ritalin in his sixth year, and the tics contin-
ued. They'd get a little better, then worse again. We asked the doctor about
what to do. She referred him to a neurologist, who diagnosed him with
Tourette's syndrome and told us that all we could do was give him Prozac to
control the tics! "Will they go away?" we asked. "Maybe...maybe not," we
were told. We were told that about 2 of 3 kids with Ritalin-induced
Tourette's outgrow it. Not great odds.*

*Thank goodness, they did disappear. We were lucky. My stepson has
outgrown the tics and most of his other difficulties. We had to weather a lot
of rough spells between then and now, but we all teamed up to try to help,
and its working. He's 12 now and a joy to have around—and NOT because
of Ritalin!*

30 Ritalin may cause insomnia.

Parents who rely on stimulants to control their children run into a catch-
22 around bedtime. On one hand, some intense kids rebound when they
come off their last daily medication dose. Their symptoms re-emerge with a
vengeance just at the time they need to be settling down for bed. If the last
dose is given too late, however, the drug may cause insomnia.

One woman had a newborn daughter and an eight-year-old girl who had
been diagnosed with ADHD. She had taken a cautious approach when it
came to medicating her child, but felt that the girl's impulsivity and hyperactivity endangered her newborn. First, her daughter was prescribed Concerta;
this form of long-acting methylphenidate caused her daughter to clench her
jaw and act like a "zombie." She was then switched to Ritalin, 5 mg twice a
day; this worked for a while, but the child began to have bad stomach aches
"ALL the time." The next drug they tried was Strattera, at 25 mg, which
helped her concentrate a bit better in school but had no effect on her impulsivity or hyperactivity. She complained that she hated her life while on this
drug. A new doctor prescribed 10 mg a day of extended-release Adderall.
The result: loss of appetite and insomnia that kept her up until two or three
a.m. She was more focused and controlled, but she'd crash when the medicine wore off and would be sleepy during the daytime. Finally, the mom
agreed to give Ritalin twice a day, and her daughter's appetite and sleeping
ability returned—but so did the stomachaches.

A mother of eight-year-old ADD-diagnosed triplet boys had herself been
diagnosed with ADD. At the time of this mother's Internet posting, all of
them were on different medications after trying several combinations and

experiencing untoward effects: the mom on an antidepressant plus dexedrine; one child on Strattera; another child on Prozac and about to try Ritalin in addition (Adderall "kept him awake all night long, chattering a million miles a minute"); and the third son's medication yet to be determined.

I wonder what we would all be doing if all of these pharmaceutical cocktails simply were not an option. Would the schools and homes of these intense children fall into complete chaos and strife? Perhaps—but probably not for long. We'd figure out some other way to deal with these issues. Would we be so ready to diagnose our children with brain disorders if these powerful drugs didn't exist or were off-limits to children? Highly unlikely. In the majority of cases, all of this pharmaceutical juggling just isn't necessary, as you'll see later.

31 The first generation of long-term Ritalin users is reaching adulthood, and case studies indicate that these adults have been permanently harmed by these drugs.

There have been reports of chronic insomnia, depression, and reduced sperm count in adults who have taken Ritalin long-term. One woman wrote on an ADHD message board: "*My boyfriend was on Ritalin for several years as a kid, and he heard that it can cause a low sperm count. Seems that he heard right.*" Other adults who used Ritalin as children report their belief that the drug has permanently altered them. Some can't explain exactly how, but instinctively they know that they have been damaged by long-term use of this drug.

When we give stimulants to children (or adults, for that matter), we alter the balance of neurotransmitters in their brains. Their brains then change in an effort to adapt to the drug's effects, decreasing production of serotonin and dopamine—creating a true biochemical imbalance where there once was none. Most of the research indicates that nervous system cells decrease their production of neurotransmitters to try to move intracellular neurotransmitter levels back toward normal, and receptor sites for these neurotransmitters become less active. This happens in adults, and *we have every reason to suspect that the problem is worse in the still-growing brains of children.* In fact, a whole scientific field—developmental toxicology—has evolved to study the interactions between drug therapies and the processes of physical, cognitive, and emotional growth.

Here is a heartbreaking Internet posting from a mother who gave her son Ritalin for several years, followed by other drugs:

"*...he is now 21, has problems waking...I took him to our physician, who now tells us that there are several case studies about the long-term* *effects of Ritalin. Since our son was one of the first cases, they are watching him closely. They are finding that Ritalin changes brain chemistry in ways that, over time, cause sleeping patterns to change for the worse. Our son will now be on antidepressants for life because of the use of this drug. The effect of years of Ritalin has "reversed" the chemicals in his brain...instead of being hyper, he's now the opposite."*

No one knows whether these effects are long-lasting or permanent, but if they are, it would explain why adults who have taken Ritalin during childhood and adolescence might suffer permanent brain changes.

32 Ritalin has been found to reduce blood flow to all areas of the brain by 25 to 30 percent.

Positron electron tomography (PET) studies performed at the Brookhaven National Laboratory in Upton, New York, show clearly what is already known about stimulants like Ritalin: they cause blood vessels to constrict. Thirty minutes after an injection of Ritalin, blood vessels clamp down and the flow of blood through them is decreased. These kinds of studies don't use high doses of Ritalin; the researchers are careful to give only enough to reproduce the blood concentrations of the drug that can be expected with the usual dose given to human patients.

Does this have any effect on the brain long-term? Yes, according to research that includes a recent study by Joan Baizer and colleagues at the University of Buffalo.[5] Dr. Baizer found that Ritalin causes long-term brain changes similar to those caused by amphetamines and cocaine. These drugs all appear to cause changes in the genetic makeup of brain cells. This could be due to blood flow restriction or other factors.

Restricting blood flow to the brain during crucial developmental periods may well have lasting effects on brain size, or on less obvious but no less important aspects of brain structure. Dr. Breggin writes:

Parents are sometimes told that methylphenidate can suppress growth (height and weight), but the explanation is usually given in a manner calculated not to frighten them. Much of the brain's growth takes place during the years in which children are given this drug; but doctors don't tell parents that there are no studies of the effect of this growth inhibition on the brain itself. If the child's body is smaller, including his head, what about the contents of his skull? And if size can be reduced, what about more subtle and perhaps immeasurable brain deformities?[6]

33 Withdrawal and rebound effects go hand-in-hand with Ritalin use.

The danger of withdrawal effects is generally understated by physicians. Ritalin—even the longer-acting form of the drug—is short-acting: it's designed to wear off at the end of the day so that the child ideally can get to sleep. When the drug wears off, the child may display withdrawal symptoms, including depression, irritability, exhaustion, even suicidal feelings. These are the same symptoms displayed by people who are addicted to "uppers" and that cause these addicts to scramble for more drugs when their current dose wears off.

If a child misses a dose, the child's withdrawal response may overwhelm the parents. The parents haven't been given detailed explanation of how to recognize a withdrawal response, and they often mistakenly interpret the child's symptoms as affirmation that he really DOES need the medication. In some cases, the child is diagnosed with additional psychological disorders and medicated with increasingly stronger drugs. When parents intuit that the drugs, not the child, are the problem, and insist on withdrawing all drugs and letting the child's physiology return to normal, they are often subjected to coercion by doctors and teachers who think they know better.

34 Shrinkage of the penis and testicles can occur in males as well as loss of libido and erectile or ejaculatory problems later in life.

Lack of libido and ejaculatory dysfunction aren't exactly worrisome problems in children. But there is some anecdotal evidence that long-term use of Ritalin in children and adolescents can set them up for sexual problems in adulthood. This makes sense, considering the integral roles the neurotransmitters play in orchestrating libido, sexual response, and orgasm. Science continues to support the theory that the brain is the most important sexual organ. Stimulants unbalance brain function.

These side effects aren't well-known and are probably not common. According to what I've heard and read from people who report sexual side effects with stimulants, it's more common to see these side effects in people who take Adderall.

Here's a posting about Adderall, which I found at www.familyeducation.com:

I am an adult male and have been taking this drug for a while. I'm not sure the positives outweigh the negatives. On the positive side, the drug undeniably has helped me to focus on nearly any task. However, I have experienced the following negative side effects: (1) The tendency to get "locked up" in repetitive or unimportant tasks, at significant times, missing the big picture. (2) Anxiety, and/or development of a "glazed-over" look. (3) Very significant shrinkage of my penis and testes. This shrinkage seems to reverse 2-3 days after discontinuing the medication. I could only find a single post on the Internet, indicating that this likely occurs because Adderall is a vasoconstrictor [causes blood vessels to constrict and decrease blood flow]. *This has been my experience at 40 mg/day, after 2-3 weeks of use.*

It is well-documented that cocaine often has a dual and daunting impact of stimulating sexual desire while making sexual performance difficult if not impossible. It is also well documented that stimulant medications like Ritalin are chemically equivalent to cocaine. Why risk diminishing the pleasure these children can experience later in life when their lives are already so complicated? Why set them further adrift?

35 There is recent evidence that Ritalin may cause cancer.

In 1995, the results of a study (funded by taxpayers, not drug companies) by the National Toxicology Program (NTP) were published. Adult mice were fed Ritalin over a two-year period at dosages comparable to those prescribed to children. The mice developed a statistically significant incidence of liver abnormalities and tumors, including highly aggressive rare cancers known as hepatoblastomas. The NTP concluded that Ritalin is a possible human carcinogen and recommended the need for further research.

While still insisting that the drug is safe, the FDA admitted that these findings signal "carcinogenic potential" and required a statement to this effect in the drug's package insert. Even the *Physician's Desk Reference* admits there is evidence on the carcinogenicity of Ritalin but states that "the significance of these results is unknown." According to Samuel S. Epstein, M.D., the American Academy of Pediatrics has endorsed use of the drug, ignoring clear evidence of the drug's cancer risks of which "parents, teachers, and school nurses, besides most pediatricians and psychiatrists, still remain uninformed and unaware."[7]

Dr. Epstein goes on to state: "Concerns on Ritalin's cancer risk are more acute in view of the millions of children treated annually with the drug and the escalating incidence of childhood cancer, by some 35% over the last few decades...."

A recent study on the same topic by Texas researchers was the first one involving humans. After only three months, every one of a dozen children treated with Ritalin had a threefold increase in chromosome abnormalities

53

associated with increased risks of cancer. The study's principal investigator acknowledged that this "doesn't mean that these kids are going to get cancer, but it does mean they are exposed to an additional risk factor...."[8] The results of even this small study make more investigation imperative.

With even this amount of evidence of a possible connection between Ritalin and cancer, why take a chance if it's not absolutely the *only* recourse available?

NOTES

1. Published in the *American Journal of Cardiovascular Pathology*, 1994; 5(1):68-78

2. www.ritalindeath.com

3. H Nasrallah, et al, "Cortical atrophy in young adults with a history of hyperactivity in childhood," *Psychiatry Research* 1986;17:241-6.

4. http://www.sntp.net/ritalin/ritalin_breggin.htm#7

5. Joan Baizer, results of study presented at the 2001 Annual Meeting of the Society for Neuroscience, San Diego, CA, November 10-15.

6. Peter Breggin, Ginger Ross Breggin, "The hazards of treating 'attention-deficit/hyperactivity disorder' with methylphenidate (Ritalin)," *The Journal of College Student Psychotherapy* 1995;10(2):55-72.

7. Samuel Epstein, M.D., from www.preventcancer.com

8. Paul Wenske, Knight Ridder News Service, article in *Virginian-Pilot*, 3-13-05

Section Three
Damage to the Relationship between Parent and Child

DO NOT WISH TO CASTIGATE PARENTS WHO DECIDE TO USE RITALIN or related medications. Parents who readily agree to medicate their children are doing so because they don't fully comprehend the risks and simply trust the advice and direct information they are given. Doctors, schools, and drug companies have done a stellar job of making these drugs seem totally necessary, beneficial and safe.

Many parents who decide to give Ritalin to their child have gone through an agonizing decision making process. They don't want to medicate their child—not necessarily because they know how truly bad these drugs are—but because they have a gut feeling that it's just wrong.

Some parents have done extensive research and recognize the risks, but they struggle every day with their child's behaviors. They are ashamed and embarrassed by the commotion the child frequently causes. Poor reports from teachers...angry reports from other parents—"Your Tommy pushed my Jimmy so hard he fell and hit his head!"...veiled contempt at the grocery store as the child careens out of control for the umpteenth time that day...all cause parents to reach a breaking point where they see the medication as a necessary evil.

Let me emphasize again that I would not be writing this book if I did not have a viable alternative to medications. The majority of parents do not have to choose between having an out-of-control child and giving her medications that can cause physical and emotional harm. (See Reason 101)

That having been said, let's look at some of the damage Ritalin and related medications, as well as the "diagnosis" of ADHD, can do to the relationship between parent and child—arguably the most important relationship that either party will ever have.

36 By controlling a child's behavior with medication, we are forever changing that child's view of himself and the view his parents have of him.

An ADHD diagnosis is stigmatizing in and of itself. Because it is widely (and incorrectly) regarded as an actual disease state, the person who is diagnosed begins to see himself as ill. The parents, too, can come to view their child as someone with a chronic illness that has no real cure, and their behavior toward the child may change in subtle or not-so-subtle ways. A child might, in essence, be "allowed" to make poor choices because "she can't help it—she has ADHD."

Here is the story of a young man who was on Ritalin from first grade until his entry into college. The names and some details have been changed. This is only one of dozens of stories like this that I have been told or read in discussion boards on the Internet.

Taking Ritalin for over 10 years has caused me irreversible damage, both socially and emotionally. My parents insist that it helped me, but I am furious at them for giving me drugs when I was really just lonely and depressed and clueless about how to relate to other people.

My parents just weren't there for me. They were both distant. On Ritalin I wasn't hyperactive—I was psychotic. I needed attention but had no clue about how to get it. I would make a fool of myself, acting out and doing all kinds of inappropriate things. Only when I found marijuana did I stop feeling so completely like an outcast—I didn't have any better social functioning, but I didn't care, either.

Then, I found out about the risks of Ritalin, which no one had told me about and which I don't think my parents knew about, either. I was enraged. I got stoned and ended up in jail for vandalism. My life is still a shambles; I haven't been able to hold a job for long and have suicidal thoughts and still no friends.

The bottom line is that I feel like a robot, a zombie without any personality. All through the years I should have been building that, my parents chose to drug me to keep me from misbehaving instead of trying to be better parents.

I can't imagine a parent who would want to have their child harboring these feelings.

The frustration that motivates parents to allow their child to be put on medication is the same frustration that can be a driving force to find and apply more powerful parenting approaches.

One of the worst repercussions of medication is that the original problems go into a holding pattern. Later in life, no matter how well-intended parents and child are about being "connected," there is really a "disconnect" that is hard to overcome in more than a superficial way. There is substantial grief and loss in this scenario.

The best outcome of childhood acting-out is that parents discover a way (yes, it exists!) to help their child feel successful and strong on the inside. Then, the same intensity that once went awry becomes a gift. The result? The parent-child relationship flourishes and the child feels essentially cherished and supported.

The same phrases, with slight variations, come up repeatedly in case studies on Ritalin. Children report that they feel "numb," controlled by the drug, "like a baby," or "dumb" because they "need" a drug to behave acceptably. Many don't have the ability to express why, but they know that they don't want to take it anymore.

Here's an exchange from an episode of the PBS *"Merrow Report"* between the interviewer and a group of 'tween and teen kids who have taken Ritalin:

MATT: *When you're not on Ritalin, you take in so much more informa-tion, such a wide array and variety, that it, life's so much greater and more interesting than when you're taking it. And when you're on it, it focuses everything down to such a fine point that nothing's fun anymore, you're not the same person that you were.*

MERROW: *Do you like yourself when you're on Ritalin...*

DAVID: *No.*

MERROW: *Why do you say that so quickly?*

DAVID: *Because it's not the real, you're not you.*

MATT: *Bingo.*

ANDREW: *It's a fake person that the medicine's creating...When people bring it up, uh, you need more Ritalin, ADD, it just makes you feel stupid. Because they, they've been putting this on you for years, my parents have been putting it on me since first grade. It just makes me feel bad, saying oh, you have ADD, you need more medicine. My mom makes it a big deal of it and stuff and I don't think it's a big deal but she tells like all of her friends he's ADD, expect bad behavior and stuff and they just think you're stupid.*

MERROW: *They think you're....*

ANDREW: *You're just like, they think you're stupid because the medi-cine, the Ritalin, is making you smart and make you pay attention, and it's not you. Because they don't, they don't let you try it yourself, they let the Ritalin do the work for you.*[1]

37 Most parents who are given a Ritalin prescription for their child are not given full and detailed information about the pros and cons of using the drug.

The vast majority are led to believe that the drug is benign. When the child complains of side effects or feeling somehow not right while on the drug, the parent may disbelieve the child, leading to problems with trust on both sides.

Many parents drug their children without having been informed that stimulants can *cause* the "disorders" they are supposed to cure. Many physicians are ignorant of this fact, too. But it's well-established—although not well-publicized—that stimulants can bring out or worsen aggression, inattention, and hyperactivity in some children. Like any form of speed, Ritalin can cause children to become anxious and to have behavior that seems erratic. Physicians may interpret this kind of drug response as escalation of the "disease," or as evidence that they misdiagnosed the child. The child may be prescribed higher doses or a stronger medication, leading to what Dr. Breggin calls "a vicious circle of increasing drug toxicity."

Parents aren't usually told of the danger of permanent brain changes following long-term stimulant use. What will the "ADHD" child who has been given Ritalin or other stimulants feel when he finds out about this potential side effect? If this isn't a breach of trust, I don't know what is.

Trust is such an essential component of connectedness with oneself and others. With diminished trust, it is hard to live life with anything approaching fluidity—hard to accept your own inner voice and hard to accept the advice and wisdom of others. There is always a degree of suspicion, anger, and anxiety.

Many families who give their children drugs to control their behavior are participating in a chain-reaction of deceit: first, they are given incomplete information about risks and benefits by the physician, and then they give the child even more incomplete information. The parents consent to drug the child based on either incomplete information or outright misinformation, and the child has no choice but to comply in most instances—even if he feels he's being lied to.

38 Ritalin represents a "quick fix" mentality.

The parents feel good because they are *doing something* about the problem, even though what they are doing is not really fixing the problem at its root—they are just temporarily obscuring it by drugging the child.

One price paid for this illusion of a fix is that the parents are now much less likely to search for alternative solutions. Another downside: the parent isn't any wiser on how to best help the child to handle her intensity and impulsivity and life force. This remains a problem before the meds kick in each day and after they wear off. Yet another downside is that the child isn't any wiser about how to love herself, to derive benefit and pleasure from her intensity and to manage the greater-than-average magnitude of her life force.

An approach that resolves this problem at the core is the only permanent solution—one that preserves and embraces the child's intensity while helping the child to control less desirable behaviors.

It brings families together instead of blowing them apart. (See Reason 101.)

39 Rather than feeling victorious over a child's problems, parents end up feeling condemned or victimized by the drug "solution."

When we resist taking the easy way out presented by medications, we are forced to see what can be achieved by other means. Many parents who give in to the medication solution feel uneasy about this decision but say they just couldn't find any other way to deal with their challenging child. That's understandable because the medical community puts down alternatives. Methods like *The Nurtured Heart Approach* are not always marketed extensively, so knowledge of their existence is typically sparse.

Parents who view medication as an absolute last resort may try it and find that they're pleased with the perceived improvements. But they are prone to feeling somewhat guilty for not having found another way.

I hope that all parents faced with these issues will try *The Nurtured Heart Approach* for two reasons: 1) it really does work to shift the child to using his intensity in wonderful ways, even for extremely challenging children, and 2) it quickly allows parents to experience that all the changes are the result of their efforts. They wind up feeling like heroes. Parents and teachers are in the best position to be the heroes, because unlike the medicating doctors or the other professionals who may see a child in an artificial context, parents and teachers have built-in context, and meaning and relationship within that context. They can have heroic impact in much more powerful ways. And the best part is that, if they become the hero, so does the child.

Any challenging child, more so than less intense kids, needs crystal clear guidance, high level inspiration and a sense of how to succeed. Drugs do not teach them these vital lessons.

Medications short-circuit the process. When behaviors appear to improve, parents feel much less compelled to search for answers and are much less likely to find the gift of this intensive kind of guidance. The child is doomed to take Ritalin or other drugs indefinitely.

Other parents are lulled into a sense of security by doctors and teachers and "patient advocacy groups" like Children and Adults with Attention Deficit Disorder (CHADD)—all of which reassure them that the drugs are benign and necessary and the only viable medical solution. But many sense that it's not the truth, even though they are told things like, "Not giving an ADHD child Ritalin is like denying insulin to a diabetic." Statements like that fly in the face of scientific evidence.

Parents can wind up feeling a myriad of mixed and unsettling emotions, all of which can easily tarnish an optimal parent-child relationship. This is amplified when the medications that seemed to work initially begin to fail perhaps because of side effects or because undesirable behaviors begin to percolate and again become problematic.

40 Children feel fear when they sense that their parents can't handle them. They do not receive modeling of a healthy sense of power; they see the parents giving up, surrendering to using drugs to control their behavior.

What parent doesn't occasionally throw up her hands and use the television as a babysitter when she can't cope with the chaos? Ritalin and other psychotropic drugs represent a similar approach: in both cases, the parent is throwing in the towel and losing interest in more constructive, less harmful solutions. Typically, once medication has been introduced, not only does the parenting style remain the same, but the level of parental intervention into the child's life diminishes.

It is easy for a child in this situation to feel that her parent has relinquished control to the medications—just as it is easy for a child who is constantly babysat by the television to feel that what the TV has to say is more important than what her parents have to say. At some level the child senses that medications are not the answer and feels deadened by their effect.

The drug-as-babysitter scenario sets the child up to give up on himself. He is likely to replicate this scenario throughout adult life. He will be more likely to acquiesce to drugs and other poor choices in the future, rather than rallying reserves of inner strength when demanding situations present themselves.

In contrast, when a parent or teacher intervenes with a more powerful approach that fosters success, not only does the child walk away with a new portfolio of first-hand experiences of achievement, he also drinks in how to be powerful and resourceful within himself.

41 Single parents are more pressured to medicate. What does this say about the true value of medications and their role in our culture?

Single parents have it rough to begin with. They often have demands that impinge on their time and resources, and no one they can share these demands with. Unless they have a strong support system, they find themselves unable to optimally balance the demands of making a living and the demands of giving their children adequate time. Their kids are more likely to end up in day care (especially with welfare reform), which has been shown to increase risk of ADHD-like symptoms: the more time a child spends in day care, the greater his or her risk of eventually being diagnosed with and treated for this "disorder."

A child living in two separate households often has less consistency and structure in his life, and this further complicates behavioral problems. Then, when the child has ADHD "symptoms," the single parent may be in a more compromised position in terms of how to deal with it. She may end up at odds with the other parent over how to help the child.

It stands to reason that the child of a single parent is at greater risk—again, not because the child's brain is different, but because her circumstances are different!

Single parents are also more likely to see the long arm of the law reach in and snatch their children away when they don't follow the party line (i.e., give medication as the first resort, and don't stop even if there are scary side effects).

Here are some excerpts from testimony given at a meeting of the Medical Board of California (MBC) in January of 2002 by Fred Baughman, Jr., M.D.:[2]

Children and adults throughout California and across the country are told they have "brain diseases" and "chemical imbalances," when, in fact, they are entirely normal. They are made into 'medical patients' even though they have no medical diseases. Thus deceived, they are labeled, drugged, shocked, restrained, and institutionalized against their will. Parents who resist are deemed "negligent," "unfit" and have their children taken from them and put up for adoption, also in the name of "medical diagnosis and treatment." Exactly how many California children and parents this has happened to, I cannot be sure, but millions of parents across the US, including parents of divorce, have suffered 'custody relinquishment' of one degree or another to allow the psychiatric 'diagnosis' and 'treatment' of their child to proceed, unhampered.

Diane Booth of Las Gatos, California, one such parent, presently seeks refugee status in Canada, in hopes of one day seeing her 7 year-old son again. As is standard across California and the US, Diane's son, Vincent, was deemed ADHD/diseased/chemically imbalanced/and in need of a 'chemical balancer'—Ritalin—by public school personnel, psychiatrists/physicians, child protective service social workers and a local judge—all speaking as if with one voice—which, of course, they do.

Diane, the only parent in Vincent's life, had the temerity to question the validity of ADHD—the 'disease' and the 'treatment'—and the fact that Ritalin, they all deemed, was not just advisable, but mandatory. And that's all it took. Vincent, still entirely normal, although labeled, was whisked off to a psychiatric hospital where his mother's interference in his diagnosis and treatment could no longer be a factor. And that's where it stands. The court is now Vincent's parent. The court sees to it that, if nothing else, no one interferes with the Ritalin treatment of his ADHD, despite the fact that the Ritalin circulating throughout his brain and body was his first and only true disease/abnormality and despite the fact that when last seen by his mother he had developed Ritalin-induced tics—involuntary movements (never before present and, therefore, not idiopathic Tourette's syndrome).

Despite the rigors of single parenting in terms of time, logistics and fiscal concerns, transforming a challenging child without medication will be *easier* in some ways for a single parent. The single parent does not have to do things by "committee" or have the full coordination and cooperation of the spouse, but instead can launch **The Nurtured Heart Approach** in any number of optimal ways, without needing permission or collaboration. This ultimately makes it easier for the parent to have the desired impact.

42 There are instances where schools call on Child Protective Services to intervene based on parents' "medical negligence." The outcome can be devastating to families.

It is becoming alarmingly common for schools to contact Child Protective Services when parents refuse to medicate their child. I met a social worker in Minnesota in 2003 whose entire caseload was comprised of children who had been removed from their homes and placed in foster care because the parent or parents were considered medically negligent.

In the web site familyrightsassociation.com, Dr. Baughman reported these stories:

- In Albany, New York, Michael and Jill Carroll wanted to take their seven-year-old son Kyle off Ritalin because of side effects (insomnia and lack of appetite). When they told his school that they wished to do this, administrators called Child Protective Services alleging child abuse. Now, the Carrolls are on a statewide list of suspected child abusers, and Kyle is still on Ritalin—because these parents do not want to lose custody of their son. Jill is especially concerned about being on a list of child abusers because she is studying to become an early childhood education worker. (Karlin, Rick, "Ritalin Use Splits Parents, School," Albany *Times Union*, Sunday, May 7, 2000.)

- Also in New York: school officials called CPS when Patricia Weathers took her nine-year-old son off of a cocktail of medications that included Ritalin, Paxil, and Dexedrine—a drug combination that made the boy hallucinate. She ended up sending her child to a private school.

- Tammy Kubiak of Buffalo, New York, took her 12-year-old son off Ritalin and two other drugs that she felt caused him to become zombie-like. She ended up losing custody. Ms. Kubiak did not believe that ADHD or ODD (Oppositional Defiant Disorder) were real diseases, and told the court so—and because of this, **they removed all of her children from her home.**

- The school of divorced mom Cindy Gallagher's child exerted pressure on her to drug and label her son, Daniel. She was threatened with possibly losing her child to CPS because of medical neglect. She took her son out of public school and began to home school. Daniel did wonderfully, but on a visit back to New York to see his sister, who was living with the father, the legal guardian provided by CPS demanded that she leave Daniel in New York pending a psychiatric review and medication. The legal guardian gave full custody to the father (whom Ms. Gallagher believes to be abusive), who soon realized he could not handle them and wanted them to go back to their mother.

Medication takes the pressure off schools to rise to the occasion and find approaches that work. As long as the collusion between schools, pharmaceutical companies (supplying misinformation about the glories of medications), and social welfare continues to exist, schools will continue to drop the ball. The good news is that a growing number of schools are refusing to take the easy (and unsafe) way out.

43 When they give Ritalin to their child, parents inflict damage on that child's ability to have healthy relationships—with family and with others.

One of the most painful aspects of the spiral of negative response that normally occurs with ADHD pertains to relationships. Even if the child seems to have "improved" by virtue of Ritalin or other stimulant medications, the child still gets a bigger response from parents, teachers, and peers when some degree of negativity is transpiring. The child still feels relatively invisible when things are going right.

This predominant force of negativity has a long-term effect on important relationships and the trust that must be at their foundation. If this is not resolved—if the child is not taught by example that he can expect to be noticed and supported when he is behaving positively—the child will be drawn to other relationships centered on negativity. As the child becomes a teen and then an adult, he will continue to believe that the only way to get noticed and to be in relationships with others is via problematic behaviors and issues.

Perhaps the saddest aspect of ADHD treatment with medication is that relationships—arguably the part of life that makes it most worth living—are likely to be troubled and rocky because of this pervasive negativity. The child who has been drugged by his parents to control his behavior may never forgive or trust them again, and his ability to trust other important people may also be damaged.

There is residual damage to relationships even if the meds are working because the child receives praise from parents or teachers (and naturally likes the praise), but at the same time builds up resentment on the basis that "it isn't the real *me* being congratulated...I don't get the credit, it's the medication."

44 The decision to medicate can give rise to marital tensions, especially when one parent wants to give the drug and the other does not.

Often, parents have differing opinions on whether a child should be medicated. Considering the huge stake both parents have in the well-being of their child, it's no surprise that the "to medicate or not to medicate" dispute might turn into a major battle.

A family with an intense child may be stressed to the breaking point when this question arises. If the parent in favor of medication wins out and the child appears improved, things might settle down for a while as the other parent capitulates, saying, "Well, I guess you were right about the meds...she does seem a lot better when she's on them." Welcome changes may appear both at home and at school. There may be more compliance, less impulsivity, more cooperation, better schoolwork, and overall a much-needed break from chaos.

In most cases, however, the parents can't help but see that the child exhibits one or more of the physical or psychological side effects mentioned in the first two sections of this book: headaches, loss of appetite, sleep issues, stomachaches, or nausea. The parents may become divided once again, with little help offered from doctors (who minimize the problem of side effects at follow-up medication review sessions) or teachers (who sing medication's praises as it brings harmony to their overloaded classrooms). The pressure is on for the concerned parent to continue along for the ride.

My experience is that it gets harder and harder for parents in this situation to combat the fear of change. The lone voice of one parent with a nagging feeling that this is just not the right approach tends to get lost in the winds of the psycho-pharmaceutical way of doing things. In the end, even if the medication does enough harm to drive the parents away from its use, the rift may continue to be an open wound between spouses who really only wanted the best for their challenging child all along.

NOTES

1. http://www.pbs.org/merrow/tv/add/chadd.html

2. Fred Baughman, M.D., from http://familyrightsassociation.com/news/ archive/2003/dec/psychiatry_and_cps.htm

Section Four
Use and Abuse of Stimulant Drugs

R ITALIN AND OTHER STIMULANTS FOR ADHD ARE "SPEED"—neuropharmacologically identical to cocaine and methamphetamine. And as with drugs like these, Ritalin is subject to widespread abuse—by schoolchildren and even by health practitioners.

This doesn't make much sense at first light, because kids with ADHD almost never like being medicated. So why would so many abusers clamor for a drug that ADHD kids complain makes them feel zombie-like and not themselves?

The difference, I believe, has to do with being *forced* to take a drug to change and control behavior, as opposed to taking a drug illicitly for the purpose of getting high or improving alertness or concentration. Also, keep in mind that the dosage of Ritalin given for therapeutic use isn't sufficient to bring on a "high" feeling.

Using psychoactive drugs to control behavior puts us in a compromised position, especially when it comes to children. This practice brings up all kinds of questions: What is the impact of teaching a child that he needs a pill to "behave?" Will that child be more likely to use illicit drugs to cope with life's difficulties later on? What effects do these stimulant drugs, which are in the same drug family as illegal "uppers" and cocaine, have on a developing brain? Do they alter the nervous system in ways that make a child more vulnerable to addiction later on?

It's likely that just the diagnosis of ADHD has an effect on a child's risk of addictive behaviors. When we condemn a child's intensity, pathologize it and "treat" it, we are already setting that child up for problems as he struggles to form his identity.

45 It may be difficult for the child to get off the medication. He may develop a psychological and physical dependency on it, and stopping may lead to withdrawal symptoms (often mistaken for a need for more drugs).

According to Breggin and Cohen, in *Your Drug May Be Your Problem: Children, like adults, vary greatly in terms of the intensity of their withdrawal response when taken off stimulant drugs. Some children experience little more than rebound hyperactivity or tension for a few hours. Others,*

66

especially after months or years of exposure to drugs, may undergo an extensive and uncomfortable withdrawal. The manifestations of withdrawal also vary. Some children may exhibit increased rebelliousness, hyperactivity, and insomnia; others may display apathy and a greater need to sleep. (p.174)

The first stage of drug withdrawal is known as *rebound*. Parents who give Ritalin to their child know about rebound; it's the hyperactivity, nervousness, and anxiety that appear a few hours following the child's last daily dose of medication. Some children who don't take their drugs on the weekends or in the summer can exhibit rebound reactions that last for days, weeks, and even longer. This rebound may seem like evidence that the child *needs* the medication; in truth, it's evidence that the child's central nervous system has become adversely and profoundly affected by this foreign substance, perhaps addicted, and is trying to find its balance again in the absence of that substance.

Other possible stimulant withdrawal reactions include "crashing" depression, exhaustion, suicidal ideation, irritability, and even psychosis. Within one to three days of stopping the drug, a child may experience sleep disturbances, hostility, anger, fatigue, confusion, and agitation. Some children may sleep a great deal or eat huge amounts of food during withdrawal.

Older children and teens may find themselves conflicted and nervous about stopping the drugs. On the one hand, they would rather not take them and, on the other hand, they may have been told for years that they have a brain disease that requires this treatment. They may wish they could "behave" and focus without the meds, but they also may not, deep down, believe that they can. They may come to trust the medication at some point more than they trust themselves....despite the side-effects.

46 The medications given to children to modify their behavior are expensive, and getting them can be inconvenient.

When obtained legally, Ritalin costs around $70 a month. Strattera costs upwards of $100 a month. These costs may be covered by insurance, but for the increasing number of people who have limited or no insurance coverage, this can be a significant expense. Of course, a child might be able to turn this into a huge profit, selling their fifty-cent Ritalin tablets to others who wish to use it illegally at $2 to $5 apiece.

Because Ritalin is a Schedule II drug—which puts it at the same level of abuse potential as barbiturates, opium, heroin, cocaine and morphine—prescriptions cannot be filled by phone, and pharmacists are instructed to ask questions that can cause Ritalin purchasers to feel like they are being investigated for drug abuse.

The DEA must approve an annual production quota for all Schedule II drugs. This raises the fear, in those who rely upon such drugs, of a Ritalin shortage. In some states, Schedule II drug prescriptions must be written in triplicate for the purpose of monitoring their use. Doctors, particularly those who prescribe Ritalin in quantity, are inconvenienced by this requirement. So are many parents who must stop by the doctor's office every time the Ritalin needs to be refilled.

Sounds like addictive behavior to me—not just physical addiction at the level of the individual children, but also psychological addiction at the level of the system that relies so heavily on medications to suppress children's intensity, exploratory urges, and high energy.

 Ritalin is a very popular street drug. It is stolen and sold on school campuses around the nation.

The problem of Ritalin abuse is an alarming one, and it is growing. Kids who are forced to take Ritalin but would rather avoid it can take it to school and sell it to others. Children, teens, and young adults have discovered that it can be used to get high (by crushing and snorting or injecting it, or taking high oral doses) or to focus better on studying for exams or other schoolwork.

When used illegally, Ritalin may be called JIF, MPH, R-ball, Skippy, the "smart drug," or vitamin R, but it's the same drug that is prescribed to millions of schoolchildren.

Rates of Ritalin abuse are similar to those of cocaine abuse: in a year 2000 study of Massachusetts school children, 13 percent of 6,000 high school students and four percent of middle school students had abused Ritalin. It's on the DEA's list of top 10 most stolen prescription drugs. Users say that it gives a great "buzz," and they warn that tolerance develops so that the dose to achieve a high must continually increase.

A PBS *"Frontline"* report on April 10, 2001, revealed the following frightening facts:

- According to a 1994 study, more American high school students abused Ritalin than took the drug because it was prescribed to them.

- Another study found that in three states, 30 to 50 percent of adolescents in drug therapy centers had used Ritalin without a prescription.

- Yet another study—this one from the University of Indiana—revealed that of 44,232 ninth grade students surveyed, 6.8 percent had used Ritalin illicitly on at least one occasion.

- The DEA's "Drugs of Concern" bulletin puts Ritalin alongside cocaine, LSD, and Ecstasy.

Some Internet postings found on Erowid.com provide enlightenment about Ritalin abuse :

Ritalin can give you a buzz…me and a friend did it in high school. We used to snort 60-70 mg each. We had a hard time getting off the stuff for a few months. We did it throughout high school, from sophomore to senior year.

Another posting replies:

Yeah, I've been doing Ritalin 10 mg white pills for a while, usually about 2 times a week or so. Then I started using 20 mg Adderall, which were these tablets with little balls inside of it. I take usually 2 sometimes 3 in the morning and it lasts all day and then I can't sleep. I have been seeing some stuff like shadows on my wall at night. I have actually been trying to stop, but it's like I think about stopping and then I just keep doing it. Any easy ways of going about stopping and getting off it for a while?(or forever) Also if I sell it, how much should I sell it for?

And here was a "helpful" reply to the above:

Take a spoon and use it to crush up the little balls. Sniff those and you will be real hella good. Or if you are really gung-ho you can melt them down and shoot it up…usually, I sniff 60-100 mg of Ritalin at once. It's a lot of powder, but once you get it done, it kicks major. Your face and your arms go numb.

 On college campuses, Ritalin use is on the rise as a study aid by students who do not have ADHD.

College students are taking Ritalin as though it were a benign study aid. Some kids are so hooked on it that they will go to any length to get it, thinking that they won't be able to achieve in school without the focus it lends them. They go without sleep because they swallow or snort Ritalin at night to study. They become addicted. Some students even fake ADHD symptoms to try to get a legitimate prescription for the drug—and many are successful.

An article by Christopher Tennant at The College Site[1] reveals that "students like the drug so much…that fraternities are stockpiling it with the same vigilance they take to ensure they never run out of beer."

The current generation of young people has been dubbed "Generation Rx" for its psychological—and often physical—dependency on prescription drugs. These kids have grown up in a world where the biochemical imbalance theory rules, and they've taken it to heart. Sad? Try this drug. Anxious? Try this one. Restless, unfocused? Ritalin is your answer. Keep on juggling until you find just the right cocktail. But stay away from those illegal drugs—and don't you dare misuse the legal ones, either!

From an article by British writer Charlotte Raven:

Things were improving when a nice Harley Street psychiatrist prescribed me a little pick-me-up. But while the Ritalin made me work like a maniac, it also made me edgy and disconnected...The wonderful thing about Ritalin is that it acts like a barrister for your denial. When the rest of you is too worn and weary to offer another reason why you shouldn't accept how f***ed up you are, Ritalin argues persuasively that the appearance of coherence it allows you is proof that you are indeed OK. I was taking eight pills a day. Wurtzel [Elizabeth Wurtzel, author of the autobiographical works *Prozac Nation* and *More, Now, Again*], *at the height of her addiction, was downing 40.*[2]

Journalist Jeremy Laurance writes, "At a conference in New York in June on the ethics of cognitive enhancement, delegates suggested students in the future might have to be dope-tested and asked to hand in a urine sample with their exam paper to prove their results were due to hard work and not pharmacology."[3]

49 Children, teens, and young adults believe that a legal drug like Ritalin cannot be dangerously addictive or otherwise harmful.

Young people already tend to feel that they're invincible; no matter what they do, they won't sustain injury or die. When they see so many of their peers taking Ritalin with a doctor's prescription and the sanction of the world at large, they feel that taking it themselves poses no risk whatsoever.

Tragically, they are wrong.

The drug is addictive and often is a gateway drug that leads to use of more intense stimulants like cocaine. In some cases, teens who are taken off Ritalin after years of legally prescribed use turn to stronger stimulants and other illegal drugs.

Illicit users often start out by taking it orally, and as tolerance develops they move to snorting or injecting it to gain the desired "high." When snorted or injected, it quickly washes the brain with high levels of dopamine, and that pleasurable "buzz" is one the user wants (needs) to return to once the drug wears off. He begins to physically crave it as his brain's delicate neurochemistry is tossed into cycles of dopamine overexposure and dopamine lack.

Taking high doses of Ritalin causes agitation, tremors, hypertension, rapid or irregular heartbeat, and even psychotic episodes or hallucinations. The DEA reports that "addiction produced by methylphenidate abuse is neither benign nor rare in occurrence, and is more accurately described as producing severe dependence." At the very least, the college or high school student who chronically abuses Ritalin will suffer from impaired judgment, anxiety, and lack of impulse control. He or she may careen back and forth between euphoria and depression.

Crushing and injecting a drug that is meant for oral use exposes the user's circulatory system to binders and other contents of medicines meant to be swallowed and digested. The FDA has received reports of death and blindness caused by the injection of crushed Ritalin tablets since the 1970s. The International Narcotics Control Board, an agency of the United Nations, reported in 1996 that "the number of methylphenidate-related emergency room mentions for persons aged 10-14 has since 1990 increased more than 10 times."[4] One 19-year-old from Roanoke, Virginia, died of cardiac arrest after snorting Ritalin at a party.

50 On any given day in some communities, more Ritalin is in schools than in pharmacies.

Serious issues have arisen about the safe handling of these drugs in school settings. In some schools, children are allowed to take their medication themselves. In some places, one school nurse has to distribute meds for an entire district, racing around to several schools during the lunch hour.

There are few safeguards preventing theft of these drugs from school nurses' offices or other locations. One RN has seen "schools where medications for middle-school students were kept unlocked in a counseling office, and kids were allowed to walk in and take their own meds."

In 1993, I was working for the state mental health system in Arizona when a shortage of Ritalin occurred. The level of panic was unbelievable—and not just among parents who pinned their own sense of security as parents upon their children being medicated. Teachers, administrators, and mental health workers were just as panicked. Many frantically tried to procure this substance—the pediatric form of "mother's little helper"—from out-of-state or through other connections.

Wouldn't it be better to help our children using resources that don't run out: our intelligence, our empathy, and our love for our children? These resources, along with the application of strategies that work, are our only hope for breaking away from our addiction to the biological psychiatry model. (See Reason 101.)

51 Ritalin is chemically equivalent to cocaine.

Parents are seldom told that methylphenidate is "speed" and that it causes the very same effects, side effects, and risks as illegal amphetamine "uppers."

Find this hard to believe? The 1989 American Psychiatric Association's *Treatments of Psychiatric Disorders* states that cocaine, amphetamines, and methylphenidate are "neuropharmacologically alike" (p.1221). This text points out that abuse patterns are the same for all three drugs; that their clinical effects in laboratory tests cannot be distinguished from one another; and that they cause similar behaviors in addicted animals. The Food and Drug Administration classifies methylphenidate as a Schedule II drug—a category with high risk of addiction that includes opium, morphine, and barbiturates.

Cocaine and Ritalin bind to the same receptor site in brain cells; cocaine unbinds more rapidly than Ritalin, making the high more intense and the craving for more of the drug more powerful. But for those who cannot get cocaine or haven't yet discovered it, Ritalin will usually suffice. Ground and snorted, Ritalin produces a high strikingly similar to the high that comes from cocaine.

52 Conflicting research exists regarding Ritalin's effects on future risk of drug addiction.

Because Ritalin is a Schedule II drug that has potential for addiction, it has long been suspected that it could act as a "gateway drug" to other, more dangerous drugs. Some researchers suggest that the use of stimulants during childhood could sensitize receptors in the central nervous system, making the child more vulnerable to addiction to other stimulants later on. Some of the research has supported this suspicion, while other research has directly contradicted it. Let's look at the two major studies that support each side of the debate.

In 1999, University of California at Berkeley professor Nadine Lambert, the director of the School Psychology Program at the Graduate School of Education, completed a landmark study on childhood Ritalin use and the risk of addiction to cigarettes and cocaine in later life.[5] She had tracked 492 children—half with ADHD, half without—for nearly 30 years, and found that Ritalin use in ADHD kids was "significantly and pervasively implicated in cocaine dependence, in the uptake of regular smoking and daily smoking in adulthood, as well as lifetime use of stimulants and cocaine."

In her study group, nearly half of the ADHD kids who were given Ritalin became regular smokers by the time they were 17 years old. Only 30 percent of ADHD kids who did not take Ritalin ended up smoking. Smokers who had ADHD and were treated with Ritalin were twice as likely to abuse cocaine compared with those who never smoked and were not treated with Ritalin or other central nervous system stimulants.

Showing the other side of the debate, Harvard professor Timothy Wilens reanalyzed data from six separate studies on ADHD, Ritalin, and risk of addiction.[6] The studies involved 674 treated and 360 untreated children ("treated" in this context means "given Ritalin") followed for at least four years. Dr. Wilens found that children who had been treated had half the risk of future substance abuse compared to those that had not been treated. In an article published in the *Chicago Tribune* in 2000, Dr. Wilens stated that "...by treating ADHD you're reducing the demoralization that comes from this disorder, and you're improving the academic functioning and well-being of adolescents and young adults during the critical times when substance abuse starts."

First, keep in mind that Dr. Wilens is inaccurate about improvements in academic function in kids given Ritalin. The research is clear on this point. It's also clear that kids on Ritalin don't have significantly improved social functioning. Kids aren't less demoralized as much as they're numb, white-knuckling it through the days. I've heard kids say that they feel like ghosts when on Ritalin. Adults look at them and they seem more focused, but the reality —at least in my experience with these kids—is that they're often having a horrible time.

Does Ritalin use change brain cell receptors, making the person more vulnerable to addiction when they try other stimulants (such as nicotine and cocaine) later on? No one knows for sure. One thing is certain: kids who have been diagnosed with ADHD are more vulnerable to drug addiction than the general population, whether they have been given Ritalin or not. It may well be that simply being diagnosed with this disorder makes a kid more likely to risk taking dangerous, illegal drugs.

It's impossible to know, based on current evidence, whether ADHD kids grow up and self-medicate because of actual biochemical changes caused by Ritalin or other stimulant drugs. More likely is that ADHD kids—whether they've used Ritalin or not—end up abusing drugs more often because the adults around them weren't able to help them in ways that enhanced inner strength and enabled them to channel their intensity positively. Frustrated and overwhelmed, feeling less than successful, these kids turn to controlled substances to feel better, and they end up getting hooked. In contrast,

73

children who come to feel strong on the inside have far greater resources to draw on to combat frustration and say no to temptations, pressure and impulses to experiment with drugs.

The media and the public have been too easily convinced by Dr. Wilens' research. No surprise, considering the stranglehold big business—including the pharmaceutical companies—has on media outlets. It is also believed that the majority of research Dr. Wilens examined was funded by pharmaceutical company dollars and agendas. Dr. Lambert's evidence that Ritalin acts as a gateway drug was not refuted by the work of Dr. Wilens.

53 Research shows that cocaine causes permanent changes in the brain's activity and structure. Since methylphenidate has the same mode of action, we have reason to suspect that Ritalin, too, causes such changes. The small amount of research to date strongly supports this suspicion.

A recent study by Dr. Nora Volkow and colleagues found that methylphenidate is actually a *more* powerful stimulant than cocaine, based on the strength with which it blocks transporters for the neurotransmitter dopamine.[7] The excess dopamine stays in the synapses, creating a feeling of being "high" or "buzzed." Cocaine blocks 50 percent of dopamine transporters, while Ritalin blocks 70 percent. This was not with a high dose, but with 0.5 mg/kg—the typical dose given to children. Following the publication of this research, Dr. Volkow stated that "...as a psychiatrist, sometimes I feel embarrassed [about the lack of knowledge of how methylphenidate really works] because this is, by far, the drug we prescribe most frequently to children." She reported being quite surprised by the study's results, saying that "the data clearly show that the notion that Ritalin is a weak stimulant is completely incorrect."

Some opinion leaders claim that Ritalin is not addictive when taken orally, that it is only addictive when repeatedly snorted or injected. But since Ritalin is a stimulant, and all stimulants are known to be addictive when taken orally, this claim seems to be wrong.

NOTES

1. http://articles.student.com/article/ritalin

2. *The Observer*, Sunday, March 17, 2002.

3. Jeremy Laurance, "Ritalin abuse hits students looking for an exam kick," http://education.independent.co.uk/news/story.jsp?story=437184

4. http://www.unodc.org/unodc/press_release_1997-02.15_1.html

5. NM Lambert, CS Hartsough, "Prospective study of tobacco smoking and substance dependencies among samples of ADHD participants," *J Learn Disabil* 1998 Nov-Dec;31(6):533-44.

6. J Biederman, T Spencer, T Wilens, "Evidence-based pharmacotherapy for attention-deficit hyperactivity disorder," *Int J Neuropsychopharmacology* 2004 Mar;7(1):77-97.

7. ND Volkow, et al, "Expectation enhances the regional brain metabolic and the reinforcing effects of stimulants in cocaine abusers," *J Neurosci* 2003 Dec 10;23(36):11461-8 (Comment on this study appeared in Brian Vastag, *JAMA* 2001; 286:905-906)

Section Five
Questionable Research: No Physical Basis for ADHD

WOULD YOU BELIEVE THAT MILLIONS OF PRESCRIPTIONS ARE WRITTEN every year to treat a so-called "disorder" that is *not real?* It's true. In the words of Peter Breggin, M.D., "...the ADHD diagnosis is not based on objective signs or criteria...it is not a specific disorder, disease, or condition." (*Talking Back to Ritalin*, p. 172-3)

Attention Deficit Hyperactivity Disorder is nothing but a collection of behaviors that have been lumped together and called a disorder by the psychiatric community. They have created a stunningly successful PR campaign that has fostered the largely unquestioning acceptance of this "brain disease" by the public. No one has demonstrated any underlying "biochemical imbalance" or neurotransmitter dysfunction in children diagnosed with ADHD versus children who are normal. As Dr. Margaret Hagen, psychology professor at Boston University, succinctly stated, the ADHD diagnosis—like many psychiatric diagnoses—is "nothing but science by decree."[1]

In the mid-1990s, a consensus meeting of psychiatrists broadened the definition of ADHD, changing the diagnostic criteria in ways that made the diagnosis more inclusive. Critics claim that this was done in collusion with pharmaceutical companies—a claim that rings true in light of the fact that Ritalin prescriptions shot up immediately following the changes made to the Diagnostic and Statistical Manual (DSM) at that meeting.

William Dodson, M.D., a Colorado psychiatrist who is paid by the makers of Adderall to promote their drug, said this in a PBS *"Frontline"* interview in April 2001:

Twenty years ago, the only child who was going to be identified, and therefore treated, was the hyperactive child who was pinging off the wall, who was aggressive, uncontrollable, and obnoxious. And so...this was the child that everybody could agree was hyperactive and who would benefit from medication.

It has only been in the last 10 to 12 years that we see that actually, the hyperactive aggressive child makes up only a small percent—20 or 25 percent—of people who have ADHD. There are far larger numbers of people who don't have any hyperactivity at all, and they are purely the inattentive subtype...The inattentive and impulsive symptoms continue unabated for a lifetime...we're doubling the apparent prevalence rate by

recognizing that the quiet, inattentive child who daydreams in the back of
the class also has Attention Deficit Hyperactivity Disorder, just without the
hyperactivity...according to [a study by Dr. James] Swanson...people are
being treated for longer periods of time. Once a person starts on the medica-
tion, we now recognize they'll benefit from the medication their entire life.

54 Attention Deficit Hyperactivity Disorder (ADHD) is not a disease.

According to the 1998 National Institutes of Health Conference on
ADHD, there is no valid, independent diagnostic test for ADHD, and there
are no data that prove it to be a brain dysfunction. Despite this lack of
evidence, ADHD is widely described as a "chemical imbalance" in the brain
that is "corrected" by stimulant drugs.

In 1963, the American psychiatric community was just beginning to
experiment with psychotropic drugs. Experimentation with drugs like LSD
demonstrated that miniscule amounts of these substances could have overwhelming effects on a person's thoughts, perceptions, sensations, and
emotions. This is where the "biochemical imbalance" hypothesis began. If a
person's brain could be rendered abnormal with drugs, then any person who
displays abnormal behavior must have an imbalance of natural biochemicals
that—theoretically—could be corrected with drug therapy.

By the late 1960s, this idea had sparked the imaginations of a lot of
scientists and cultural critics. If this biochemical imbalance theory turned out
to be fact, what would stop medicine from developing drugs to provide
optimal neurochemical states in every person, normal or not? Could we
solve some of the world's problems by changing personalities with pills?
That seemed within our reach.

As the years passed, the notion that mental illness is caused by a biochemical imbalance gained widespread acceptance. This was not because of
rigorous, repeatable, and peer-reviewed scientific research. It was due to a
phenomenon known as "theory begging" within the psychiatric community.

Theory begging is, simply, the repetition of a theory so often that it
becomes accepted as fact within the profession, without actually having been
proven.

In the 1980s, the American Psychiatric Association (APA) compiled a list
of behaviors and called them "diagnostic criteria" for a condition they called
Attention Deficit Disorder (ADD). In 1987, ADHD was voted into existence
by the APA and added to the updated Diagnostic and Statistical Manual of
Mental Disorders (DSM-III), the "bible" used to make psychiatric and
psychological diagnoses. Within a year, 500,000 people, mostly children, had

been diagnosed with this brand-new disease. Today, approximately seven million American children have been treated with Ritalin and similar drugs for ADHD—without any demonstration that they actually have a disease. It would be one thing if these drugs were completely safe and did no harm, but this is absolutely not the case.

There is no test to support the chemical imbalance theory—not for any mental illness. Diagnoses of disorders such as ADHD, anxiety disorder, depression, bipolar illness, and alcoholism are made based on observations and reports from friends, family, and teachers. Millions of people have been told that they have a biochemical imbalance that needs to be "corrected" with medication. What they really have are symptoms—behaviors, really— that are being classified as disease states. With direct-to-consumer drug advertising and so-called "awareness-raising" campaigns, many people try to explain away their problems by diagnosing themselves with psychiatric disorders and march into physicians' offices asking for this or that drug.

Psychiatry can't have it both ways. They can't medicalize a disorder that cannot be defined through laboratory tests but only through observation.

55 ADHD is not a Ritalin deficiency.

When there is the illusion of improvement in a child's ability to focus and sit still with Ritalin, it is because he is drugged—not because an imbalance has been corrected. Children and adults without ADHD symptoms show similar "improvements" when they take these drugs. Rapoport et al (1980) reported in the *Archive of General Psychiatry* that their research demonstrated that Ritalin has the same basic effect on normal individuals as on those with the diagnosis. Even strong drug advocates do not dispute this.

I say "illusion" because this is exactly what it is when a child seems to improve when taking Ritalin. Adults eager to force the intense child into a mold that doesn't fit him understandably breathe a sigh of relief when the child's intense behaviors lessen. In the parlance of the psychiatric drug culture, however, this is called improvement. To *improve*—according to Webster's Dictionary—is: 1. to make better; 2. to make more valuable by cultivation, construction, etc.; or, to do or make better than. The child on Ritalin is not improved; he is only made to appear more socially acceptable.

Some recent studies have suggested that Ritalin improves focus and concentration by increasing levels of two neurotransmitters—dopamine and serotonin—in the brain. According to one such study, done at the Brookhaven Center for Imaging and Neurosciences, adults given dosages equivalent to those given to children "activate motivational circuits" and "make tasks more interesting" while suppressing "background firing of neurons not associated with task performance," making for a "clearer signal" in the brain of the person who has taken Ritalin.

These brain changes, described in language purposefully designed to make the imprecise tweaking of neurotransmitter function sound both precise and benign, take place in virtually every person who takes a stimulant drug, *whether or not they have been diagnosed with ADHD.* The best proof of this comes from two places: scientific studies on children who do not have any psychiatric diagnoses, and from the fact that college and high school students across the U.S. are using Ritalin illegally to improve their ability to concentrate on studying and other schoolwork.

Ritalin has been said to have "paradoxical" effects on children who are hyperactive. In other words, it's a stimulant, but it appears to calm kids who need to be calmer. This is another attempt to make ADHD sound like a medical disorder, a chemical imbalance that is re-balanced by the drugs. But Ritalin doesn't differ in its effects on "normal" and ADHD children. Normal children become zombie-like and have narrowed focus and OCD-like behaviors when on Ritalin, too. They don't become hyperactive. This drug doesn't discriminate between people with ADHD and people who have not been given this label.

The use of Ritalin can't be justified by saying that it alters neurotransmitter concentrations; this statement may hold some degree of truth about its biological action, but it does not at all prove that there was any imbalance to begin with. And the language that is used to describe Ritalin-induced changes in brain activity is extremely deceptive. What we are doing is drugging children whose behaviors bother us—and this will remain the truth, no matter what language we use to describe it.

56

The diagnostic checklist for ADHD is almost identical to the one used to identify children as Gifted and Talented.

Here are two diagnostic checklists. One is designed to help discern children who are gifted; the other, to diagnose ADHD. Can you tell which is which?

Poor attention, boredom, daydreaming in specific situations	Poorly sustained attention in almost all situations
Low tolerance for persistence on tasks that seem irrelevant	Diminished persistence on tasks not having immediate consequences
Judgment lags behind development of intellect	Impulsivity, poor delay of gratification
Intensity may lead to power struggles with authorities	Impaired adherence to commands to regulate or inhibit behavior in social contexts
High activity level; may need less sleep	More active, restless than normal children
Questions rules, customs and traditions	Difficulty adhering to rules and regulations

If you guessed that the checklist on the right is for ADHD diagnosis and the one on the left for identifying a child who may be gifted, you guessed correctly. You probably see from this comparison, however, that making this distinction is not easy.

Gifted children may be described as ADHD by a teacher in a subject they don't like, while they focus and achieve well in other subjects. They may be seen as ADHD in school but not at home or in out-of-school activities that they enjoy. ADHD "experts" claim that the truly ADHD child has problem behaviors virtually everywhere, although "the extent of their problem behaviors may fluctuate from setting to setting, depending largely on the structure of that situation."[2] In classroom settings, a child who is gifted and has trouble focusing, sitting still, or staying on task is probably bored from waiting for his classmates to figure out what he has already figured out. Disruptive behavior can result when these kids—often two to four grade levels above their peers academically—become challenged by a too-slow pace of learning.

As if this weren't vague enough, it is also said that ADHD and giftedness often coexist in the same children! How many gifted, intense, challenging kids are currently being drugged for a supposed "attention deficit?" And what effect will this have on their gifts? We'll probably never know.

My experience is that the giftedness of almost all intense children, even those who initially appear to be academically deficient, can be easily cultivated when you have an encompassing enough approach that shines the light of success in the child's eyes and an approach that enables adults to transport that child into a new and healthy way of seeing the world. Intense children have so much more propulsion than the normal child that can be channeled into greatness.

But this cannot be achieved with conventional techniques.

I've met so many children who were considered deficient in the academic and social aspects of school functioning, but who turned out to be high achieving and quite adept at social functioning when exposed to an approach that shifted their "portfolio of who they really are" to one of success.

 The wholesale drugging of children springs in part from modern society's intolerance for discomfort, and the habit of blaming others for our own discomfort.

Our reactions to children's intensity are just that—*our reactions*. Tolerance levels vary. Our own fear and frustration at children's intensity can open us to important changes in ourselves and the way we parent, if we are willing to be uncomfortable. Frustration is highly motivating and leads us to research and explore alternatives.

In his book *Blaming Our Genes*, Ty Colbert writes:

"The fact that the hyperactive child annoys us is not wrong...what is wrong is how we deny our own reaction and in the service of this denial, draw the false conclusions that end up violating these individuals...Reactions to such individuals should be a starting point for further careful investigation...Our feelings of fear, terror, and anger are a legitimate starting point, but they must be seen as a window or path to a deeper truth. Perhaps at times the other person needs to take responsibility for his/her behavior, but more importantly, if we as individuals, professionals, and as a society do not first take responsibility for our own reactions, we will always violate the rights and inner security of the other person."[3]

My experience bears this out completely. I would much rather work with a family who has not yet taken the medication route as it taints and dilutes their motivation to put aside the methods they know. It makes it much harder to get them to try new recommendations in an all out manner.

On the other hand, the family that is completely frustrated is ready and willing to implement the new approach as if their life depended upon it. Ultimately, if the family is not led astray by the illusion that medications are producing some improvement, that frustration is a blessing.

58 There is no clear demarcation between ADHD and normal. The DSM criteria for adults are even less specific than those for children. In other words, an ADHD diagnosis is in the eye of the beholder.

When asked by the press about the substance of the National Institutes of Mental Health (NIMH) conference on ADHD held in 1998, panel member and pediatrician Mark Vonnegut, M.D., replied, "The diagnosis is a mess." David J. Kupfer, M.D., panel chairman and a psychiatry professor at the University of Pittsburgh, stated that "there is no current validated diagnostic test."[4]

There is enormous variation between states and between different types of practitioners when it comes to diagnosing ADHD. Family practitioners diagnose and prescribe meds more quickly than do psychiatrists or pediatricians. There are several different diagnostic tests available, but there is no standard test used across the board, and they are all ultimately subjective assessments in any case.

According to the Consensus Statement published after the NIMH conference, "Some practitioners invalidly use response to medication as a diagnostic criterion... The quickness with which some practitioners prescribe medications may decrease the likelihood that more educationally relevant interventions will be sought." In other words, if the child seems to calm down with the drugs, some practitioners see this as corroboration for the diagnosis. With a "universal enhancer" like Ritalin—a term used to describe drugs that appear to improve certain aspects of function in most people, whether they have a "disorder" or not—*this is a decidedly unscientific approach to diagnosis and treatment*.

The Consensus Statement[5] goes on to say:

...some practitioners do not use structured parent questionnaires, rating scales, or teacher or school input. Pediatricians, family practitioners, and psychiatrists tend to rely on parent rather than teacher input. There appears to be a disconnect between developmental or educational (school-based) assessments and health-related (medical practice-based) services. There is

often poor communication between diagnosticians and those who implement and monitor treatment in schools. In addition, follow-up may be inadequate and fragmented.

It is unconscionable that we have drugged so many millions of children based on such a shaky foundation. How could this have happened?

In terms of the diagnostic tests that are available, one variety is the "continuous performance tasks" tests, which measure ability to pay attention during a series of repetitive actions. Mary Eberstadt, in her article "Why Ritalin Rules," describes one such test: the "Gordon Diagnostic System, a box that flashes numbers, whose lever is supposed to be pressed every time a particular combination appears."[6]

However, children are almost always diagnosed based on reports from teachers and parents, and a (usually) brief session with a physician that only serves to back up the opinions of those who wish to find ways to subdue a challenging child.

A test for adult ADD, published in Thomas Hallowell's book *Driven to Distraction,* asks 100 questions such as: *Are you impulsive? Are you easily distracted? Do you fidget a lot? Do you change the radio station in your car frequently? Are you always on the go? Do you have a hard time reading a book all the way through?* This is all extremely subjective.

If psychiatry is going to diagnose millions of people with a mental disorder, it had better come up with some reliable and consistent ways to test for it as well as a solid dividing line between "disordered" and "healthy."

59 Research indicates that the "awareness-raising" campaigns of biological psychiatry have been a success: Parents tend to over-identify ADHD "symptoms."

Relying on parental reports of ADHD-like behaviors may lead to over-identification of the disorder. In other words: parents' perceptions of what behaviors are pathological and what behaviors are a normal part of childhood may not be the best indicator of whether that child "has" ADHD. These kinds of reports—usually in conjunction with reports from teachers—are the basis for many ADHD diagnoses and prescriptions.

In one study, 253 mothers reported on the ADHD symptoms of their preschool children (aged two to six years).[7] Based solely on parental report, 9.5 percent of the sample—24 children—met the DSM-IV criteria for ADHD. Average ratings of hyperactivity, impulsivity, and inattentiveness were about midway on a one-to-seven point scale, with impulsivity—"on the go or acts as if driven by a motor"—the highest-scored variable. The authors state that "males and children of less-educated parents were more likely to receive endorsement of ADHD symptoms."

What does this study mean? It is a vivid illustration of the subjective nature of ADHD. Description and definition of so-called "symptoms" as diagnostic of ADHD depend enormously on the mindset, background, and belief systems of the parents, teachers, and other influential adults in the child's life. These apparently hold more sway than the actual objective behaviors of the child.

This study also tells us, as do some others described in this book, that parents are getting their "information" about ADHD-like symptoms from somewhere. One can certainly conclude that it comes largely from television, magazines, chats with other parents or teachers, or other such sources perceived as knowledgeable authorities. In other words, awareness-raising campaigns led by pharmaceutical companies are convincing parents that their children's problem behaviors are caused by ADHD.

And less educated parents seem more inclined to be swayed by awareness raising aimed at the general public. These parents are also less likely to understand the risks of these drugs. This shows the possibility of socioeconomic differences in the diagnosis and treatment of this disorder. Parents with more education and financial resources might have more motivation and confidence in themselves and in turn might more readily seek non-drug solutions.

 The language used by drug proponents is sinister.

Ritalin is said to "harmonize brain chemicals," to "help children be more agreeable and less argumentative" (Barbara Ingersoll in *Your Hyperactive Child*[8]), when what we are really doing is not helping or harmonizing them, but instead giving them addictive psychotropic drugs to control their behavior. In the *New Yorker,* journalist Malcolm Gladwell enthusiastically states that "we are now extending to the young cognitive aids of a kind that used to be reserved exclusively for the old."[9] He neglects to mention that most children who are given this advantage would much rather not have it, or that these cognitive aids work by making a child obsessive-compulsive, spaced-out, or zombie-like. It's one thing to give drugs to an adult who is capable of true informed consent; it's another thing entirely to force them on children who are the least empowered members of our society.

Other experts claim that by increasing levels of extracellular dopamine, we are "activating motivational circuits" and "suppressing background firing of neurons not associated with task performance," providing a "clearer signal" within the brain. This type of medical jargon does little to educate the public about the true qualities of stimulant medications, and it can be downright frightening to parents who are seeking accurate (and understandable) information about their child's health.

Physicians who support the use of Ritalin describe it and related medications in ways that make the drugs sound benign and necessary. Edward Hallowell, M.D., says that meds "act like internal eyeglasses, increasing the brain's ability to focus on one task over time."[10] Others have compared stimulant drugs for ADHD children with hearing aids for the hard of hearing, or aspirin for headache. Supporters of drug use claim that it's actually cruel to withhold this kind of help from children who need it, just as it would be cruel to deny a nearsighted child the use of glasses. One colleague who had been treated for depression as a child was told by her psychologist that not giving her antidepressant drugs was akin to withholding insulin from a diabetic.

This is all rationalization—doublespeak designed to candy-coat the real effects of the drug. It's absurd to compare drugs that hold such potential for harm, and that work by altering brain chemistry, to eyeglasses or hearing aids, or to a life-sustaining substance like insulin. *Unlike administering insulin, which is a natural substance in every human body, there is no such thing as a Ritalin deficiency in the body. It is not a naturally occurring substance but rather a Class II narcotic.*

Besides: the evidence that Ritalin is effective over the long-term is far from compelling. Initial impressions of improvement may seem dramatic, but over time, those improvements can't be relied upon, and the evidence is strong that the risks of the drug outweigh the chances for long-term benefits.

61 Some brain imaging studies show minor differences in the size of certain parts of the brains of ADHD and non-ADHD subjects, but this is hardly evidence supporting the widespread use of stimulant drugs.

Recent brain imaging studies do show differences between the size of parts of the brains of ADHD children and non-ADHD control subjects. (In earlier versions of these studies, these differences were at least partially *caused by stimulant medication.*) In an interview aired on the PBS news show *"Frontline,"* F. Xavier Castellanos, M.D.—one of the most well-respected ADHD researchers around—said that "the posterior inferior vermis of the cerebellum is smaller in ADHD...it's taken about five years to convince myself that's the case. That's about as much as I know—*that* I'm confident about." The *Frontline* interviewer asks, "What does that mean?" Dr. Castellanos answers, "I don't know what it means, but it's true, and it's a fact."[11]

He concedes that it will probably be three to five years before anyone knows what this research really means. We don't even know whether the brain size differences cause the behaviors of difficult children or result from those behaviors.

The cerebellum is a region at the base of the brain, associated with muscle tone, balance, and other basic non-thinking functions. Dr. Castellanos goes on to explain that the cerebellum contains more neurons (brain cells) than the rest of the brain combined, but that it has never been seen as very important because *it can be removed* without any terrible consequences. In his research, severity of ADHD symptoms strongly correlated with brain size. Another way of saying this: the more severe the symptoms, the smaller the child's brain.

Dr. Castellanos, who is a member of the child psychiatry branch of the National Institutes of Mental Health (NIMH), knows well the practical limitations of his research and that differences in various brain areas aren't something you can "treat" with medication. (In fact, the drugs may well cause further shrinkage...not the ideal treatment in this regard!) It is not his fault that people with a vested interest in pushing drugs are misstating and misusing his research to do so.

Brain scan research on these two population groups has also found differences in brain size (a four percent difference), particularly in the prefrontal cortex, and in the basal ganglia (about a six percent difference). In both cases, as with the cerebellum, no one knows the implication of these minor differences. The parts of the brain that differ in childhood follow the same growth curves over time in ADHD and non-ADHD subjects. This may well simply be what greater intensity looks like in terms of brain structure. So far there is no compelling evidence that this is any indication of disease. We also don't know if interventions of teaching and parenting approaches that really work with these children counteract this difference. However, what we do know is, difference or not, children considered to have this syndrome respond remarkably to upgraded styles of intervention.

Keep in mind that research has revealed other distinctions when it comes to brain size:

- The brains of women are smaller than those of men.
- Brain size varies dramatically between people of different body sizes.
- Some research has shown that certain parts of the brains of homosexual men differ in size compared to those of heterosexuals.
- Nutrition during very early life has much to do with future brain size.
- Controversial research has shown that the average size of the brains of people of Asian, African, and Caucasian descent differ (Asian the largest, African the smallest, and Caucasian somewhere in between).

- It has been well established that early childhood experience powerfully affects future brain size. Neglected children have significantly reduced cortical volume compared to children who are well cared for.

Dr. Castellanos also points out that when parents are faced with the choice of whether to give Ritalin to their child, the uncertainty about the drug's long-term effects needs to be acknowledged and openly discussed by the prescribing physician. Nine times out of ten (a generous estimate), this doesn't happen. Parents are sent home with a prescription without even skimming the surface of what is and what isn't known.

Dr. Castellanos and his colleagues are doing excellent and thoughtful work to try to discover a biological basis for this "disorder"—or, as I would rather see it said, to try to discover how the brains of more intense people might differ structurally from those of less intense people. But in the end, this doctor openly admits that he is uncomfortable with how little is known about how stimulants work and what their long-term risks might be. He states that the cup of knowledge on this front is "not even half full. It's about a tenth full."

62 Even if there is a biological basis to ADHD—which there may turn out to be—the human brain has remarkable plasticity, and there is every reason to believe that thoughtful non-drug interventions, begun at an early age (when Ritalin is usually started), could move the brain into a more balanced state without the use of medications.

According to the researchers at the John F. Kennedy Center for Research in Human Development at Vanderbilt University, brain plasticity describes the way in which "circuits in the brain change—organize and reorganize—in response to experience or sensory stimulation." Most of the research in the field of brain plasticity relates to helping those who have suffered brain injury, finding ways for them to regain lost physical function and thinking ability. If we can "rewire" the brains of adults who have had strokes or paralyzing injuries, we most certainly can help children with ADHD without feeding them drugs.

However, Ritalin is currently seen as so benign and effective that it is the first-line therapy. Given this mindset, there is little reason and few resources for scientists to do much work into neural plasticity and how it could help people to move out of destructive intensity and into more positive manifestations of that intensity. It's becoming evident, however, that the real risks of giving these drugs to children are so great that they should only be used as a very last resort. If the scientific, medical, and educational communities were to recognize this—if they were prohibited from using Ritalin unless a child was so out of control that he posed a genuine threat to the safety of himself and others—we would most likely see a further increase in this field of research.

When a human being is first born, there are about 2,500 *synapses* per neuron in the cerebral cortex, the part of the brain responsible for thought and learning. A synapse is a connection between one nerve cell (neuron) and another nerve cell, across which the exchange of neurotransmitters like dopamine and serotonin carry information. As we learn from our environments, these connections multiply. A two- or three-year-old has about 15,000 synapses per neuron. Then, over the rest of that toddler's life, synapses are selectively removed, which explains why a child's mind is so incredibly fertile and why an old dog has trouble learning new tricks.

Everything we learn, every stimulus from the environment, actually physically changes our brains. A child's brain is enormously flexible, and the right therapeutic techniques (see the 101st Reason) take advantage of this flexibility. Daniel Siegel, M.D., considered by many to be the foremost 21st century expert on brain functioning and author of *The Developing Mind: How Relationships and the Brain Interact to Shape Who We Are,* makes the case that plasticity is largely a function of interactive or social learning. In other words, the brain can make incredible gains in terms of functional growth through the active avenues of how parents and teachers choose to interact with a child.

Some research has been done with neurofeedback and other alternative modalities for children with ADHD, with symptom control equal to and greater than the "improvements" seen with medication. As long as Ritalin and other stimulants are being prescribed so freely, however, these alternatives will receive little attention.

Instead of forcefully altering synaptic connections with stimulants, we can work with the child's nervous system in a more natural way—helping her brain evolve into a more socially acceptable intensity—a *positive* intensity rather than a negative one.

63 A federally funded study found that the more time children spend in daycare, the more likely they are to end up having ADHD-like behaviors.

In 1960, only 30 percent of children grew up in households where both parents worked. Today, around 70 percent of kids live in two-parent households where both parents work at jobs outside the home. More children than ever before are growing up in households with only one parent. As they try to juggle work and time with children, many adults find themselves in the quandary of knowing that their kids need more time with them, but fearing that if they don't maintain work as high priority, they may end up unable to support their families.

As a generation, today's kids spend more time in daycare than any that preceded them. Many parents think little of putting a child as young as six weeks of age into a daycare setting so that they can return to work. Many have no alternative. According to a study published in the July/August 2003 issue of the journal *Child Development,* the more time children spent in child care from birth to age 4-1/2, the more adults tended to rate them as disobedient, noncompliant, assertive, and aggressive. The study was part of the National Institute of Child Health and Human Development (NICHD) Study of Early Child Care and Youth Development.[12]

Not surprisingly, the study found that higher-quality day care—care that involved plenty of one-on-one interaction and stimulation from a caring adult—yielded fewer problems than day care in large centers where kids got less direct interaction. But even the best of care didn't appear to replace this kind of attention from parents. Whether the care was of the highest quality or of the lowest, the amount of time spent in day care was associated with later problem behavior.

If we continue to refuse to place any responsibility for ADHD-like, challenging, intense behaviors on the decisions we make—if we continue to call it a "neuropsychiatric disorder" that needs to be treated with drugs instead of targeting vital differences in the way we choose to parent and teach—we will never solve this problem. It will continue to grow and expand, and more and more kids will think they need to be on stimulants or other drugs for life. It's not fair to parents or the child, and fundamentally it's not the right thing to do.

A friend who is mother of four wrote:

When I take my little ones to the park to play while my older two are in school, I always see other kids there with nannies or babysitters or in groups with day-care workers. Most of the nannies and sitters are college-aged kids who have little to no clue about how to consistently or firmly discipline young children. Day-care workers have more training, but they are over- whelmed with the number of kids they are caring for.

I see the children in their charge getting away with all kinds of behaviors that they would (hopefully) never get away with when a parent was in charge. The sitters or nannies just let things slide. They put out fires, try to stop the crying or put a band-aid on the cut or stop the siblings from fighting, but they aren't concerned with the long-term implications of what they're doing—only with getting through the day without any of the children in their charge getting hurt or having serious problems.

It isn't the sitters' fault; they don't typically have the knowledge or the deep intuitive need to do what's right by these kids. But I can see two things happening with the children: first, I see them having a great old time, like they're pulling one over on the substitute teacher. But then I see this deep sadness in their eyes. I see them craving and missing firm and loving guidance—something they instinctively know that they need. And they're confused by its absence.

The good news is that styles of teaching and childcare make all the difference in the world. Tolson Elementary School in Tucson, Arizona, used to have all kinds of disciplinary problems until the year 2000. Then the principal found out about *The Nurtured Heart Approach* and insisted that all staff use this style of working with children. In the four-plus years of using the approach prior to the writing of this book, not one child has been referred by the school for an ADHD evaluation and not one child put on stimulant medications. Can this simply happen by chance in a school of over 500 children in a largely disadvantaged area? Can you have a childcare worker or childcare agency that is extraordinary as well? The answer is yes, because in the same time period, all of Tucson HeadStart, well over 2,000 new children per year in 80 classrooms, used *The Nurtured Heart Approach* with the very same outcome: no children referred for evaluations and no children put on stimulant medications.

Of course parents today need nannies and daycare and other alternative arrangements, so the answer is in finding someone or some place that is already applying extraordinary strategies or is willing to learn. Children can ultimately thrive in these situations when caregivers know what they are doing. The secret is not in entertaining children, but in knowledgably helping children to feel successful.

Same with parenting: I've met so many parents who spend lots of time with their child and still wind up in the thick of problematic behaviors.

The secret again is not in the sheer amount of time but in the way parents knowledgably help the child experience success. Not just the simple statements of "thank you" and "good job" but rather more encompassing and more profound levels of success. The surprising thing is that approaches that accomplish this are far easier than the demanding work of handling problems and taking a child down the road of medications.

64 The meteoric rise in ADHD diagnoses has coincided with increases in time children spend with electronic media—television, video games, computers.

We cannot discount the role these media play in shortening children's attention spans, and we should not drug children to try to make up for it.

A study published in the April 2004 issue of the journal *Pediatrics* casts a poor light on TV-watching by young children. Researchers evaluated two groups of children, aged one and three, with varying levels of exposure to television and found that, for each hour of TV they watched per day, the kids had a 10 percent increase in ADHD-like symptoms at age seven. The scientists theorized that TV may over-stimulate the developing brains of very young children, even permanently "rewiring" the circuits that enable the child to learn and pay attention.[13]

The American Academy of Pediatrics has recommended that children under the age of two not be exposed to television or computers at all, and that children two and older should watch no more than one to two hours of TV a day.

Parents aren't listening. In a survey of 1,000 American families with young children, the Kaiser Foundation[14] found that children aged six and younger spend an average of two hours a day in front of a TV or computer screen; that two of every three children live in households where the TV is on for at least half the day; and 36 percent live in homes where the TV is on most or all of the time. More than one of every four American children under the age of three has a television in their room, and 43 percent of children under age two watch TV every day.

Parents may not readily see how television foments ADHD-like changes in children, and we need to take a really good look at the price we ultimately may pay, despite what might be our understandable interest in our children staying glued to the tube while we conduct our busy lives. Hopefully, continuing research in this area will make the side effects all the more evident and drastically cut down the amount of TV America's youth watches. This should, in turn, reduce the number of children who are given medication to help them focus in school and to control impulsive behavior.

Some parents marvel at how their children become entranced by TV—to the point of literally having to shake them back into reality when they're watching. (One acquaintance of mine refers to this as the "TV coma.") Some seem to think that this is a sign that the child is learning, or that this is something that's good for the child. The truth seems to be that the rapidly changing, brightly colored, attention-grabbing images and sounds of modern television programs appear to actually *shorten children's attention spans*. One might compare it to the effects of Ritalin on intense children: it's a stimulant that so overwhelms the child's brain that he calms down. Both create zombie-like children who lose their spark, their creativity, their life force—at least in the short-term.

Studies of newborn rats show that exposure to different levels of visual stimuli literally changes the architecture of their brains. This raises the possibility that if there are differences in brain structure between ADHD and "normal" children, some children may be more vulnerable to the effects of television and high levels of visual stimuli than others.

Most modern children's television programming is a mile-a-minute barrage of colors, sounds, and movement. You can virtually feel these shows affect circuits in the brain! Don't expose children to these over-stimulating places and things until you sense they can really handle it. The much higher level of inner strength that results from *The Nurtured Heart Approach* will give you more options. (See Reason 101.)

65 Research comparing psychosocial interventions with medication is flawed and biased.

Several studies published since the year 2000 seem to indicate that children on Ritalin who receive no psychosocial intervention (therapy, parent education, specific interventions similar to the one I have designed and implemented) do just as well as children who take Ritalin along with this kind of intervention. Such studies all share one major flaw: they do not look at the long-term differences (more than two years) between children who take Ritalin and children who do not. Chalk that up to more of what we don't know about long-term use of stimulant drugs. They also rarely compare intensive psychosocial interventions (such as *The Nurtured Heart Approach*) alone, without medication, to medication alone.

In a study conducted by the National Institutes of Mental Health (NIMH) in 1999, drug proponents believed that they had open-and-shut evidence that Ritalin was safe, effective, and a necessary part of ADHD treatment.[15] The study had lasted 14 full months and had compared children in several different parts of the nation, all of whom received either meds, meds plus behavior therapy, "community care" (care by their doctors or schools; many in this group got Ritalin) or behavior therapy only. Sixty-four percent of the children who got meds in this study suffered from adverse drug effects, as reported by parents and teachers. The children did not rate themselves improved. The research team responsible for the study were longtime, staunch advocates of psychiatric drugging of children. Thirty-one percent of the children in the study were already taking Ritalin when it began, suggesting that their parents already had faith that drugs were the best way to go.

Dr. Breggin tears the study limb from figurative limb in *Talking Back to Ritalin*, citing flaws that are impossible to explain away: *...In summary, the NIMH Ritalin study was a scientific fiasco, even a hoax, conducted by highly biased advocates of medication. It failed to adhere to the most important, essential scientific standards for clinical drug trials, including* *double-blind procedures and placebo controls.* (p.147)

Many of the studies that are referred to by Ritalin proponents evaluate medication alone and/or medication plus psychosocial interventions. The problem is that there is no "gold standard" psychosocial intervention—in other words, no such intervention tested in these studies could be construed as excellent. This inconsistency sets up the interventions to fail when compared with the deemed "improvements" seen with Ritalin.

Worst of all, these studies make no distinctions between interventions. Unfortunately, so many approaches, including many specifically recommended by ADHD experts, actually reward continued negative behaviors.

As you will see if you try *The Nurtured Heart Approach*, the nature of the approach and the power of the approach to create success make all the difference in the world.

NOTES

1. "Experts debunk DSM," at www.cchr.org/issues/dsm/experts/

2. RA Barkley, *Attention deficit hyperactivity disorder: A handbook for diagnosis and treatment*, Guilford Press, New York: 1990.

3. Ty Colbert, *Blaming Our Genes*, pp. 124-126, Kevco Publishing, California:2001

4. Paul Recer, "Treatment of attention deficit disorder still uncertain," *The Oregonian*: 11-19-99

5. ibid

6. Mary Eberstadt, "Why Ritalin Rules," http://www.policyreview.org/apr99/eberstadt.html

7. GA Gimpel, BR Kuhn, "Maternal report of attention deficit hyperactivity disorder symptoms in preschool children," *Child Health Care Dev* 2000 May;26(3):163-76.

8. Mary Eberstadt

9. "Running From Ritalin?" *The New Yorker*, February 1999.

10. www.insiderreports.com

11. FX Castellanos, et al, "Developmental trajectories of brain volume

abnormalities in children and adolescents with attention-deficit/hyperactivity disorder," *JAMA* 2002 Oct 9;288(14):1740-8.

12. J Brooks-Gunn, WK Han, J Waldfogel, "Maternal employment and child cognitive outcomes in the first 3 years of life: the NICHD Study of Early Child Care. National Institute of Child Health and Human Development," *Child Development,* 2002 July/August;73(4):1052-72.

13. JM Healy, "Early television exposure and subsequent attention problems in children," *Pediatrics* 2004 Apr;113(4):917-8.

14. www.kff.org/entmedia/entmedia102803nr.cfm

15. MTA Cooperative Group, "14-month randomized clinical trial of treatment strategies for attention-deficit/hyperactivity disorder," *Archives of General Psychiatry* 1999;56:1073-86.

Section Six
Ritalin and Other Stimulants Don't Help a Child Heal

Behaviors are signals that should be interpreted and understood, not suppressed.

—Peter Breggin, M.D.[1]

MEDICATION, ULTIMATELY, ISN'T THE ENEMY. On the contrary, to some parents and teachers, it appears to be a godsend—shifting a difficult child into one who is much easier to live with, practically overnight. The medications do give the impression of improvement, and improvements are strongly sought after when a child's intensity is going awry at home, at school, or both.

This is understandable when a child is acting out or underperforming, causing great frustration to parents and teachers. If medication can "grease the wheels" as beautifully as we are led to believe it can, why not use it? If it's really as effective as the PR describes it to be, why not put kids on it as soon as we see problems arising?

Side effects aside—after all, they may not happen to every last child who uses the drugs, and it might be a risk worth taking if a child is really out of control—there is another problem that medication advocates are loath to address: *stimulant medications don't heal a child's problems.* They are only a stopgap measure, like handing a beer to someone who needs to relax at the end of the day or a double espresso to someone who needs help waking up in the morning.

Of course, we don't give these things to children, because they could adversely alter a child's developing brain. Few drug proponents mention that stimulants and antidepressants and the other drugs used to control children's behavior may also cause toxic and adverse effects in the brains of children.

Drugs don't heal. They alter a child's behavior only for as long as he is on them. Their effects wear off after a few hours. The toxicity of the medication may linger but the improvements are *gone.* The child is literally back to ground zero. There's no personal growth, just dependency.

Drugs actually *inhibit* healing. By giving the impression that all is well, they destroy the motivation of parents, teachers, and other involved parties to join forces and give the child the kind of intensive support and guidance that will truly bring out the best in the child.

The changes that occur in a child's ways of thinking and behaving while on stimulants are widely viewed as positive.

On closer examination, however, these children are hardly "improved."

66 Stimulants work in children in the same way they work in rats: by "inducing stereotypical behavior"...i.e., by reducing the number of behavioral responses.

Stereotypical behavior is defined as repetitive, simple, and meaningless activity. This information comes from the *Oxford Textbook of Clinical Pharmacology and Drug Therapy*. Its authors say that "it is beyond our scope to discuss whether or not such behavioral control is desirable" (p.141). This renowned clinical pharmacology text states that stimulants induce stereotypical behavior and hints at some level of disapproval by saying that it's beyond their scope to discuss whether or not such behavioral control is desirable.

That stimulants induce stereotypical behavior is confirmed in my own observations over the years of hundreds of children on stimulant medications. Examples of this type of behavior, repeated over and over again, might be washing up or looking in the mirror or erasing a mistake.

While writing this book, I was haunted by the feeling that I personally needed to do a short trial of Ritalin in order to feel what it was like from the inside out. I discussed this with my physician who agreed to supervise me over a ten-day course of treatment. I describe my personal experience in a detailed journal of those ten days in the epilogue of this book.

Words do not begin to fully describe how strange it is to find yourself in the throes of this compulsion toward stereotypical behaviors. It's like someone has put your heart on hold and all you can do is ride it out by doing all these doable but meaningless activities until you feel like yourself again.

I was lucky in that I knew that I would be off this substance at the end of 10 days, unlike children, who rarely have a say in what must feel to them like an endless spin cycle...something they feel but can rarely put words to that repeats itself every day.

I was also fortunate in that I had a strong foundation of inner strength and wonderful support to get me through. I can hardly imagine how hard it would be for a young child to go through this without the same. No wonder most of these children deeply resent when someone tells them how much better they are now that they take medications.

67

The NIMH (National Institutes of Mental Health) points out that studies demonstrate that Ritalin has short-term effects such as reducing "classroom disturbance" and improving "compliance and sustained attention," but it also recognizes that the drug seems "less reliable in bringing about associated improvements, at least of an enduring nature, in social-emotional and academic problems, such as antisocial behavior, poor peer and teacher relationships, and school failure."

While medication subdues the child's problem behaviors, most likely by causing a level of over-stimulation that the child experiences as overwhelming, which in turn appears to produce a desirable effect, this is only part of the picture. We now know that medications don't really improve academic performance or peer relations long-term. Research supports this, although most clinicians have touted the opposite for years based on earlier flawed studies.

My experience as a clinician strongly suggests that, in contrast to the medications, interventions that really teach the child how to feel great about himself, exert self-control over impulses and better utilize inner strength and resolve *will* powerfully transform attitude, schoolwork and peer relations in an enduring way.

In a study by the MTA (Multimodal Treatment Study for Attention-Deficit Hyperactivity Disorder) Cooperative Group,[2] researchers evaluated 579 nine-year-old children who had been diagnosed with "combined type" ADHD. The researchers evaluated the effects (at 14 months) of each of the following methods: medication only; psychosocial treatment only; a combination of both treatments; and community care (only supplying parents with a list of community resources for dealing with ADHD). They looked at each method's effects on ADHD symptoms, oppositional/aggressive symptoms, social skills, and internalizing symptoms (such as depression and anxiety) based on parent and teacher ratings. The parents also completed questionnaires on parent-child relationship, while a battery of tests measured academic improvement, and other measurements evaluated peer interactions.

The psychosocial intervention component of this study was intensive.[3] Parents attended 27 group and eight individual sessions. The children spent five days a week for eight weeks (during summer vacation) in a nine-hour-per-day program that employed intensive behavioral interventions. There were point systems, consequences, social reinforcement, modeling, group problem solving, sports, and social skills training. Teachers also underwent special training, spending 10 to 16 sessions learning how to deal with these intense kids. They got help for 12 weeks from part-time assistants who worked directly with the ADHD children. Daily report cards were passed from teachers to parents.

Reduced symptoms were seen in all four groups over time. As expected, medication plus psychosocial intervention brought about the largest reduction in symptoms, with the medication-only group showing about equal improvement. But one important finding in this study was that the combined treatment (meds plus psychosocial intervention) was significantly better at reducing so-called "non-ADHD" symptoms: oppositional/aggressive behavior, internalizing, and social problems as rated by teachers, parent-child relations, and reading skills. Another MTA study found that in children with "comorbid anxiety," psychosocial treatment alone proved to be as effective as medication in controlling ADHD symptoms.[4]

When we rely on drugs to subdue "symptoms," we don't take the needed steps to help these intense kids positively grow into their intensity. Drugs may seem cheaper and less difficult to implement than psychosocial interventions in the short run, but they are much more expensive over time. Some say that this "disorder" is such a big problem that we're better off just using the drugs and not bothering with all these other interventions.

If the drugs are just as good at reducing the symptoms as these time-consuming and intensive interventions, why not just use them? Because an intervention such as *The Nurtured Heart Approach* addresses the *whole child* and improves his ability to function happily and healthily. **Drugs don't.**

68 There is no information on the repercussions of drug therapy lasting for more than two years.

The NIH and Ritalin's manufacturer (Novartis) claim that the long-term effects of stimulants remain in doubt. Most children take Ritalin for at least a year. According to PBS's *"Merrow Report"*:

Hundreds of studies on stimulant medications have been conducted, but few have looked at long term side effects. Measuring the long term effects of pediatric medications is prohibitive because of legal and ethical dilemmas surrounding the use of children as test subjects. The federal Food and Drug Administration labeling for Ritalin includes the specific warning, "Sufficient data on the safety and efficacy of long term use of Ritalin in children are not yet available."

In a study published in the *Journal of Abnormal Child Psychology*, researchers evaluated 62 children who had been on Ritalin for periods ranging from less than six months up to four years.[5] They looked at teachers' reports, number of failed grades, special education services, and two individually administered achievement tests to deduce whether their symptoms had been "cured" by treatment. The results: the children's hyperactivity had decreased, "but remained higher in these children than in normal peers. Behavioral and social problems were less pervasive than academic under-achievement."

The biggest blow to Ritalin in this study was the fact that the duration of stimulant interventions did not alter the child's course in any significant way. Any benefits of drugs were only seen within the first months of therapy. The benefits did not increase over time.

Real and enduring personal growth is not taking place. What parents and teachers want for children in this situation is to see them use their intensity in a wonderful and heart-centered way—shifting the child into greatness without the need for medications. We just haven't had many well-publicized ways of achieving this in the past. Fortunately, now we do.

69 The drugs don't normalize all behaviors; kids on drugs still have higher levels of behavior problems.

Stimulant drugs and antidepressants can give the superficial impression of a big change in a child's behavior, especially when they are first being used. They can seemingly change a child from an out-of-control "problem" into a milder-mannered version of her former self, one that is better able to follow directions and sit still more readily.

But, by and large, kids who use stimulant drugs aren't transmogrified (a word from that classic comic strip *Calvin and Hobbes*—surely the parents of the mischievous Calvin would be pressured to medicate their son if he were in school today!) into model citizens. They still have behavioral issues. They are still more symptomatic than their peers.

In a 1990 comprehensive review of ADHD treatment studies, as published in the *Journal of the American Academy of Child and Adolescent Psychiatry,* researchers revealed that:

1. Stimulants create the appearance of improvement in the areas of behavior, performance, and attention.

2. There is little evidence of improvements in sustained attention, retention of information, anger control, or scholastic achievement in children given stimulant drugs.

3. There is no difference between ADHD kids given meds or not given meds in terms of grades failed or achievement test scores.[6]

Both medicated and non-medicated "hyperactives" were less likely to attend junior colleges and universities; they failed more grades than non-hyperactive kids; and they dropped out of school more frequently.

The fact that so many behaviorally challenging kids persist with challenging behaviors while on medication—despite some perceived improvement—is a strong indication that their issues spring not from a need for pharmaceutical intervention, but a need for something else: parenting and teaching methods tailored to their heightened requirements for relationship and boundaries. Instead of acknowledging this, we increase their medication dosages, or give them new diagnoses and new meds.

Parents and teachers may be thrilled to experience what looks like a diminished level of acting out, but the truth is that they continue to focus on the child's problems rather than shifting that focus onto the child's successes. Children know and resent this and long for the real shift—not the same old garbage.

70 Kids on drugs show little improvement in academic and social skills.

The experience many families have with Ritalin and other drugs given to children is similar to the experience people have with cocaine (which is chemically equivalent). Everything seems rosy for a while, but invariably, the other shoe drops. If you've ever known someone who has experimented with cocaine, you know that at first, they feel like they are walking on water, that there's nothing they can't accomplish. Then their lives begin to fall apart...and eventually and inevitably, there's a huge price to pay.

With Ritalin, parents and teachers (not the child being drugged) are often initially thrilled with the immediate impression of improvement. Over time, their pleasant surprise is transformed into something altogether less positive. Although doctors who prescribe Ritalin and other stimulants will tell you that the science on these drugs is solid, *there is no unflawed scientific evidence of improvement in children who take stimulant drugs,* academically or otherwise. There is only the illusion of improvement.

Overall, the research does not show that ADHD kids on stimulant drugs improve their academic performance. They may sit still better, they may appear to focus better, but their grades and test scores don't reflect any real increase in retention of material or positive changes in the realm of thinking ability.

Drug makers have tried time and again to show academic improvement with stimulants, but they have repeatedly come up short. One study, published in 2001 in the journal *Experimental and Clinical Psychopharmacology,* found that adolescents given three doses of Ritalin showed some improvements in "note-taking quality, quiz and worksheet scores, written language usage and productivity, teacher ratings, on-task and disruptive behavior, and homework completion." The main problem here: how much can we really tell from just three doses?

This study also found that the lowest dose (10 mg) worked best, and that higher doses were not more effective. In fact, in some of these teens, the higher doses were *less* effective.[7]

According to a group of concerned scientists from Montreal University, "Medication does not improve complex abilities like reading, or social interaction. Results in school can be improved but the medication cannot correct any learning disability. No improvement has been noted for any significant emotional problem...There exists no evidence of long term improvement for children submitted to psychostimulant prescription regarding an improvement of their academic results or a decrease of their antisocial behavior."[8]

The use of Ritalin and other stimulants in children is often justified on the basis that the child needs "help" to socially interact with peers in an acceptable way. Parents are told that if they don't medicate, their child will have unsatisfying social interactions and be rejected by peers, which will exacerbate their behavior problems.

But *no scientific evidence shows that stimulants improve a child's ability to socialize*. There might be diminished impulsive or threatening interactions—certainly a good thing—but these interactions are often replaced with a zombie-like demeanor and stereotypical, meaningless, repetitive behaviors. Their need for human interaction decreases rather than flourishes.

One more comment here on the topic of the highly sought after areas of "sitting better" and "having better focus." On many occasions I have been invited to observe classrooms. Often these are classrooms where teachers have a fair amount of training and where they consider themselves to be quite positive. The problem, as you will read in reason 101, is that most conventional ways of being positive are inadequate and far from being as powerful as they can potentially be.

The most common positive comments I hear at schools, beside very generic ones like "thank you" and "good job," which are too vague to be truly influential with challenging children, are comments like "thanks for sitting quietly" and "thanks for paying attention." I rarely hear complex comments that truly celebrate a child's greatness. It's not that these common statements are bad, but they barely scratch the surface of the real inner wealth we can easily help a child to feel.

We only need a mind set and strategies that allow us to address the child as a whole person.

Sitting quietly is only a tiny bit of a whole person. It's almost as if we can reach inside and massage a child's heart in a loving way when we make the quantum leap to an approach that allows us to provide appreciation, recognition and acknowledgment in a more profound and spiritual manner.

For example: "Billy, I really appreciate the thoughtfulness and consideration you are using in choosing to leave your sister alone this afternoon. It didn't just happen...you decided not to argue or fuss and that shows respect and a very good attitude. Keep up the good work."

Statements like this become a powerful first-hand experience of success and introduce the child to a new sense of self-esteem and a new sense of their inner wealth and greatness.

71 Pharmaceutical solutions preclude solutions that involve dietary and lifestyle changes, which have been successful for many families.

There is a doctor-designed, extensively researched *elimination diet* that carefully cuts out all synthetic additives, preservatives, artificial sweeteners, and dyes/colorings from the child's diet. It's called the Feingold Approach. While many intense children do not have strong reactions to these ingredients, there is a subset of so-called "ADHD" kids who do. These children make remarkable turnarounds when the artificial ingredients are removed from their diets.

"But my child won't eat vegetables or fruit!" you might be thinking. "There's no way we'd be able to stick to that kind of diet." Before you rule the Feingold Approach out entirely, realize that the team that runs the Feingold Association has compiled a 100-page list of acceptable foods. They do intensive research, investigating every food they can find and determining whether it's appropriate for their diet plan. A child on the Feingold diet can have burgers and fries, hot dogs, and much, much more—but the parents need to be careful to choose varieties of these and other foods that are free of the additives that can spark difficult behaviors. Parents for whom this plan works rave about how their children have been transformed—without drugs.

The Feingold plan is not easy to implement in our junk-food saturated world, but it is worth trying. Here are some of the studies that show its effectiveness in children who are candidates for psychiatric drugging:

- In the June 2004 volume of *Archives of Diseases of Childhood*, researchers tested the Feingold diet on three-year-old children with hyperactive symptoms. The children's symptoms significantly improved when additives and preservatives were withdrawn, and worsened when they were added back into the diet. It took only 20 mg of artificial coloring to worsen the symptoms—not much, considering that green ketchup contains 150 mg per tablespoon![9]

- In the journal *Annals of Allergy,* another study demonstrates that 73 percent of children responded favorably to the elimination of reactive foods and artificial colors.[10]

- In 1977, before ADHD was called ADHD, a research team looked at the Feingold diet's efficacy in "hyperkinetic" children. Of 59 children with "hyperkinetic, minimal brain dysfunction syndrome," 32 tolerated the Feingold diet well, and 11 were markedly improved.[11]

- Another study published in the journal *Archives of Diseases of Childhood*—this one in 1993—looked at 78 children placed on a Feingold elimination diet. Fifty-nine percent had improved behavior. Further study of those children showed that 19 had significant intolerance of one or more of the specific additives that were removed from their diets.[12]

If you are intrigued by this, you can get further information about the Feingold diet at www.feingold.org, or by calling (800)321-3287 (in the U.S.) or (631)369-9340 (outside the U.S.). You can get food lists, newsletters, and a lot of helpful information through the web site. Another great resource for supplements and other holistic nutrition is www.drcabin.com.

Nutritional supplements have helped many families wean their intense children off stimulant drugs, or to avoid them altogether. A significant body of research has linked ADHD symptoms to deficiencies of omega-3 fatty acids, found in fish and flaxseeds. These fats are crucial for proper brain development, and they are lacking in nearly every Westerner's diet. You can learn more about how to supplement your child's intake of these fats by referring to Marcia Zimmerman's book, *The ADD Nutrition Solution: A Drug-Free 30-Day Plan* (Owl Books, 1999) or Dr. Andrew Stoll's definitive work on omega-3s and brain function, *The Omega-3 Connection* (Simon & Schuster, 2001). Many health food stores carry omega-3 supplements specifically designed for children. You can also buy them on the Internet; check out Dr. Julian Whitaker's site, www.healthydirections.com.

Other research indicates that adding supplements of B vitamins and the minerals magnesium, manganese, and calcium can improve the behavior and focus of difficult children. Be sure to use supplements specifically designed for children. The Feingold diet may require you to use specific types that don't have additives, so check their list before you buy if you are interested in trying their approach. Herbs such as passionflower, valerian, and lemon balm are gentle natural sedatives that have been used safely for hundreds, even thousands, of years. They have a much better safety profile than Ritalin!

I have every reason to believe that programs of micro-nutrition and homeopathy have a strong amount of merit as well. Exercise, too, is a terrific natural "sedative" for energetic, distractible children. Case in point, from an Internet posting:

A lady I know was told by her son's school that he HAD to take Ritalin. She knew better. Instead of putting him on Ritalin, she had him swim laps in her pool for about 30 minutes before school each day. That did the trick. He became a straight-A student. Now he flies fighter jets for the Navy.

Be aware that healthy alternatives are often not given merit by the medical community. I personally feel the optimal solution involves emotional and psychological nutrition along with optimal physical nutrition. These are a winning combination. Normal medical recommendations typically leave all of this out of the equation in favor of stimulant medications…a big mistake.

72 When a child's behavior improves while taking Ritalin, adults may mistakenly believe that they have found a solution, and they stop searching for real solutions.

Some prominent opinion leaders in the field of ADHD have literally given up on interventions by parents, claiming that they aren't worth the effort because they don't really work. Many claim that these parenting interventions are basically all alike and that they are no substitute for medication.

This is good news to some parents, because it takes them off the hook of having to put so much effort and time into changing the way they parent. They find themselves with only one alternative—drugs—rather than a confusing array of other, less medically-sanctioned choices. And then, when the child becomes easier to handle after taking the meds, the parents and teachers all too often see this as an affirmation that the child needed the drugs. They breathe a sigh of relief and get on with their lives…until they realize that the drugs don't really solve anything as much as they mask the old problems and create new ones.

Effectiveness of Ritalin is not diagnostic of ADHD or any other disorder! Not even the foremost Ritalin proponents can say that it is. To suggest that medication is the end-all solution for "treating" this "disorder" requires a sort of tunnel vision—a vision that eliminates the troublesome problems that I describe herein: that meds don't engender long-term improvement; that meds may well be far more dangerous than we expect them to be; and that we have no reason to expect that ADHD children whose parents and teachers don't seek new and more effective ways of dealing with them will ever heal.

73

Drug therapy for ADHD focuses on solving problems (diminishing negativity) rather than on enhancing the positives. Building the new "portfolio of inner wealth" is the only way to truly help the intense child shift into an entirely successful way of living his life.

Research into long-term treatment of ADHD suggests that we're dealing with an incurable disorder and that we may as well not fool around with costly, time-consuming educational and behavior modification measures when they just don't work.

Of course, if we didn't have medications, or if we honored how dangerous these meds can be, we'd simply try to change the other two types of intervention . . . to perfect them, to *make* them work to the best of our ability. Maybe we'd take these interventions to a higher order where we positively affect the whole person instead of our typical attempt to just deal with target behaviors (code for problems). Given the results many people have seen with *The Nurtured Heart Approach*, I believe that the best possible intervention has already been discovered.

Even if drugs help to calm a child's discomfort-causing behaviors, the child continues to be reinforced in one important area: when he is "behaving" due to the drug's effects, he still gets less attention, energy and relationship than when he is behaving badly. A far greater amount of the energy of adults is brought forth in response to misbehavior, while good deeds and good attitude are expected and therefore under-energized. Nothing has essentially changed.

Some therapeutic approaches to ADHD can actually worsen the disorder—because *they still focus on the negative*. All the focus goes toward issues and problems, and little or none goes toward "hijacking" the child into success. The latter requires powerful strategies that are heart-centered rather than conventional behavior modification.

Delving deeper and deeper into the child's problems does little to help the child. In the long run, the people responsible for that child's welfare throw up their hands and say that therapy just doesn't work...and they go on believing that drugs are the answer. For a child who already has the impression that he gets more out of life via adversity, a focus on problems will simply deepen his existing impression.

Experts agree that the symptoms of so-called ADHD children tend to go away under certain circumstances. Most telling is the fact that these symptoms tend to dissipate when the child receives the undivided (positive) attentions of an adult. Peter Breggin, M.D., has half-jokingly renamed ADHD as DAD—Dad Attention Deficiency. One parent I know told me that when she turns her "laser beams"—her name for undivided focus—on her

ADHD son, he becomes significantly calmer.

The Nurtured Heart Approach takes this a step further by helping the child know that positive behaviors will reliably be perceived as a success—the "laser beams" my friend spoke of—and that she need not go to the trouble of misbehaving to get this kind of attention. In fact, over a surprisingly short amount of time, the process becomes internalized and the child can provide positive attention for herself.

This essentially changes the entire nature of the child's inner relationship. Instead of a lifetime of living out a script of needing to replicate negativity in order to feel most alive, the child can settle into a much more harmonious life script of success and tranquility. I believe that this is what we are *really* fighting for and that this is what parents and teachers *really* want.

74 Drug labeling specifies that stimulants are not appropriate therapy for a child who has symptoms "secondary to environmental factors."

What this means is that the medical community and pharmaceutical companies agree that Ritalin and similar medications are to be used for neurological, biochemical and genetic circumstances, not for symptoms due to environmental factors. One could argue (at least from the evidence presented in this book and in similar sources) that, in the vast majority of children who display ADHD-like symptoms, those symptoms are rooted in the child's environment. In other words, they are actually the result of environmental and *not* biological factors. The natural conclusion to be drawn, then, is that stimulants are not appropriate for them.

In fact, that is precisely one of the key points I hope you will glean from reading this book. My clinical experience working with children displaying ADHD-like symptoms is that, because of the environmentally-bound way in which they view the world—having formed the impression that they get so much more relationship and energy from the significant adults in their life through "adversity"—they will never respond to normal, conventional and traditional approaches to parenting. And because they don't, they are labeled ADHD and put on medications.

But I have proven, through *The Nurtured Heart Approach*, that ADHD children can be transformed without subjecting them to the risks of stimulant drugs. The question that has to be posed is: "If the very same child is using his intensity in wonderful ways within a month of this new intervention, was it really a biochemical, neurological or genetic condition, or was it really environmental to begin with?" It follows then that, according to the Ritalin label, stimulant medications should *hardly ever be prescribed,* because the child's symptoms are almost always linked to environmental factors; and it follows that the diagnosis itself is called into question.

The drastic methods of *The Nurtured Heart Approach* are, in essence, a way of comprehensively changing the child's environment. We do so by incisively altering the quality of the relationship, energy, and behaviors we use to interact with these children.

75 Drug sensitivities can vary dramatically; it is crucial to carefully attend to adverse effects that can become psychosis, suicidal ideation, and increased aggression.

Children on Ritalin may become sad, tearful, depressed, apathetic, or tired. On the flip side—which may be sad for adults to see, but may seem preferable to the out-of-control hyperactivity that preceded it—there's the dreaded evening rebound. The child who finally can sit still in school becomes even more hyperactive at night than he was before he started on Ritalin. And if the drugs cover the child until bedtime, insomnia becomes an issue.

Beyond these problems is the possibility of even worse adverse effects. There may be psychosis that may involve hallucination of small insects or objects, or it may be expressed as paranoia, excessive distrust or suspiciousness. Some experience mania—grandiose thoughts and plans, bizarre notions of invulnerability, poor judgment, paranoia, and a quick reflex toward violence. (Doesn't this sound remarkably like typical side effects of Ritalin's cousin cocaine?)

Early signs of these problems may go unnoticed because the child's behavior has changed so much that the parents aren't sure where the drug effects end and the adverse effects begin.

Once the parents recognize that the child is sensitive to the medication and is having unacceptable adverse effects, he may already have met one of two disastrous fates: He may have been diagnosed as psychotic or bipolar by a psychiatrist and put on anti-psychotic drugs; or he may have committed a terrible act against another or against himself.

Is this common? Interview the tens of thousands of children around the country who are in some form of out-of-home placement: group homes, residential treatment facilities, hospitals and incarceration facilities. You'll find that the vast majority have been summarily prescribed Ritalin as a first course of treatment and, as symptoms and side-effects progressed, stronger drugs were administered, obviously to great detriment to the child.

Of course we can blame the child and his family, but that would be a great injustice. When you give them an approach that really works, the situation turns around in no time flat. So the child, the parents and the teachers aren't the culprits; it's the methods they have at their disposal.

76

Drugs do not cure ADHD. They do, however, prevent the child's root problems from being addressed, and such issues become harder to address as the child grows into a teenager and then into an adult.

I'll say it again, because it's a crucial fact that is rarely addressed: *Drugs do not cure ADHD.* Mainstream psychiatry claims that drugs don't cure ADHD because ADHD is incurable. The truth is that you can't cure something that is not a true disease in the first place.

In my practice, we treat thousands of children with these symptoms, but we help them before medication comes into play. We consistently experience that, when parents and teachers are given an approach that is more interactive in healthier ways, these same children with symptoms of intensity (impulsivity, disruptiveness, inattention) quickly shift. They become children who are intensely wonderful.

This is how, despite my classic training in recognizing the syndrome that is considered ADHD, I began to question whether these children really have a disorder in the first place.

If they become distinctly wonderful children in three to four weeks, is the pre-existing diagnosis really valid?

There is no research that shows ADHD symptoms are simply outgrown. You can't drug a child through her childhood and expect her to "snap out of it" at a later point in life. That is a myth. When we alter a child's developmental arc by drugging her, we are disrupting the building of the foundation of her personality and her self-image.

Only by doing whatever is necessary to deal with the root of the issue—which has nothing to do with any "biochemical imbalance"—can we help that child build a solid, steady foundation. And that child is going to feel supported and loved by all those who worked hard to help him find his way rather than betrayed by those who didn't like his behavior and used pills to control him.

Children with intense behaviors are at a crossroads: they are asking for help, guidance, and support in the only way they know how—by acting out. The child is waving a figurative flag, requesting a new level of interaction beyond anything received in the past. Medication kills the messenger. It ignores the canary in the coal mine.

It's easier to help a young child who acts out in difficult ways than to help a teenager. When problems are not addressed during the early years of a child's development, they may become more ingrained parts of the child's personality. Although teens can certainly be transformed as well, it may require a great deal more determination and effort.

One study found that 80 percent of children with ADHD symptoms retained those symptoms at the end of eight years in spite of medication, behavioral modification, and educational modification—the three-pronged approach most recommended by the therapeutic community. My interpretation: first, that medication hinders the progress that can be made with the other two approaches; and second, that traditional approaches to behavior and educational modification are typically not effective with these children anyway.

Medications do not stop the child from waving the flag of acting-out but rather make the child more prone to giving up on the adults in his life.

If it's more structure they are "dying" for and if it's not forthcoming in positive ways, they eventually will go shopping for the more convoluted versions available in the neighborhood. Alcohol and drug abuse, involvement in the juvenile justice system or in gangs, or getting pregnant as a teen are all highly structured experiences. They take over your life and dictate your existence.

Not killing the canary is a much better choice. (See Reason 101.)

NOTES

1. www.breggin.com/RitalinAH2.html

2. MTA Cooperative Group, "A 14-month randomized clinical trial of treatment strategies for attention deficit/hyperactivity disorder," *Archives of General Psychiatry* 1999;56:1073-1086.

3. WE Pelham, T Wheeler, A Chronis, "Empirically supported psychosocial treatments for attention deficit hyperactivity disorder," *Journal of Clinical Child Psychology* 1998;27:190-205.

4. MTA Cooperative Group, "Moderators and mediators of treatment response for children with attention deficit-hyperactivity disorder," *Archives of General Psychiatry* 1999;56:1088-96.

5. L Charles, R Schain, "A four-year follow-up study of the effects of methylphenidate on the behavior and academic achievement of hyperactive children," *J Abnorm Child Psychol* 1981 Dec;9(4):495-505.

6. D Jacobvitz, et al, "Treatment of attentional and hyperactivity problems in children with sympathomimetic drugs: a comprehensive review," *J Am Acad Child Adolesc Psychiatry* 1990 Sep;29(5):677-88.

7. SW Evans, et al, "Dose-response effects of methylphenidate on ecologically valid measures of academic performance and classroom behavior in adolescents with ADHD," *Exp Clin Psychopharmacol* 2001 May;9(2):163-75.

8. D Cohen, Ph.D., I Clapperton, M.D., M.Sc., CSPQ, P Gref, M.D., FRCPC, and Y Tremblay, M.D., CSPQ, FRCPC: "Critical analysis of research report: Attention Deficit and Hyperactivity Disorder. Perceptions of the actions and use of psychostimulants," issued April 1999.

9. B Bateman, et al, "The effects of a double-blind, placebo-controlled, artificial food colorings and benzoate preservative challenge on hyperactivity in a general population sample of preschool children," *Arch Dis Childhood* 2004 Jun;89(6):506-11.

10. M Boris, F Mandel, "Foods and additives are common causes of the attention deficit hyperactivity disorder in children," *Annals of Allergy* 1994 May;72:462-8.

11. A Brenner, "A study of the efficacy of the Feingold diet on hyperkinetic children. Some favorable personal observations," *Clin Pediatr (Phila)* 1977 Jul;16(7):652-6.

12. CM Carter, et al, "Effect of a few-foods diet in attention deficit disorder," *Arch Dis Child* 1993 Nov;69(5):564-8.

Section Seven
The Dangers of Polypharmacy

Pharmacological treatment of children with psychiatric disorders is increasing, despite the limited availability of supporting evidence for its effectiveness...Little data exist to support advantageous efficacy for drug combinations.

> —National Association of State Mental Health Program Directors in the *American Academy of Child and Adolescent Psychiatry,* September 2001[1]

Our usage exceeds our knowledge base. We're learning what these drugs are to be used for, but let's face it: we're experimenting on these kids.

> —Glen Elliott, M.D., University of California at San Francisco Psychiatric Institute[2]

ONLY FIVE PSYCHIATRIC DRUGS HAVE BEEN FDA-APPROVED for use in children: methylphenidate (Ritalin, Metadate CD); dextroamphetamine; imipramine (a tricyclic antidepressant); sertraline (Zoloft); and fluoxetine (Prozac). All others are used "off-label," meaning that they are used in children without having been subjected to clinical studies required for FDA approval for a specific use.

Off-label prescription is a very common practice in modern medicine. It is especially rampant in pediatric populations. There are ethical issues surrounding experimentation on children that preclude thorough pediatric testing of prescription drugs.

Of course, using untested drugs on millions of children might pose a more serious ethical dilemma, but this hasn't quite hit the radar screen of modern American medicine.

Children aren't just small adults. Their bodies and brains are not the same as adult bodies and brains. They don't always react to medications in ways that can be predicted by the effects of those medications on adults.

This is especially true with psychoactive drugs. For example, recent evidence shows that selective serotonin reuptake inhibitors (SSRIs) such as Paxil and Prozac dramatically increase suicidal tendencies in children.

What's even worse is that it's an accepted practice to administer two or more psychoactive drugs to a child at a time.

111

77

When side effects show up, kids are often given additional medications to control those side effects.

Drugs given to treat ADHD can *cause* stimulation, eliciting symptoms much like those attributed to ADHD. This often leads to increases in dosage or the addition of extra medications.

Let's say little Benjamin is given Ritalin or Adderall to treat his supposed ADHD. He can't sleep, so the doctor prescribes a sleep-inducing drug like clonidine (actually a drug approved to treat high blood pressure). The child then begins to feel depressed, and the doctor adds an SSRI to treat what really is a medication side effect. If the child is lucky, this is as far as it will go, but if Benjamin then starts to show pronounced mood swings from being given all these meds, he may be diagnosed with bipolar disorder and given lithium or Depakote. This previously slightly inattentive or hyperactive child then might really begin to have bizarre thoughts and behaviors, at which point he may end up on antipsychotics—drugs that can cause permanent damage and certainly additional toxicity, and drugs that he may be led to believe he needs for the rest of his life.

It is frightening to see how many children are winding up in this bipolar trap. The trend began around the late 1990s and has taken on a head of steam. I know at least one doctor who administers this diagnosis left and right. You could take a group of kids who clearly have the symptoms that have come to be labeled as ADHD, and have clear consensus on this "diagnosis" from a panel of therapists, yet this doctor will see it as bipolar disorder. How scientific is that? Truly, it's mind-boggling.

Bipolar disorder is serious business, treated with powerful drugs that carry a heavy burden of side effects. Once a child has been given this diagnosis, she is well on her way to becoming a victim of the system and a chronic mental patient—unless her family comes upon an extraordinary approach that has the power to create a transformation. I wish I could say that every family has had access to *The Nurtured Heart Approach*, but that is not yet the case.

Children may be given SSRIs or other antidepressants, powerful antipsychotics such as Haldol or Mellaril, or medications to help them sleep at night. Since each of these meds has its own side effects, the child ends up on a medication treadmill that is, in the end, a subjective guessing game rather than a scientific process.

One parent posted the following on the discussion forum at www.difficultchild.com, the web site for *The Nurtured Heart Approach*:

The doctors started my son on Wellbutrin for about six months when he was six and a half. I kept telling the doctors that he became withdrawn and depressed while on the drug. I was getting worried. This was not my son's normal behavior. The doctors insisted that this was normal and that I should give it more time. They also wrote him a prescription for Ritalin and Paxil to take along with the Wellbutrin. They said that this would somehow "balance out" his depression. Well, I hate to admit it, but I lost my temper, and told her (the doctor) that maybe it was she and my son's teachers who needed medication.

BTW [by the way], my son has been off of all meds for three years now, and he's as normal and happy as can be.

78 Medications sometimes stop working.

When this happens, dosages and diagnoses escalate, and the child ends up on multiple medications along with a diagnosis that could well destroy any potential for a normal, happy life.

The body has a miraculous ability to accommodate to substances that are foreign to it. This is why the Ritalin that appeared to be working for a period of time may one day cease to have the desired effect. The family and doctor, upon reviewing this situation in the next medication monitoring session, may increase the level of the original medication or add yet another. A colleague of mine in the Midwest reports that virtually every child she sees as a psychiatric nurse is on what she calls a "medication cocktail" of *four or more medications*.

How can even the brightest specialist know which medication is producing what result?

This piling-on of potent psychotropic medications is a direct result of the flawed biopsychiatric model that got the child on Ritalin in the first place. I am willing to bet that few (if any) parents are ever warned of this possibility.

Following is a case in point, prepared by Brenda, a client of mine, discussing her daughter's situation. She writes:

When Donna-Belle was 5 and in kindergarten, her teacher called one day and told us that we needed to have her evaluated for ADHD. "She is not paying attention, she is distracting the class" was basically what we heard. The teacher was not being mean-spirited and had our daughter's best interests at heart, but that phone call impacted the next four years of our lives in amazing and not always good ways.

About a year and one-half later, after several rounds of testing and trying to "fix" the problems with tougher rules and punishments, and searching for the doctor who could FIX her, the doctor decided to start Donna-Belle on an

ADHD medication. We saw almost immediate changes in her behavior and thought we had found the miracle drug of the century. Five days later, our daughter was only sleeping one hour a day, which meant we were only sleeping one hour a day! While her behavior was still improved, she was becoming physically exhausted; the doctor's answer was to add a different drug to help her sleep. (At this point we were still thinking the doctor knew everything and that we needed to listen to him without question.) This combination didn't work so he changed the first medication to something different. That medication did nothing to control the ADHD behaviors and so another change came several weeks later. This new medication came with a different side effect. In less than six weeks, my daughter, who is little to begin with, lost about 10 to15 pounds. She had no appetite, and no amount of begging, pleading, and threats could get her to eat more than a couple of bites at any meal or snack. The answer to this was to add a pill to make her hungry! By this time we had her taking so many medications that she had her own pillbox! (I will grant that some of the pills were supplements to give her the missing vitamins and minerals that I have found in my research many of these special kids may be missing in their systems.)

But the more we worked on treating Donna-Belle's ADHD, the more we noticed other very troubling behaviors becoming very prominent. Violent mood swings and raging became a nearly daily event. She had no doors on her room because she had pulled them off the hinges during rages. I frequently was covered in bruises from her raging and having to be physically restrained. The more she raged and became angry, the more the doctors increased her medications and added mood stabilizers. We also increased the intensity of our interventions. We got a private counselor for her, and then we got a family counselor to come to the house on top of that. The counselors began discussing putting my little 8-year-old girl in residential care because she was so out of control, and the doctors continued playing what we had come to call "pharmaceutical roulette" with our daughter.

I was spending about 40 hours a week researching on the Internet, in chat rooms, in the library, searching for something to help my little girl, and I came to the conclusion that I was also looking for something that was HOLISTIC. Not a new pill or shot or even a doctor.

We found your Nurtured Heart Approach, and within about six weeks began to implement it. That was in early January 2005. By late January, we had removed the mood stabilizers (with the doctor's knowledge, so we were sure that we didn't take her off anything too quickly). With your help, Howie, we then fully implemented the program, and in early February Donna-Belle came off of the ADHD medication (she was developing a severe shake and tic that prevented her from being able to write or hold a pencil even). Within a very few days, her behavior was changing. She tested the new program, but there was only one rage and a few "age appropriate" tantrums.

Our daughter has become a totally different child. She is very active, yes, but that is not bad! She uses her energy and her power in positive ways, to get more positive attention.

Donna-belle has always had issues with the word NO ... tantrums and fits would ensue from the slightest hint that she would not get her own way. It was not long before I was thrilled to see the first time I can ever recall that my daughter used problem solving to "get what she wanted" (actually a compromise) instead of throwing a tantrum. And then as I combed her hair, she said to me, "You know mom...I am liking myself now... I don't love me yet, but I don't hate me anymore!" I nearly started crying. This was the biggest step, in my mind ... going from self-hate and loathing to liking herself, which will only continue to improve as she sees that the world now is workable.

79 Ritalin is sometimes a "gateway drug" to the SSRIs, including Prozac. Selective serotonin reuptake inhibitor (SSRI) drugs such as Paxil and Zoloft have been linked with suicidal behavior in children.

Prozac, Zoloft, Celexa, Lexapro, Paxil, and other drugs in the SSRI class have slightly differing actions in the body, but they all work in fundamentally the same way. Naturally produced serotonin (a neurotransmitter) that has moved into a gap (synapse) between two nerve endings is prevented from being reabsorbed. This has the effect of extending the action of that bit of serotonin, and this in turn has the effect of improving mood. These antidepressants have a better side effect profile than any of those that came before them (most notably, the tricyclic antidepressants) but they are certainly not the wonder pills many have made them out to be, especially in the pediatric population.

Many experts—including Peter Breggin, M.D., who has been quoted extensively throughout this book, and Joseph Glenmullen, M.D., a clinical instructor in psychiatry at Harvard Medical School and a psychiatrist in private practice who authored the controversial *Prozac Backlash*—feel that the degree to which these drugs are being prescribed to both adults and children is unfounded and potentially disastrous.

Here are some statistics that you might find astounding:

- According to the MEDCO Drug Trend Report, the use of antidepressants in the pediatric population rose 27 percent between 2000 and 2003.[3]

- In the first three months of 2003, the number of children using antidepressants increased by 15 percent.[4]

- Between 1998 and 2002, the rate of antidepressant prescription in children under the age of five—a population for whom there is virtually zero evidence that these drugs are necessary or helpful—doubled.[5]

- According to a study by Express Scripts, 0.16 percent of girls and 0.23 percent of boys **under age five** were on antidepressants by the year 2002.

- Antidepressant prescriptions for children of all ages rose 68 percent for girls and 34 percent for boys between 1998 and 2002. Nearly seven percent of girls between the ages of 15 and 18 were on these drugs in 2002. [6]

Evidence from controlled clinical trials (studies comparing drugs to placebo or to each other), clinical reports (reports from clinicians who use drugs to treat their patients), and epidemiological studies (studies that examine the effects of various factors on populations) shows us unequivocally that SSRIs—in the words of Dr. Breggin—"commonly cause or exacerbate a wide range of abnormal mental and behavioral conditions." Most frightening is the very real risk of increased suicidal ideation and behavior that is a known side effect of most of the SSRIs. Recent evidence shows that children are particularly vulnerable to this effect. In fact, the British Committee of Safety in Medicine outlawed the use of any SSRI drug aside from Prozac in children under 18 because of increased risk of suicidal behaviors.[7]

An FDA advisory panel on February 20, 2004, heard the following testimony from families and patients who held SSRIs responsible for suicide attempts, violent behavior, and other dramatic and negative changes in personality and behavior:

- One child's family doctor saw that the teen had mild social anxiety and depression, and so prescribed the selective serotonin reuptake inhibitor Paxil. When the 16-year-old became more depressed, even suicidal, the doctor switched him to Effexor, a different antidepressant in the same class. Within three weeks, his dose rose from 40 to 300 mg daily. The boy took a rifle to school and held several classmates and a teacher at gunpoint for 45 minutes.

- A 12-year-old girl had been taking Paxil for three weeks when her personality began to change dramatically and her grades began to drop. A few months later, she committed suicide by hanging herself in her family home.

- A 16-year-old on SSRIs for three weeks became dangerously manic.

- A 17-year-old on SSRIs experienced agitation, insomnia, hallucinations, and paranoid delusions about the devil.

- A 15-year-old uncharacteristically struck a classmate in the face while on an SSRI, but had no signs of aggressive behavior once taken off of the drug.

- A 13-1/2-year-old heard a "weird ego-alien" voice telling him to kill himself while he was on an SSRI. The voice and his angry, explosive outbursts over minor matters went away within 10 days of stopping the drug.

Other case reports show that these kinds of symptoms went away once the drug was stopped and returned when the drug was started again.

Is this new information? No. The danger of increased violent behavior, suicidal thoughts, agitation, hostility, anxiety, and mania with these drugs has been known since the early 1990s. These drugs often cause *akathisia,* a sometimes excruciating agitation that can become so agonizing that the person commits violence toward himself or others. Estimates for rates of akathisia in users of Prozac range between 9.7 and 25 percent of people who use the drug.

In a 2002 study by Timothy Wilens et al, 22 percent of children (18 and under) suffered from psychiatric adverse effects while taking an SSRI.[8] These adverse effects went away when the drug was stopped. When these children were placed back on SSRIs, the adverse effects rate shot up to 44 percent. On August 22, 2003, Wyeth Pharmaceuticals issued a letter of warning to health care professionals in both the U.S. and the U.K., explaining that research had shown unacceptably high levels of hostility and suicide-related adverse events such as suicidal ideation and self-harm in children who take SSRIs. Finally, on December 18, 2003, Eli Lilly (the maker of Prozac) issued letters to British health care professionals, saying that Prozac is not recommended for treatment of children at all.

The brains of children are still forming. It's obvious that neurochemical-altering drugs like SSRIs, just as with stimulant drugs, cause both short-term and long-term adverse effects. And all too often, these drugs are prescribed in tandem—one to control behavior, and the other to control Ritalin-induced depression or anxiety.

According to Thomas J. Moore, a researcher and author of a paper on psychoactive drug usage that draws on two major health surveys performed by the U.S. government, 89 percent of children in these surveys were taking an antidepressant drug for a medical use for which there was no FDA approval. Most common was the off-label use of antidepressants for the treatment of attention deficit and conduct disorders. In other words, these drugs are not only being used to treat depression secondary to ADHD, but also as a first-line therapy for the "disorder."

Moore's research also revealed that 25 percent of the children who were on psychoactive meds were using a drug that the manufacturers now state should not be used in children. He also found that 10.3 percent of the children on drugs were taking three or more medications intended to affect the central nervous system.[9]

80 Children who become more aggressive, hyperactive, or inattentive while using Ritalin may end up on neuroleptics such as Haldol and Mellaril.

Stimulants are known to cause aggression, hyperactivity, and inattention in some users. Rather than withdrawing the offending medication, doctors may add additional drugs, unscientifically tinkering with the child's neuro-chemistry until his behavior becomes less threatening to adults. According to Dr. Joe Woolston, Director of Children's Psychiatric Inpatient Services at Yale-New Haven Hospital in Connecticut, "Every week I see at least one child who is on a regimen of something like Ritalin, Depakote, Haldol and Zoloft. It's just a ridiculous medication regimen." He calls this "a brand-new chapter" in child psychiatry. "The problem is people are using medications instead of doing full evaluation and treatment. Medication should be part of intervention, but it can't be stand-alone."[10]

Antipsychotic (neuroleptic) drugs are incredibly potent and dangerous, but today they are being handed out to children at an alarming rate as their diagnoses are ramped from ADHD to depression to bipolar disorder to psychosis. Thorazine, Risperdal, Mellaril, Haldol, Zyprexa, and Prolixin are a few of the neuroleptic drugs prescribed in a misguided attempt to tweak neurotransmitter levels.

Never mind the fact that these drugs work by downregulating the dopamine system, the neurotransmitter system that is *enhanced* by stimulant drugs. How scientific is it to stimulate a system and then downregulate it (in other words, to give another drug to lower the amount of stimulation)?

The brain responds by enhancing the sensitivity of the dopamine system. In a fair proportion of people who take neuroleptics, this leads to permanent neurological ill effects. There's tardive dyskinesia, characterized by tics, spasms, and abnormal movements; there's tardive akathisia, an especially intense, torturous form of restlessness that pushes the person into constant motion and suffering; and there's neuroleptic malignant syndrome (NMS), a potentially fatal brain disease that resembles viral encephalitis.

Rare but possible serious side effects of Risperdal, a neuroleptic:

NEUROLEPTIC MALIGNANT SYNDROME (NMS): characterized by symptoms such as muscle rigidity, altered mental status, irregular pulse or blood pressure, rapid heart beat, profuse sweating, kidney failure, and rhabdomyolysis (a rapid breakdown of muscle tissue). There is no medical agreement about how exactly to treat NMS. Patients who are put back on antipsychotics after a bout of NMS have been known to experience recurrences.

TARDIVE DYSKINESIA: potentially irreversible, involuntary movements. It is impossible to predict who will develop TD in response to antipsychotic drugs. The longer a person takes these drugs, and the greater the dose, the higher his or her risk of developing TD; but the syndrome can develop after brief treatment periods at low doses, as well. No treatment exists. The syndrome may go away partially or completely once the drugs are withdrawn. Antipsychotic treatment itself may suppress (partly or completely) symptoms of TD, masking the syndrome's development until the drugs are stopped.

Risperdal's labeling recommends that only those who have diseases known to respond to antipsychotic drugs should be given this medication. ADHD is not such a disease. It also recommends that it should be a last-resort treatment after less harmful treatments have been tried.

Neuroleptic malignant syndrome (NMS) is considered to be rare, but according to the FDA's criteria, it is actually a common side effect of these drugs. According to Lazarus, Mann, and Caroll, who performed a review of the research on this topic, between .02 and 3.23 percent of patients in psychiatric hospitals who are treated with neuroleptics fall prey to this syndrome.[11]

By FDA standards, an adverse effect that occurs in one percent of those treated with a drug is "common" or "frequent." According to some research,[12] between 1,000 and 4,000 deaths per year can be attributed to NMS. (If this sounds crazy to you, remember that over 100,000 deaths per year are directly attributable to adverse effects from properly prescribed prescription drugs.)

These are, obviously, not drugs that we should be giving to children. Those who would do so are simply not looking at the risk-benefit relationship in a clear fashion.

81

Proponents of Ritalin may casually advise users and parents of users to ignore the body's signals that something is wrong (i.e., side effects).

Carol E. Watkins, M.D., and Glenn Byrnes, M.D., Ph.D., put it this way: "We can treat annoying side effects so the individual can continue to take the stimulant." Here are some excerpts from these doctors' web site, which is entitled "Ritalin Helps, but What Are the Side Effects?" Note how casually these respected doctors recommend that parents and patients ignore the body's signals that something is awry, advising patients to simply obliterate side effects with additional drugs.

Jittery feeling: Eliminate caffeine or other stimulant-type medications. [Like Ritalin?] *A small dose of a beta-blocker (a type of blood pressure medication) can block tremor or jitters.*

Sleep difficulty: ...the sleep problem is sometimes due to the AD/HD, not the medication. If the sleep problem is truly due to medication effect, give the last dose earlier in the day. Sometimes clonidine or guanfacine help one settle down for sleep.

Irritability: Sometimes irritability may be due to the AD/HD or another psychiatric disorder. If the irritability is truly due to the stimulant, there are several options. Reduce the stimulant dose, switch to a different stimulant, add clonidine/guanfacine or use another class of medications to treat the AD/HD.

Depression: This may be a delayed effect of a stimulant medication. It may be more common with the long-acting stimulants. Screening for a history of depression, and treating co-existing depression can minimize this. If the depression truly is related to the medication, one may switch to another class of medications to treat the AD/HD. These second-line medications would include the tricyclic antidepressants and buproprion (Wellbutrin).

NOTES

1. www.nasmhpd.org/general_files/publications.med_directors_pubs/ polypharmacy.pdf

2. Jeffrey Kluger, "Medicating young minds," *Time Asia* 2003 Dec 8; 162 (22)

3. MEDCO's Drug Trend Report and Symposium at http://www.drugtrend.com

4. Medco Health Solutions, Inc., news release 2/1/05

5. www.express-scripts.com/ourcompany/news/outcomesresearch/on-linepublications/antidepressant

6. MB Keller, ND Ryan, M Stober, et al, "Efficacy of paroxetine in the treatment of adolescent major depression: a randomized, controlled trial," *J Am Acad Child Adolesc Psychiatry* 2001; 40(7):762-772.

7. "New guidelines for prescribing antidepressants," UK, 12-6-04

8. TE Wilens, et al, "A systematic chart review of the nature of psychiatric adverse events in children and adolescents treated with selective serotonin reuptake inhibitors,: *J Child Adoles Psychopharmacol* 2003 Summer; 13(2):143-52

9. http://drugsafetyresearch.com/download/med_use_antidep.pdf

10. From a Reuters press release by Kevin Drawbaugh

11. A Lazarus, SC Mann, SN Caroll, "The neuroleptic malignant syndrome and related conditions," *American Psychiatric Press*, Washington DC, 1989

12. Maxmen and Ward, 1995, p.3

Section Eight
The Conspiracy to Drug America's Children Into Submission: Doctors and Drug Companies

The way to sell drugs is to sell psychiatric illness.
> —Carl Elliott, Bioethicist, University of Minnesota[1]

The whole business of creating psychiatric categories of 'disease,' formalizing them with consensus, and subsequently ascribing diagnostic codes to them, which in turn leads to their use for insurance billing, is nothing but an extended racket furnishing psychiatry a pseudo-scientific aura. The perpetrators are, of course, feeding at the public trough.
> —Thomas Dorman, M.D., internist[2]

A S YOU KNOW IF YOU'VE READ THIS FAR, the evidence that ADHD has any basis in brain chemistry or brain abnormalities is much too scant to be put forth as fact. Despite this, the drug companies that make and market Ritalin (Novartis) and the new non-stimulant ADHD drug Strattera (Lilly) report to physicians and the public that "Attention-Deficit/Hyperactivity Disorder (ADHD) is a neurological brain disorder that manifests as a persistent pattern of inattention and/or hyperactivity-impulsivity that is more frequent and severe than is typically observed in individuals at a comparable level of development." (From Strattera.com, a web site of Lilly Pharmaceuticals)

Lilly's site promoting Strattera claims that ADHD's cause is unknown, but that "Overall studies have concluded that heredity explains, on average, the majority of ADHD-like behavior exhibited by children, while environmental factors explain only approximately 20% of this type of behavior...Increasingly it has become clear that ADHD is a neurological disorder that requires a medical diagnosis and treatment."

In other words, we don't know for sure, but ADHD *might* be a genetically transferred neurological disorder. Sure, it *might*, but there's also a great deal of compelling evidence that it *isn't*.

On its web site (ADHDinfo.com) promoting Ritalin, Novartis claims that "Stimulants are designed to restore the natural balance of the chemicals in the brain affected by ADHD."

Stimulants don't restore any kind of natural balance—they promote an *imbalance* that replaces hyperactive behavior with overly focused, zombie-like behavior.

Physicians aren't encouraged to see this side of the story. For the most part, they only see information that is designed to promote the use of drugs to treat this "disorder." The Novartis site's Information for Healthcare Professionals section advises that "primary care doctors should establish a treatment plan that recognizes ADHD as a chronic condition"—meaning a condition for which there is no cure and for which medication may be needed indefinitely. It goes on to state that "40 to 80 percent of children with ADHD continue to meet the criteria into adolescence, and 50 to 65 percent continue to meet the criteria of ADHD into late adolescence and early adulthood."

Doctors are, by and large, hardworking people who have the best interests of their patients at heart. They are incredibly overworked and stressed in today's climate. Managed care, fear of malpractice suits, and high costs are squeezing doctors beyond what many can handle. It's far easier and less time-consuming for them to prescribe medication to a child presenting ADHD-like symptoms than it is to do a detailed evaluation or to provide direct transformational treatment. In many instances, the child has been brought to the doctor's office for the sole purpose of getting a prescription for stimulant drugs, and pressure will mount on her if she resists doing so.

Pharmaceutical companies, on the other hand, have become more preoccupied with their bottom line than with helping people become well. They promote their products with direct-to-consumer advertising; they disguise advertising as education, effectively pushing their products on physicians and the public by disseminating biased information about the nature of ADHD; and they fund so-called "patient advocacy groups" like Children and Adults with Attention Deficit Disorder (CHADD) that promote the use of medication.

82 Doctors giving psychological evaluations to children may not have the proper training to do so accurately.

Many parents report that their child was handed a prescription for Ritalin after a single 15-minute visit with the doctor. In 75 percent of evaluations of behavior problems by family doctors or specialists, meds are prescribed that same day.

The doctor doing the initial medication evaluation may not have had training in techniques and strategies that allow for what I would consider to be an accurate evaluation. Generally, physicians have no idea how to interact with the child in a way that will enable them to "see around the corner" and perceive whether this child might be a candidate for an excellent outcome without medications.

When I had my therapy practice, I would welcome a new family in the waiting room, orchestrate introductions, and then make my way over to the child for a vital component of the assessment. I would use a number of the techniques described at the end of this book and observe the child's response. Typically, by the time I ushered the family into my office, I was able to say the following with full confidence:

"I know you are here today because of your concerns about issues at home and school. I also know from what you said over the phone that others have been leading you to think that your child may have ADHD, and that there is some pressure right now to consider medications. I have good news for you: I just did what I consider to be a very reliable assessment in the waiting room, and I have every belief that ADHD is not something you need to concern yourself with at this point in time.

"Your child responded beautifully to the approach I took in the waiting room. Based on my experience, if I can teach you this approach successfully, the changes you'll see in the next few weeks will amaze you. I am confident that your child's intensity will be a source of joy instead of distress within a month's time."

From that point on, the family's experience is not one of diagnosis and disease and prescriptions, but one of growth and learning together. They save enormous amounts of money and time.

One of the more painful moments I've experienced in my years as a therapist happened when I attended a medication evaluation with a family with whom I had just begun to work. This child had responded perfectly to my approach in my initial assessment and was responding well to his parents' initial use of the approach I had taught them. Then, I went to the psychiatrist with them for an appointment that had been arranged months in advance and saw immediately that this doctor had a terrible style of interacting with the child. He sat behind an obscenely large desk the entire time and only talked to the child to scold him. There were no appreciative comments on any of the child's acceptable behaviors—which, by the way, were plentiful.

This doctor sent a strong and immediate message to the child that he was, in effect, invisible when he did not break the rules. The child saw that he got far more energy from the doctor when he created adversity, and plenty of adversity transpired in that brief meeting. I could almost see the doctor raising the dosage he would prescribe in his mind as the minutes ticked away. He was trained to assess and treat pathology.

Ironically, this same doctor, who was renowned for prescription writing for almost every child he saw, ended up coming to me for help with his own child years later. Hopefully, the successful work we did with his child drastically influenced his subsequent work with other children. This was not an isolated incidence.

Remember that there is no accepted diagnostic test for ADHD. I've heard so many parents say that their children were given prescriptions for Ritalin and an ADHD diagnosis after a brief interview where there is virtually no direct interest shown in the child, but rather a review of what the parent and teacher provide by way of the Connor's Scale or other such subjective assessments considered by the medical community to somewhat empirically assess the existence of ADHD.

Most diagnosticians try to adhere to the criteria in the updated Diagnostic Statistical Manual of Mental Disorders (DSM-IV). At least eight of these "symptoms" must be present from before the child is 7 years of age, and they must persist for at least six months. As you will see here, all of these criteria are extremely subjective.

DSM-IV Criteria for ADHD Diagnosis

A. *Either 1 or 2:*

1. Six or more of the following symptoms of inattention have persisted for at least six months to a degree that is maladaptive and inconsistent with developmental level:

   a. Often fails to give close attention to details or makes careless mistakes in schoolwork, work, or other activities

   b. Often has difficulty sustaining attention in tasks or play activities

   c. Often does not seem to listen when spoken to directly

   d. Often does not follow through on instructions and fails to finish schoolwork, chores, or duties in the workplace (not due to oppositional behavior or failure to understand)

   e. Often has difficulty organizing tasks and activities

   f. Often avoids, dislikes, or is reluctant to engage in tasks that require sustained mental effort (such as homework)

   g. Often loses things necessary for tasks or activities (toys, assignments, pencils, books, or tools)

   h. Is often easily distracted by extraneous stimuli

   i. Is often forgetful in daily activities

continued next page

125

DSM-IV Criteria for ADHD Diagnosis *(continued from previous page)*

2. Six or more of the following symptoms of hyperactivity-impulsivity have persisted for at least six months to a that is maladaptive and inconsistent with developmental level:

Hyperactivity

a. Often fidgets with hands or feet or squirms in seat

b. Often leaves seat in classroom or in other situations in which remaining seated is expected

c. Often runs about or climbs excessively in situations in which it is (in adolescents or adults, may be limited to feelings of restlessness)

d. Often has difficulty playing or engaging in leisure activities quietly

e. Is often "on the go" or often acts as if "driven by a motor"

f. Often talks excessively

Impulsivity

g. Often blurts out answers before questions have been completed

h. Often has difficulty awaiting turn

i. Often interrupts or intrudes on others (such butting into conversations or games)

B. Some hyperactive, impulsive, or inattentive symptoms that caused impairment were present before age 7 years

C. Some impairment from the symptoms is present in two or more (such as in school or work and at home)

D. There must be clear evidence of clinically significant impairment in social, academic, or occupational functioning

E. The symptoms do not occur exclusively during the course of a pervasive developmental disorder, schizophrenia, or another psychotic disorder and are not better accounted for by another disorder (such as a mood, anxiety, dissociative, or personality disorder)

ADHD Types Using DSM-IV criteria

ADHD, predominantly inattentive type
   Meets inattention criteria (section AI) for the past 6 mo

ADHD, predominantly hyperactive-impulsive type
   Meets hyperactive-impulsive criteria (section A2) for the past 6 mo

ADHD, combined type
   Meets criteria for section AI and section A2 for the past 6 mo

ADHD, not otherwise specified
   Prominent symptoms of inattention or hyperactivity-impulsivity that do not meet the criteria for ADHD
   In partial remission

What constitutes "excessive talking"? What constitutes "easily distracted," "difficulty remaining seated," or "fidgeting"? Physicians, parents, and teachers may all have different expectations here. For example, behavior seen as annoyingly fidgety by a teacher might not bother the parent at all.

I'll concede that, with some children, there's no confusion about these issues. It's obvious that he is not good at sitting still or paying attention under some circumstances. But almost without exception, so-called ADHD children are able to focus and sit still under other circumstances—proof positive that there is not a brain dysfunction or lack of capacity at play, but most often a square peg that doesn't fit into a round hole. Once we change the shape of the hole, the peg can be a great fit. This can be done by employing the approach described at the end of this book.

Data from a number of studies have shown that about 50 percent of kids who are diagnosed with ADHD will also end up being diagnosed with ODD (oppositional defiance disorder) or CD (conduct disorder). It is rare for a child to be diagnosed with CD or ODD without also being diagnosed with ADHD, however.

Interesting, isn't it, that instead of considering the notion that these kids might have perfectly good reason to be angry, we call their anger a "disorder" and give them drugs to treat it?

The way I see it, kids are at risk of going from ADHD to ODD to CD because *no one is listening* and *no one is giving them what they need to improve their behavior.* **And apparently the medications are not preventing this progression.**

According to the DSM-IV, ODD differs from ADHD in that it involves behavior considered to be deliberate and willful. ADHD kids often annoy, disobey, and fail to follow through, but the belief is that they can't help it. With ODD, the behaviors are intended to be contradictory.

Conduct disorder (CD) is a more severe type of behavioral disorder than ODD that is also more likely to develop in children with ADHD. According to DSM-IV, the essential feature of CD is "...a repetitive and persistent pattern of behavior in which the basic rights of others or age appropriate social norms or rules are violated."

Psychiatrists warn that ODD, if left untreated, may well evolve into CD, a more serious "disease" that has a very poor prognosis. Among its symptoms: The child has little empathy or concern for others' wishes or feelings and does not feel guilty or regretful about his misdeeds. He may jump to the conclusion that others' intentions towards him are hostile and may react aggressively in response. Children who are irritable and have a hard time tolerating frustration...who become sexual very early...who use and abuse drugs and/or alcohol...and who end up poor academic achievers who drop out or are suspended from school fit the profile of the child diagnosed with CD.

Psychiatry points out that while ADHD and CD share some "associated features," they are truly distinct disorders that overlap little. The actual symptoms used to diagnose each condition are distinct. Parents are warned not to attribute antisocial behavior that fits in with the CD diagnosis to the child's ADHD.

This does lend some authority to the "co-morbid" (or co-existing) diagnosis, but what all this says to me is that the ADHD child whose cries for a different kind of attention are not heard will start to act out in more and more destructive ways. We're not talking about two co-existing disorders, but about patterns of behavior that grow in intensity and destructiveness when not properly attended to.

83 Doctors are trying to help, but most are limited to the perspective that ADHD is a disorder of the brain and that medications are the only solution. Many find themselves under huge pressure from schools and parents to prescribe medication.

Most doctors have limited training in alternatives to medication. Every major organization that has released position statements on optimal therapy for ADHD has clearly stated that medication *and* therapy are required to yield good results, but it's the rare ADHD child who gets the therapeutic intervention she really needs. Because of the current medical belief that ADHD is a disorder of the brain, there is little room to see that any non-medical intervention can provide a complete remedy.

It's also important for parents and educators to recognize that much of the information that physicians get about ADHD comes from pharmaceutical industry marketing. The long arm of the drug companies reaches into medical journals, articles in lay magazines, television commercials and news programs, and seminars and research presentations backed by these companies. Doctors are often actually paid to attend medication seminars, and drug industry representatives show up in doctors' offices with study results (funded by their employers, crafted carefully to yield positive results) and free samples for the doctors to distribute to their patients. To say that the makers of ADHD drugs have a vested interest in ensuring that doctors see ADHD as best treated with medication is an understatement.

As much as doctors wish to provide relief for the child and her family, they can only do so with the tools at their disposal. If their toolbox consists only of medications, they are limited to the tools at hand, and the children they treat have only one option.

Schools send families to physicians for the sole purpose of getting a difficult child on medication. They say that the school "cannot meet the child's needs within the regular classroom setting without medication," meaning that if the child doesn't get his prescription, that child will be put into an alternative needs setting or even into a different school. The expectation is that the doctor will readily hand over a prescription.

This can put enormous pressure on even the most dedicated doctor![3]

Those who refuse, or who insist on a long, thorough diagnostic process, are seen as a roadblock rather than a caring and dedicated professional who wants the best for each and every child he sees.

In his article "Ritalin: Better Living Through Chemistry?" internist Leonard Sax, M.D., writes of his own experience:

I've seen this happen many times. Sometime around the end of first grade or the beginning of the second, the boy's parents are summoned to the school for a "team meeting." This formidable encounter typically consists of the parents at one end of the table, with the boy's guidance counselor, plus one or two of the boy's teachers, plus the principal, and sometimes the school psychologist sitting at the other end. "Johnny [or Brett or David or Justin] isn't reading at grade level," the counselor tells the parents. "He doesn't pay attention," the teacher adds. "He may have ADD," the psychologist warns. "We think you should speak with your child's doctor about getting your son on Ritalin."

...The parents bring their son to see me. I'm supposed to decide whether this six-year-old boy needs to be on Ritalin...As the boy's doctor, I have two choices. I can accept the recommendation of the counselor, teacher, principal, and psychologist; write a prescription for Ritalin; and move on to my next patient. Total time elapsed: five minutes. Or I can question the recommendation of the school professionals, do my own assessment of the child, interview the parents at length, and question the need for Ritalin. Total time elapsed: sixty minutes, maybe longer. Meanwhile, I have other patients in the waiting room, eyeing the clock, asking the receptionist why Dr. Sax is running so far behind. What choice would you make in my position?[4]

I now know doctors who rarely prescribe medications at the first visit for two reasons. First, they have developed their own way of interacting directly with the child in a manner that allows them to see a way around medication, at least for the time being. Second, they have therapists on staff that have been trained in my approach, and deliver this as part of the services their clinics offer. These doctors ultimately feel better about their ability to *heal* the situations of their patients and the patients' families. They still can manage to make an income by way of the evaluation and check-ups, but now they are having an enormously positive impact on their community.

84

Doctors are, by and large, not trained in the use and effectiveness of alternatives to medication and tend to be biased toward pharmacological solutions.

Medical schools and internships focus on pharmacological and high-tech solutions to every problem. Med school research and continuing education for physicians are funded by the pharmaceutical companies, who gear their efforts toward promoting drugs.

And let's not forget that physicians are now operating under the strain of managed care. Often, they are pressed into "standard of care" decisions because of pressures from insurance providers or medical group practices to which they belong.

Any physician who tries to go in another direction—embracing alternative methods, perhaps using nutrition or supplements to help their patients, and saying no to drugs unless they are absolutely necessary—is likely to experience a great deal of criticism and even problems with their licensure or malpractice insurability. Physicians are asked to do far more than any one person can reasonably do, so it's understandable when they decide to toe the party line.

There's an old saying in medicine that "when you hear hoofbeats, think horses, not zebras." Look first for the simplest solution. If a patient presents with a rash, first think contact dermatitis, not flesh-eating bacteria. If a patient has a cough, first think bronchitis, not tuberculosis.

Modern psychiatry in particular has started thinking zebras all over the place. Child acting out? Think *brain dysfunction*, think *ADHD*, think *bipolar disorder* or *depressive disorder* or *anxiety disorder* or any one of the dozens of DSM-described diagnoses. Don't think *child who needs more attention* or *child who needs a different kind of attention or learning environment,* or *child with problems at home that need to be resolved,* or *child who is easily overwhelmed and needs more support or different quality of support.* Because then we wouldn't be able to "fix" the child's problems with medication!

Modern physicians also are asked to adhere to the Hippocratic tenet of *first do no harm.* By writing prescriptions right and left without any real evidence to support what they're doing, they risk going against this tenet—the most basic rule of all for doctors to follow. If we "fix" someone by "breaking" them—essentially what we do when we confuse the neurochemical circuitry in a child's brain without any evidence that there is an imbalance to start with—we are doing harm.

85

Pharmaceutical companies influence what doctors learn from journals and continuing education, and they also fund most drug research.

Many of the more "mainstream" ADHD resources, such as the CHADD (Children and Adults with ADD) web site, advise readers to avoid alternative treatments like biofeedback, naturopathy, diet and the like because they are unproven and of questionable efficacy. Instead, they promote the approaches that are supported by the studies published in medical journals: what they refer to as a multimodal approach...code for a combination of medications first and foremost, along with behavior modification regimens at home and school.

There is a fundamental problem with the system that creates research. Someone has to pay for every research study that is performed, and each one can cost millions of dollars. Do you think that the folks who support biofeedback, naturopathy, or dietary approaches have pockets anywhere near deep enough to fund such a study? Of course not—and so the research rarely gets done. On the other hand, pharmaceutical companies have the monetary resources to fund study after study—and to essentially hire teams that will give them the results they want.

Also keep in mind that physicians' offices are frequently visited by representatives from pharmaceutical companies. These salespeople are there to do one thing: sell their latest, most costly products to these doctors. They often give doctors skewed versions of the research into these new drugs, and they may leave free samples for the docs to pass out. Pharmaceutical reps tempt overworked physicians with fancy gifts, meals out, or trips to exotic locales in exchange for meetings to hear the pitch about the latest wonder drug. Drug companies spend an average $13,500 in marketing *per doctor per year.*[5]

Do you think the biofeedback, naturopathy, or diet therapy folks are going from doctor's office to doctor's office peddling their wares? Do you suppose they have the resources to offer Dr. So-and-So an all-expenses paid trip to the tropics? Of course not. It simply isn't done.

Pharmaceutical companies also fund much of the continuing education that doctors need to maintain licensure, so these seminars are often strongly biased toward drug therapies. Pharmaceutical companies are also the major funder of medical journals, where medical research is published and where physicians learn about the latest advances in medical science. Pharmaceutical companies shape the content of these journals, influencing the subject matter and strategically placing advertisements for their products.

Finally, let's not underestimate the effectiveness of drug company lobbyists in Washington, D.C. For every legislator in D.C., there are six drug company lobbyists, pushing to promote their employers' interests when policies are made. Alternative medical approaches don't stand a chance in this environment.

Doctors are, of course, human, and any one of us put in their place would find it difficult not to be swayed by the smooth persuasive tactics employed by the pharmaceutical industry. Some might take the perks and refuse the drugs in the end, but certainly these represent a fraction of doctors practicing today.

86 **Pharmaceutical companies hire research teams that implicitly guarantee the results the company wants. You don't stay on the payroll unless you produce research that supports the company's agenda—and there is strong evidence that these agendas are about money, not about helping people who are ill.**

If you are a researcher, and you receive a grant to do an ADHD/medication study, it is more likely than not funded by a pharmaceutical company. Chances are that if the results of your study do not support the use of the company's product, you will never see another dime of their funding dollars. There is plenty of evidence to support experimenter bias in drug research.

In one recent study, published in the highly esteemed journal *Lancet,* researchers at the Centre for Outcomes Research and Effectiveness in London, England, evaluated two sets of data on the use of SSRIs in children between the ages of five and 18. They first looked at the data that had been published in a peer-reviewed study; they then looked at data from the same studies that had been excluded from the final versions of the studies—the versions that eventually reached publication. Their analysis of the **published** data indicated that the risk-benefit profile of Prozac in this pediatric population was fairly decent, while the risk-benefit profile of Zoloft and Paxil were uncertain.

In the analysis of the **excluded** data, however, Zoloft and Paxil's risks began to look more serious and their benefits more questionable.

In other words: the researchers who created the studies got rid of data that didn't support the conclusions they were trying to reach.

Here's what a *Lancet* editorial had to say:

The story of research into selective serotonin reuptake inhibitor (SSRI) use in childhood depression is one of confusion, manipulation, and institutional failure. Although published evidence was inconsistent at best, use of SSRIs to treat childhood depression has been encouraged by pharmaceutical companies and clinicians worldwide. Last month, the Canadian Medical Association Journal *revealed excerpts from an internal GlaxoSmithKline memorandum demonstrating how the company sought to manipulate the results of published research. Concerning a study of paroxetine [Paxil] use in children, the memorandum states 'it would be unacceptable to include a statement that efficacy had not been demonstrated, as this would undermine the profile of paroxetine.'*

...In a global medical culture where evidence-based practice is seen as the gold standard for care, these failings are a disaster. Meta-analysis of published data supports an increasing number of clinical decisions and guidelines, which in turn dictate the use of vast levels of health-care resources. This process is made entirely redundant if its results are so easily manipulated by those with potentially massive financial gains.[6]

According to Victor Cohn and Lewis Cope in their excellent book *News & Numbers: A guide to reporting statistical claims and controversies in health and other fields* (University of Iowa Press, 2001), a meta-analysis is "the statistical analysis of several low-power research studies to integrate the results. In effect, it adds several studies together to try to come up with stronger conclusions." It's easy to see how this technique could be manipulated to bring out the best possible outcome in favor of a drug.

An acquaintance in the pharmaceutical industry told me that the makers of one ADHD drug had a goal for fiscal year 2004 of increasing the number of prescriptions for that drug from 20 million to 25 million.

Does this kind of agenda match the agenda of a family looking for safe answers for their intense child?

87 Pharmaceutical companies fund organizations like CHADD, which on the one hand support the notion of ADD by calling it a biologically based disorder that should be treated with drugs, and then on the other hand attempt to "de-stigmatize" the disorder.

CHADD (Children and Adults with Attention Deficit Disorder) portrays Ritalin as a benign, mild stimulant that is not associated with abuse or serious side effects. Millions of parents rely on CHADD's web site for information and support when dealing with their supposedly ADHD children. Adult "ADDers" are also reliant upon information from CHADD. These people, for the most part, do not know that CHADD gets most of its financial support from Ciba-Geigy, nor that this creates a significant conflict of interest that biases the information they are receiving.

The Department of Education is in on the con, too. Here's part of an article at eagleforum.org:

In 1994, the U.S. Department of Education, Office of Special Education Programs, under contract HS92017001, gave the Chesapeake Institute of Washington, D.C. the funding to produce two slick videos: "Facing the

*Challenges of ADD," featuring actress Rita Moreno, and "One Child in
Every Classroom" with Frank Sesno as moderator...In a PBS documentary
following eight months of investigation, a Department of Education
spokesman was asked if he was aware that the parents who spoke so enthusiastically about Ritalin on the videos were board members of Children and
Adults with Attention Deficit Disorder (CHADD), and if he knew that
CHADD has received cash grants of $900,000 plus in-kind services from
Ciba-Geigy, the manufacturer of Ritalin. Obviously embarrassed, the
bureaucrat denied such knowledge.*[7]

Statements by CHADD are inconsistent with scientific literature. There is
a section of the organization's web site (which ironically claims to separate
ADHD fact from fiction) stating that it has been proven that ADHD is a
biopsychiatric disorder that has little or nothing to do with parenting styles
or other environmental factors. Even to non-scientists, their side of the story
doesn't ring true. And scientists who are critical of widespread overuse of
stimulants and other psychiatric drugs in pediatric populations have very
vocally denounced the "facts" put forth by CHADD.

This is a slick organization, well-funded and with a wide reach. They
hold powerful influence over parents and, it seems, even over the
Department of Education. The International Narcotics Control Board,
however, isn't fooled: it has expressed concern that CHADD is actively
lobbying for the use of Ritalin in children.[8]

88 The creation of new drugs—for ADHD or for other psychiatric or physical "disorders"—is motivated more by profit margins than by public health needs.

Drug companies sell psychiatric drugs by selling the disorder, which may
or (as is the case with ADHD) may not be real. This is called "raising
awareness" by the drug companies, but in reality they are creating a market
for a drug. In *Talking Back to Ritalin,* Peter Breggin states that "the psychiatric medicating of children is now a significant source of income, identity,
and authority in the field of pediatrics, family practice, neurology, and
psychiatry." (p.23)

New drugs are automatically patent-protected for 17 years. For that span
of time, drug makers have no competition from generics or from others who
would profit from their new pharmaceutical formulation. In theory, this
period of patent protection allows the drug's maker to pay itself back for the
costs of research and development, enabling them to charge as high a price
as necessary for the drug without fear of anyone else charging less. In
practice, however, the patenting system is being played like an orchestra by
greedy pharmaceutical companies.

When a drug first comes out, the maker's marketing machine celebrates it as a great boon to humanity, even if it's only slightly chemically different from another drug. In most instances, new drugs are far from revolutionary; they are a molecule away from being identical to some other drug. Nine times out of 10, they aren't shown to be superior to drugs that have been around for years. Still, the hoopla created by direct-to-consumer and medical journal ads and pharmaceutical representatives convinces the world that this new drug is *better* than the old ones. So the system or the individual is willing to pay drastically higher costs to have the new drug, or to try the new drug when another didn't work for them.

Fast-forward to 17 years later. The drug company has probably been feverishly working to tweak the drug in some way for a few years now— perhaps create a longer-acting version, or some new delivery system, or some other molecular change that would allow for a new patent. Then, when their old patent is set to run out, they have a fabulous new product to replace it. Chances are good, too, that other drug companies have seen this day coming, and they have probably tried to create a new drug that could compete.

Case in point: ADHD drugs. According to Karen Thomas, a writer for *USA Today*:

Moms accustomed to being sold lunchbox notions and cold remedies are starting to see ads for powerful drugs to control their children's behavior in an escalating marketing push that has some child advocates and government officials twitching...drug companies are launching an aggressive battle to win the beefiest slice of what is shaping up to be a billion-dollar industry for treating ADHD with stimulants such as Adderall, Concerta and Ritalin...Those drug treatments with single-dose formulas—pills taken once a day, instead of two or three times a day—are rising quickest. Prescriptions for Adderall have increased 1,017% since 1997. In less than a year since becoming available, Concerta, also a single-dose drug, captured 11 percent of the market. The use of Ritalin, which requires two or three doses daily, is declining quickly and steadily.

Enter a reinvented Ritalin...Novartis, the maker of Ritalin, hopes the FDA next month will approve Ritalin LA, a long-acting formula that lasts for six hours—the length of a typical school day.[9]

All of the stimulant drugs work in the same way to quell children's intensity and narrow their focus. There are minor differences in the way children react to the various versions, for reasons no one quite understands, but these differences are rarely as significant as drug makers would like us to believe. Even long-acting drugs—which are promoted for "covering your child's ADHD for the entire school day"—aren't that much of an improvement over old-fashioned, take-your-dose-at-lunch Ritalin.

135

Drug makers whose top priority is the bottom line are scrambling to try to distinguish their products from the others, but there is essentially very little difference. In their attempts to come out on top, the drug companies that make some of these drugs have been reprimanded by the DEA for their deceptive advertising tactics in magazines such as *Ladies' Home Journal* and *Parade*.

89 Off-label prescribing is the rule rather than the exception.

Drugs are approved by the FDA for specific uses, but are often prescribed "off-label"—i.e., for uses other than those for which they have earned FDA approval. FDA approval is generally a rigorous process designed to ensure drug safety and efficacy. It takes years and requires several well-conducted studies. (In recent years, however, the government and pharmaceutical companies have conspired to make drug approval easier to get, and drug companies continue to refine the art of designing studies and hiring researchers that all but guarantee to get them the results they need to earn an approval.) Off-label prescribing is much less founded in hard science than on the intuition and clinical expertise of individual physicians and word-of-mouth between them.

Of the 10 drugs most prescribed off-label to children in 1994, three were psychiatric medications: Prozac, Zoloft, and Ritalin (which was approved for children over six, but was prescribed 226,000 times to children under the age of six that year—technically, off-label prescribing).

Off-label prescribing relies on the judgment of individual doctors, who often try a drug that is not approved for a specific problem when they learn that a colleague has done so with some success. This is not a very scientific way to prescribe drugs, and all too often it gets out of hand, with word-of-mouth replacing the gold standard of FDA approval—which is garnered through millions of dollars' worth of studies that are, hopefully, rigorous and concise enough to reveal any reasons why the drug should not be taken by millions of people.

Even when a drug has been approved to treat a specific disorder, it can only be officially approved to treat people in the age groups that were included in the pre-approval studies. Clinical drug research is rarely performed on children. It's seen as unethical to experiment on children, and no drug company wants to be left holding the bag when a child is seriously harmed or killed while participating in that company's drug study. (Recently, the FDA helped drug companies get past this fear by offering to extend patent protection on drugs if those companies would test them on children.)

Of course, when we don't thoroughly test drugs on a selected population of children and instead prescribe the drug off-label, we are in essence experimenting on every child who takes the medication. Most frightening is the trend toward off-label prescribing of antipsychotics and SSRIs to children as young as two.

We need to wipe the slate clean and start fresh, with a new respect for the harm these drugs can do, as well as the help they can offer when they are prescribed only when *absolutely, positively needed.* We need to stop mass experimentation with the minds of children and embrace non-pharmacological means for helping children thrive.

An unpublished study I conducted when I was director of a family therapy clinic known for its exciting outcomes using *The Nurtured Heart Approach* followed the treatment of a group of children coming to our clinic who clearly met the diagnostic criteria for ADHD. During a 10-month period in 1998, our clinic worked with 211 children and their families. Of the 160 children who were not already on medications, only eight were subsequently referred for psychiatric evaluations and only four were actually prescribed medications subsequent to the evaluation. This represents less than a 3% rate of utilization of medications. In contrast, given the severity of the presenting symptoms of these children, I am certain that, had they seen a medical doctor for an evaluation first, the vast majority would have been prescribed stimulant medications as a first course of treatment. As things turned out, the vast majority had remarkable and wonderful outcomes without resorting to medication.

90 Health insurers are vastly more likely to cover the cost of ADHD medication than therapy, and this plays a huge role in the decision to use only meds to "treat" an intense child.

Counseling is expensive. It can range from $60 to well over $100 per hour. To benefit, some children require extensive hours of this kind of help. Many of the approaches used in counselors' offices are off the mark, so it can happen that parents and child invest time and money and faith in the process—all for naught.

Increasingly, health insurers are refusing to pay for counseling, or are only paying for a small portion of it. Electing the services of a therapist can cause premiums to rise, or can cause serious problems if and when the insured party has to find a new insurance plan. Medication may turn out to be the only intervention that the family can afford, because it is almost always covered by insurance.

Here's what the NIMH's Peter Jensen, M.D., had to say on PBS's *"Frontline"* on April 10, 2001, about the evolution of ADHD diagnoses due to changes in health insurance:

The other big factor, I think, that took place during that time [1990-1993; to increase ADHD diagnosis and medication] *was health care reform. And health care reform hit mental health with a vengeance in many ways. Because what it said to mental health was, 'We're cutting way back on the kind of therapies that we're going to offer, and we're going to set a total number of sessions. And we're going to say when you can get sessions and why...' So what we hear from many parents was that they could not any longer go see a therapist for 50 or 60 sessions a year, every week or twice a week.... More and more, doctors were being asked to say, "We can only approve therapy sessions if you've also given a trial of medicine." Or parents were being told, "We can only give therapy if the child is also getting medicine."*

In an article in November 1998, Phyllis Gray discusses some of the social issues behind the use of Ritalin, particularly health insurance factors:

In addition, the market-driven restructuring of the health care industry has also contributed to the increase in Ritalin usage. It is much cheaper for Health Maintenance Organizations (HMOs) to treat ADHD with drugs rather than therapeutic interventions and other behavioral therapies. A typical month-long prescription of Ritalin is $30 to $60. A typical therapeutic intervention might range from $1,500 to $3,000 annually or two to four times as much as the cost of Ritalin for a year.

Most managed care plans also limit psychiatric treatment or behavioral therapies to time frames that are much too short to have any effect on ADHD.

In addition, HMOs, managed care and health insurance companies all pressure doctors to spend less time with patients. Few doctors have the time for the type of evaluation required to diagnose a child with ADHD: observing the child, discussing with the parents, teachers and other caregivers. Routine appointments in a clinic are placed 15 minutes apart and most doctors do not even spend that much time with the patient. Furthermore, the changes in diagnostic standards have meant that physicians are no longer required to witness symptoms, but can rely on reports from untrained school authorities and parents.[10]

NOTES

1. *Asheville Global Report*, www.agrnews.org/issues/131/nationalnews.html

2. www.cchr.org/publications/dsm_facts.htm

3. Lawrence Diller, "Just Say Yes! to Ritalin," www.alternet.org/story.html?StoryID=9838.

4. http://www.worldandi.com/public/2000/november/sax.html

5. "Requiring drug companies to disclose marketing expenditures to physicians," www.consumersunion.com/campaigns/learn_more/001813indiv.html

6. J Green, "Depressing research," *Lancet,* 2004 Jun 19;363(9426):2088.

7. http://www.eagleforum.org/educate/1996/july96/focus.html

8. http://www.fightforkids.com/chadd_lie.htm

9. "Parents pressured to put kids on Ritalin," posted online at www.resultsproject.net/USA_Today.html

10. http://www.wsws.org/news/1998/nov1998/rit-n04.shtml

Section Nine
The Conspiracy, Continued: Teachers and School Systems

...To the degree educators are expected to diagnose children, they are being distracted from their main duty which is to provide our children a quality education. Our schools are the only institution entrusted to attend to the academic needs of our children and their mission must not be diluted.
I urge this committee to do everything in its power to get schools out of the business of labeling children and back to the job of teaching.
—Patti Johnson, Colorado State Board of Education[1]

TEACHERS, LIKE PHYSICIANS, ARE—FOR THE MOST PART—HIGHLY MOTIvated to help children succeed. They are rarely given the tools and training to deal with the kinds of intense children they are encountering in their classrooms. Ten to 20 percent of new teachers quit by the end of their first year, and I contend that this is because they are so blown away by the demands and conditions they must work under. Even the most wonderful, motivated teacher can feel squashed by a single student who won't stop disrupting the classroom or being destructive toward others.

If the teacher has only the normal methods of classroom management at her disposal, she isn't equipped to deal with intense, difficult children. Normal ways of managing unruly behavior in classroom settings are more likely to worsen the problems teachers face with these kids.

Teachers, of course, typically believe in Ritalin, especially when they are given the impression by doctors and pharmaceutical companies that these drugs are totally safe.

I have asked over 10,000 teachers this question over the past three years: "Did your university training prepare you for the kind of children you actually now meet in the classroom?" Less than a dozen have said yes.

If teachers are given the right tools, tools that work reliably for even the most challenging children, most will use them.

In the school in Tucson where *The Nurtured Heart Approach* is being used, there has not been one medication referral since it was put into practice.

School systems, too, seek to help children thrive and learn. Unfortunately, they also have to find ways to fund their schools and pay their teachers in an increasingly tight economy. Drugging children is considered to be less expensive than decreasing class size, training teachers in new methods for dealing with challenging kids, or making other changes that might be helpful enough to make drugs largely unnecessary.

How can teachers be expected to cope without recommending Ritalin when classrooms have 30 to 35 children, when "mainstreamed" special education students are placed in regular classes because of cuts in special education programs, and when funding for teachers' aides, specialists, counselors and special education teachers is decreasing by the year?

Perhaps we should refer to it as "Teacher's Little Helper!"

The irony is startling. The school in Tucson paid only $1,000 for two in-service trainings during a one-month period. The first two-hour training was for the teachers and other staff, and the second was for the parent community once the principal established that *The Nurtured Heart Approach* was indeed a successful model.

This remarkable principal was brave enough to do what the vast majority of those in educational leadership are afraid to do. At the risk of incurring the wrath of her staff (who were using various approaches that contributed to the school being ranked one of worst in the district prior to the year 2000), she mandated the use of *The Nurtured Heart Approach* by evaluating the teachers largely based on their success using it.

In nearly five years since this act of heroism, the school went from over 30 suspensions per year to none. It had much higher results on standardized tests. There were no referrals to juvenile court. Referrals for special education placement declined from 15% to 5%. Teacher turnover went from an everyday occurrence to a rare occurrence. And there were no referrals for ADHD evaluations and medications.

This occurred in a school of more than 500 minority students in a largely impoverished area where over 80% of the students receive free or reduced price lunch.

There has been no further cost since the initial trainings, an amount comparable to the annual cost of Ritalin for one child (with interest) for these five years.

The cost in human capital is also far less than the typical school's maddening demands of handling adversity all day long...even the adversity of children supposedly subdued by stimulant medications.

And the cost is a lot less than the costs of another Littleton, Colorado.

91 Many school systems demand that parents of intense children put their kids on medication or risk having their child put into special education classes or removed from the school altogether.

As of 2003, seven states had laws in place prohibiting schools from coercing parents to drug their children or expelling children whose parents chose not to give them drugs for ADHD. Even with such laws in place, there is plenty of room for more subtle pressure on parents to go the drug route when their children don't "behave." And the majority of states still allow outright coercion when it comes to medicating children who are deemed difficult or unfocused.

Schools are not doctors, nor are they pharmacies. And behavior problems aren't medical disorders to treat with drugs; they are cries for attention and nurturance.

Educators have come to believe that medication is the only viable alternative when intense, difficult, or distractible children end up in their classrooms. When educators pressure parents to medicate their children, they are stepping way out of the bounds of both their rights and their expertise. The only people who have the right to make a decision about medicating a child are the child's parents, in concert with their physician.

It seems unbelievable that teachers and public school administrators could be making decisions as serious as that to start a child on Ritalin. Believe it— it happens every day. Part of the reason for this is that the PR on Ritalin is so good. It has been portrayed as benign and helpful, and as hugely effective, and most educators believe this portrayal. If they saw their own child go through what so many kids on these drugs go through, they would have a very different perspective on the safety and effectiveness of stimulants. And if they saw that a far better outcome is all the more possible without drugs, that the same intensity is a gift when handled differently, that new perspective would take an amazing leap forward.

A concerned grandmother posted the following at www.familyeducation.com:

I am very involved in my grandchildren's lives. When my grandson hollered out that he 'needs a pill,' I asked him why on Earth he would say something like that. He replied that his teacher told him to tell us that his dose needed to be increased (for the third time that year) or that he was going to fail his grade. The second time the dose was increased, it was done by his teacher without asking his parents!!!

Another posting from a parent:

My son was on Ritalin from kindergarten through the second grade. The doctor and I decided together that the side effects were making him ill, and that he should stop. At the next meeting I had with his teachers, they told me that they would charge me with 'educational neglect' if I didn't put him back on his meds. I refused. Within a week, I received a letter from my doctor with a prescription for Ritalin. The letter said that my son's teacher had requested that my son be put back on Ritalin. I was outraged and made complaints about the teachers trying to practice medicine. Nothing was done to discipline either teacher. I'm sure they see me as a crazy overprotective mom who doesn't know what's best for her kid.

I have heard now of classrooms where literally half of the children are on stimulant medications. That could not happen without a teacher who was spending more time looking for and rewarding symptoms than looking for solutions. Great teachers never complain about their intense kids because within a week or two at most these same children typically become their best and brightest kids.

Teachers need to learn new ways to deal with so-called "ADHD kids" while also learning more about the dangers of the drugs used to treat ADHD. Only then will the reliance on pharmaceuticals begin to ebb. As far back as 2000, some states were beginning to propose legislation designed to prevent schools and teachers from recommending that children be put on medication. I hope this trend will turn into the rule rather than the exception.

92 Ritalin provides an easy way out for teachers and schools that can't handle intense students.

Rather than change school systems to accommodate the needs of all children who attend them, we choose to drug children so they can better fit into the current, dysfunctional educational model.

Here's a note I received from Prue Addy, a mother and therapist from Bend, Oregon, whose child came close to being sucked into the biopharmaceutical vortex that schools have become:

I wanted to share with you that our seven-year-old son goes to a "magnet" school. It's part of the public school district, but very different: more active, more community, and grades K through eight interact throughout the day. We love it. However, our active and bright seven-year-old needs some extra help, and so we okayed the IEP [individual education plan] *process. Everyone went on a witch hunt. Was he autistic? Autistic spectrum? Asperger's? ADD? ADHD? Since I am a licensed Marriage and Family Therapist and know diagnosis, I was clear that our son fit into none of these categories. We were very clear with the school psychologist that Ritalin was not an option for us at any time. There are so many other avenues to try.*

What happened next was nothing less than typical of what schools seem to be doing these days. During the final IEP meeting, this school psychologist tried three times to hook us into Ritalin. She said, "You know, kids like your son, if they don't get on Ritalin, well...when they have their first drink of alcohol, they love it." A little later, she said, "You all said you would do what it took to help your son, and it may be he needs Ritalin." And then she

143

said, a few minutes after that, "I don't mean to scare you, but your child may become bipolar!"

Oh my God, I pointed my finger at that woman and told her to stop, right there and then. She backed down. But how many people does she do this with? Where are the lawsuits for this kind of misdirection, for these leading questions, the singular focus on drugging kids? I have consulted with schools for years as a specialist in behavior. I know that this goes on all the time. Still, I wasn't prepared for the tenacity with which they push these drugs.

Nancy Reagan may have said "just say no," but the parents in this country are saying "yes, yes, yes!" My poor husband was so upset. He was shaken, he said to me, because "if you had not had the professional background you do, I would have run to the pediatrician's office for drugs Monday morning!"

This phenomenon is so tragic...

I'll end on a wonderful note, however. I began volunteering at my son's school almost full-time. His dad and I "dance" with him (we do not have the struggles they have at school), and when I saw what the teachers were doing—they were so lacking in boundaries with him, talked too much and got so frustrated with him—I was able to guide them into the same kind of dance, into better ways of keeping this gifted boy engaged.

For five weeks now, he has been "dancing" there too, and the principal has me speaking to staff about many of the things in your book and others to help "contain" and lead our son to successful behaviors. Staff members were so relieved to understand our son more, and to give themselves room to be the wonderful people and excellent teachers they are.

Prue's letter is so congruent with my own experience of being in similar school meetings and seeing the extent of the pressure levied for medications. And Prue so aptly describes how staff members are relieved to really understand these children and to have strategies that transform their intensity into greatness. Teachers enter the field with such high hopes, and it's so much fun to see them emerge as the heroes who have the joy of creating success in the lives of these children. And the same strategies that work with these children help the "average" child flourish at even greater levels than normally expected.

 Teachers are not doctors or diagnosticians.

One parent wrote on an Internet discussion board:
When my son was in Kindergarten, his teacher told us he was suffering

from Fragile-X syndrome [a genetic condition that involves mental retardation]. *She said she read about it in a magazine. It's sick that any 'teaching professional' would dare to diagnose a child that way...My son is just fine, by the way.*

According to a study by psychologist and family physician Leonard Sax, M.D., 50 percent of ADD cases are diagnosed by teachers and another 25 percent are diagnosed by parents. Dr. Sax interviewed 400 child psychiatrists, pediatricians and family doctors in the Washington, D.C, northern Virginia, and suburban Maryland areas to determine this.[2]

He found that children's physicians were often pressured to "rubber stamp" the diagnosis with a prescription for Ritalin. Dr. Sax reports that "in the great majority of cases, teachers were the first to suggest the diagnosis. Doctors are busy; they've got a room full of patients...seldom do they do their own investigation. They just take a paper from the school saying, 'We think Justin has ADD, would you please prescribe Ritalin,' and the doctors do it."

Dr. Sax reports one case where a doctor did evaluate the child and determined that the school's conclusions were not correct—the child didn't have ADD. The school principal actually called the doctor's superior and asked how the doctor could dare question the school's diagnosis, insisting that the doctor be disciplined! The doctor ended up being called into his superior's office to defend his actions. In his interviews, Dr. Sax was told of half a dozen similar incidents.

Who is providing this diagnostic training to school personnel? This knowledge wasn't acquired at the medical school the teacher attends in her spare time. Are pharmaceutical companies paying schools for the honor of enlightening the staff? It probably isn't so, but I can't help but wonder sometimes.

94 Teachers, like doctors, mean well; they need only be given the right methods for dealing with intense children.

It seems that children are not the same as they were 20 years ago. Ask any educator who has taught for years and they will tell you that on day one of each school year, they have a greater number of intense children and that their rate of intensity is greater. If so, it's no wonder that teachers see an increased need to promote the medication solution.

If our only answer remains Ritalin or other stimulant medications, then my pediatrician friend and colleague in North Carolina, Bose Ravenel, M.D., stands to be correct when he jokingly predicts that the real meaning of President Bush's slogan "No Child Left Behind" is that eventually every child will be on medication.

In my experience, once teachers see the impact they have with a more powerful and extraordinary method like *The Nurtured Heart Approach*, they not only use it with challenging children, but with all children. There is a downside, however; they wind up being sought out by parents, colleagues and administrators and asked to take in yet another difficult child.

Ironically, teachers who become masters of this approach can have a dozen or more of these "symptomatic" children and the day is nothing but wonderful. The challenging children become the best children. Their intensity is soon the source of greater-than-average levels of success. The teachers feel great—energized at the end of the day instead of burned out.

I have received messages from teachers around the world thanking me for this approach, and the letters typically rave about how good it feels to be living their dream of having a positive impact on children's lives, to be influential in transforming challenging children in particular, and to no longer be locked into recommending medication.

95 The Ritalin solution is an offshoot of "teaching to the test."

In the April 2004 Carnegie Foundation newsletter, Lloyd Bond writes that "a recurring criticism of tests used in high-stakes decision making is that they distort instruction and force teachers to 'teach to the test'... The public pressure on students, teachers, principals, and school superintendents to raise scores on high-stakes tests is tremendous, and the temptation to tailor and restrict instruction to only that which will be tested is almost irresistible."[3]

Teachers are pressured to push students to perform better on standardized tests, and they are being forced to "teach to the test" more than ever before. Schools and teachers are strongly judged by the test results. When children are drugged, they may be better able to deal with the boredom of being taught the answers to standardized tests than with a setting where real learning, critical thinking and problem-solving are going on.

Proponents of giving children drugs for behavioral control insist that *not* giving the drugs is, in itself, harmful when a child is out of control. They paint a picture of the drugged child as better able to do well in school and have positive interactions with peers and adults. As you've seen throughout this book, this picture is not an accurate one. By giving the child a drug that suppresses intensity and replaces it with OCD-like or zombie-like behaviors, we don't help him achieve better in school or have improved peer relationships. All we do is get his intensity out of the way. There's no doubt that this helps overstressed, overloaded teachers do their jobs, but at what cost? I hope this book adequately argues that the cost is too high.

Teachers and children need new ways to interact to bring out the best in all children. (See Reason 101.) Standardized testing is necessary, but certainly overemphasized, and hopefully this will change over time. We medicate children so we can continue with the current educational system, rather than face the fact that we're barreling in the wrong direction. We need to do the hard work necessary to change this.

The irony is pointed out once again by way of looking at a school that has produced an alternative solution. At Tolson Elementary in Tucson, the heroic principal, Maria Figueroa, although highly academically oriented, does not allow teaching to the test. Rather, she has her teachers teach to **success.** She has found that if one's focus is primarily on creating strong first-hand experiences of success (the old method of waiting to "catch successes" fails compared with having methods that "create successes"), then the children begin to display successful ways without twisting their arms. They want to participate positively in class, want to do their homework, and want to do well on their tests regardless of their home situations.

96 School systems are being forced to spend enormous amounts of money on special education teachers, equipment, and resources for ADHD kids.

Approximately six million American children are considered to be "special ed," and their numbers continue to grow. Parents who want the best for their children struggle to get services through the schools that will enable their children to achieve at a level equal to that of their peers. Cash-strapped schools, on the other hand, continue to place new roadblocks in the way of those who would put more costly demands on them for special education services. According to administrators Sheldon H. Berman and David K. Urion, in *School Administrator:*

Local school districts nationwide are experiencing increases in special education costs. In states that are placing a high priority on education reform, the special education cost increases are rapidly compromising the ability of districts to effectively fund the implementation of these reforms. Policymakers point to two major causes of the increase in costs. First, they claim schools are funneling too many children into special education to ease the burden on the classroom teacher of addressing behavioral and learning problems. Second, they point to the increased advocacy on the part of parents and physicians.

Based on these assumptions, policymakers tend to recommend that states impose financial disincentives for increases in special education populations. They believe these disincentives will force school districts to apply more rigorously the eligibility requirements, leading to smaller special education enrollment and less special education spending.[4]

By the early 1990s, one in every four dollars spent on education in the New York City school system went toward special education services. In a report dated March 2002, the National Association for the State Boards of Education revealed that the per-student cost of special education in the 1999-2000 school year was $12,474—almost twice the cost of a general education student. The federal government is supposed to provide funds to cover 40 percent of the cost of special education, but according to a National Education Administration report, the feds only provide half that, or 20 percent. This leaves state and local school districts dealing with a $10.6 billion shortfall. At the same time, while so many school programs are being cut for lack of funding, special education tends to be exempt from these cuts.[5]

Not all of these special education students are ADHD, of course, but growing numbers of them are. And there is no doubt that some students are placed in special education merely because they have been labeled with ADHD symptoms. The rise in ADHD diagnoses is rapidly increasing the burden on overtaxed school systems, thus reducing the resources schools could be using to give truly disabled students what they deserve. If the principles of *The Nurtured Heart Approach* could be implemented in schools in a widespread manner, we could keep intense kids out of special education—and not have to hire additional special ed teachers.

Once a child is on Ritalin, there is typically less communication between the parents and the school.

Some education scholars warn that public schools are taking over the roles that should be played by family. Families are typically far more invested in their children's ultimate welfare than schools, and so it follows that they should be entrusted with their child's best interests, even though some schools act as though they know better and are the authority on a host of important and controversial subjects such as morals and sexuality not to mention ADHD drugs.

The power of schools and teachers to label a child with a "disorder" such as ADHD represents another brick in the wall that separates parents from their ability to do what they think is best for their children. Schools in most states can insist that a child be put on psychotropic, potentially addictive drugs—even against the will of the parents. Then, once the school has pharmaceutically squashed the spirited child into submission, parents often hear little more than silence, punctuated by the occasional "I think Tommy needs his dosage increased." Once the behavior issues are downplayed by the effects of the medications, special attention seems less warranted. But the child's need for such attention hasn't gone away.

Parents of many special education children who are taking Ritalin—and of many who are not taking stimulant drugs but who have qualified for special educational services due to ADHD "symptoms"—complain that once their child finally gets the special education resources they feel entitled to, they fail to get adequate feedback as to their child's progress. They may get a notation on the child's report card that he is making progress, but they don't really know what this means. IEP (Individualized Educational Plan) meetings don't always give parents the full picture either. Parents in this situation should have more than adequate feedback in order to discern whether special education and IEP interventions have led to a point where medications can be diminished or discontinued entirely.

NOTES

1. U.S. House of Representatives Subcommittee on Oversight and Investigations Hearing, 9-29-00

2. "Teachers diagnosing ADD in 50% of cases: study," www.healthyplace.com/Communities/add/Site/story_diagnosis.htm, August 31, 2003.

3. www.carnegiefoundation.org/perspectives/perspectives2004.Apr.htm

4. S Berman and D Urion, "The misdiagnosis of special education costs: district practices have no bearing, but medical and social factors accelerate spending," *School Administrator*, 2003 March.

5. Charles Sykes, *Dumbing Down Our Kids,* St. Martin's Griffin, New York, NY:1995.

Section Ten
The Conspiracy, Part III: the Government

I N 1999, AFTER THE COLUMBINE MASSACRE, President Clinton and First Lady Hillary convened a White House Conference on Mental Health at Howard University in Washington, D.C. The point of the conference was to "raise awareness" about the problem of mental illness and to help those who are diagnosed with mental illness to avoid being stigmatized when they seek treatment. It was said at that gathering of experts that "one out of ten children suffer from some form of mental illness...but fewer than 20 percent receive proper treatment."

"Raising awareness" is usually code for "creating a market for drugs." The conference gave the stage almost completely to experts who promote the notion that mental illness is entirely biological—that it is not the product of nurture, but of nature.

How do we treat biological illness? Can we change biology with therapy? No—we have to use drugs. It isn't anyone's fault. It's DNA; it's bad wiring in the brain; it's something awry in the recipe for the neurotransmitter soup that bathes the nervous system; it's some parts of the brain being too small, others not small enough.

The Conference was a brilliant moment for the makers of psychoactive drugs, legitimizing the use of their products for children at the very highest level of American government.

But the press releases from this conference neglected to mention a very important point: at least one of the Columbine shooters was *already being treated for a "mental illness" with medication.* Many other children who have lashed out in violence were taking psychoactive drugs during or close to the point at which they committed their crimes.

We can't rely on government to tell us what should be done for children with psychological issues any more than we can rely on pharmaceutical companies. They are so deeply in each other's pockets that they can't see what is really going on, and America's children are suffering because of their collaborative blindness.

Word on the streets as of the beginning of 2005 is that this very collaboration is cooking up the next supreme recipe for fiscal gain at the expense of children and families: mandatory mental health testing. Though this plan is ostensibly designed to help, its real goal is to expand the utilization of medication.

Pharmaceutical companies contribute heavily to certain political campaigns and now it's payback time. Unfortunately, your child or some other child you care deeply about might be caught in that very barbed net.

98 In other nations, including Great Britain, Sweden, and Norway, authorities are much more conservative about prescribing Ritalin and other drugs to children.

Physicians who work in England's National Health Service are not allowed to give methylphenidate in routine practice because it is not on the approved drug list. (They can prescribe amphetamines, which have a similar effect, but this is a rare practice that is discouraged.) Sweden prohibits the drug's use; it was taken off the market there in 1968 due to concerns about abuse.

Ninety percent of the world's Ritalin is used in the United States. This fact provides strong support that there is a cultural or social cause underlying ADHD. Unfortunately, the U.S.'s overuse of Ritalin appears to be the start of a worldwide trend. Other nations that have been more conservative are starting to prescribe it and other stimulant drugs with increasing frequency and to pathologize certain behaviors just as North Americans do. Australia uses nearly as much Ritalin on a per capita basis as the U.S., with Canada not far behind. But for the most part, other nations look upon the Ritalin trends in this country with disbelief—and, sometimes, horror.

Early in 2005, Canadian regulators ordered England-based Shire Pharmaceuticals Group to withdraw its best selling product from the Canadian market. That product was Aderall XR, which the drug company reported had been linked internationally to the deaths of 16 children and six adults. In the U.S., the FDA's reaction was to issue a public health advisory on its web site, but it planned no immediate changes to the drug's labeling or approved use.

99 Parents whose families are on public assistance are significantly more likely to have a child or children diagnosed with ADHD. They can get help with medical care and possibly additional assistance for having a child that has been labeled with a disability.

Children who are part of families with at least one member receiving welfare or TANF (Temporary Assistance for Needy Families) income are more likely to have some sort of physically or psychologically limiting condition (examples: obesity, diabetes, asthma, ADHD, learning disability) than children of families not on public assistance.

Here are some interesting statistics:

- Studies of hundreds of families show that 31 percent of families on welfare or TANF have a child with at least one limiting condition, while 18 percent of families not on assistance have one such condition.

- Another study found that in the year 2002, 14 percent of children in families receiving welfare had been diagnosed with ADHD, while only 7 percent of non-welfare children had been diagnosed with the disorder.

- A third study of a large group of American children led the authors to conclude that 11 percent of children on public health insurance have been labeled with an ADHD diagnosis, while only 6 percent of children under private insurance have earned the same label.[1]

Does this mean that children who are from lower-income families are genetically predisposed to chronic conditions or biological brain diseases? Of course not. Does it mean that environmental and social factors conspire to put these children at increased risk of health and behavior problems? Not necessarily.

The chilling truth is that a child on public health assistance or other forms of welfare is more likely to be shuttled into what Joseph T. Coyle, M.D., of Harvard Medical School, calls "an 'assembly-line' healthcare approach increasingly designed to move patients through the system quickly and cheaply, particularly for those receiving public assistance."[2]

This is less of a problem when it comes to treating conditions with known biological causes, like diabetes, obesity, and asthma, than when it comes to ADHD. The parents of these children are likely to have less education and less understanding of their options when they are told that something is wrong with their child's brain.

But there's one other important element at work here: Government assistance creates incentives for low-income families to obtain diagnoses like ADHD for their children. Parents can get extra help for their children and for their families if their children are diagnosed with a disabling disease.

It isn't beyond the realm of possibility that some parents on public assistance—who may initially resist thinking of their child as mentally ill—might warm to the idea once they see that they'll get more help from the government. This approach is often encouraged by case workers and social service personnel, though it does more damage than good.

100

Government agencies and national organizations continue to disseminate false information about the biological nature of psychological disorders—encouraging people to think of themselves as mentally ill and in need of drugs and to feel as though this is an acceptable way to live.

According to the White House Conference on Mental Health held in June 1999, one out of ten children suffers from some form of mental illness... but fewer than 20 percent of them receive proper treatment. Given this government-stated belief, and given public officials who are so enmeshed with the pharmaceutical industry, it's little wonder that Ritalin and other drugs are being prescribed so often.

Biological psychiatry is firmly entrenched in this country. It has been accepted wholeheartedly that ADHD is a biological disorder, despite the fact that there is no conclusive evidence to back this theory up. The National Institutes of Mental Health (NIMH), the government's authority on mental health, says that there is "little compelling evidence at this time that ADHD can arise purely from social factors or child-rearing methods. Most substantiated causes appear to fall in the realm of neurobiology and genetics."

A slam-dunk for biological psychiatry? Not quite. The NIMH statement goes on: "This is not to say that environmental factors may not influence the severity of the disorder, and especially the degree of impairment and suffering the child may experience, but that such factors do not seem to give rise to the condition by themselves." (www.nami.gov) You can see from their language that they would *like* to be able to ascribe ADHD to biological causes, but they simply don't have enough support to do so. What they end up saying is that the "disorder" is an interaction between nature and nurture. Reality is that some children are not wired to sit still in a chair for five or six hours a day. We're not talking about a disease, we're talking about normal differences between people.

Lahey and Willcut state in *Validity of Diagnosis* that "there is no evidence of a natural threshold between ADHD and 'normal' behaviors. Thus there is little evidence to suggest a natural boundary for this diagnostic category." They also point out that "diagnostic categories of mental disorders are social constructions" (Bandura, 1969).

Perhaps 'social constructions' might be further defined to include the handiwork and collaborative efforts of governmental agencies and their agendas, educators and their sphere of influence, drug makers and their fiscal concerns, and the medical community and their biases. Unfortunately these collaborations continue to lead to greater use of medications.

The core issue is not what *causes* ADHD, however—although an understanding of the cause could eventually make a difference in preventing the problems of this so-called disorder. The core issue is, how do we help children who, for whatever reason, can't seem to control their impulses, sit still, pay attention or use their intensity well? Finding a biological cause is all about justifying the huge scale at which drugs are being handed out. If we can move past this, and see that the drugs' risks we already know about far outweigh their benefits and recognize that we don't truly know about their long-term safety, then we can start looking at ways to truly heal and help intense children to succeed without giving up the intensity that is so central to who they are.

The National Alliance for the Mentally Ill (NAMI), an organization with government ties, describes itself as a "nonprofit, grassroots, self-help, support and advocacy organization of consumers, families, and friends of people with severe mental illnesses, such as schizophrenia, schizoaffective disorder, bipolar disorder, major depressive disorder, obsessive-compulsive disorder, panic and other severe anxiety disorders, autism and pervasive developmental disorders, attention deficit/hyperactivity disorder, and other severe and persistent mental illnesses that affect the brain." Its web site (www.nami.org) further states that "mental illnesses are biologically based brain disorders. They cannot be overcome…"

This is simply not true when it comes to ADHD. As my work has proven over and over, the right approach can make all the difference in the world. So, without further ado, I give you Reason 101: *The Nurtured Heart Approach.*

NOTES

1. www.childtrendsdatabank.org/pdf/76.PDF.pdf

2. www.gsdl.com/news/connections/vol8/conn20000315.html

Reason 101

Why Ritalin is Almost Always Unnecessary: The Nurtured Heart Approach

TOLSON ELEMENTARY IN TUCSON, ARIZONA, is a Title I school of more than 500 students, 80 percent of whom qualify for free and reduced lunch programs—largely disadvantaged kids who are statistically at higher risk of ADHD. Tolson had over 30 school suspensions in the year preceding its introduction to *The Nurtured Heart Approach*. This was the highest number of suspensions in the school district. This one elementary school accounted for a full eight percent of the total number of suspensions (336) in a district made up of 60 other elementary schools.

Between 2000 and 2005, the school implemented *The Nurtured Heart Approach* (NHA) school-wide. Since *The Nurtured Heart Approach* was put into motion, Tolson has had a complete turnaround: no suspensions, no referrals to the court system, no referrals for ADHD evaluations, and no new children on ADHD medications.

Plus there was one other benefit: Tolson's standardized test scores have risen dramatically since *The Nurtured Heart Approach* was implemented.

This intervention works, and here's why: children who systematically experience their "inner wealth" will create success because they want to be great students and want to make positive choices.

This is true no matter what the child's home situation.

That inner wealth is what *The Nurtured Heart Approach* is all about.

I wouldn't be so dead-set against Ritalin and other ADHD drugs if I didn't know of an approach that works to bring difficult children out of "bad behavior" and into a space where their intensity is transformed into something wonderful.

It is possible to preserve the marvelous qualities of the intense child while helping him move into more than socially acceptable patterns of behavior.

I've seen it work over and over again. Thousands of times.

This is an approach I developed through trial, error, intuition and inner guidance. It's never stopped being 100 percent worth the effort. When I view parents and children seeing how they can work together to make life better and easier without robbing the children of their spark, it's all I can do to not stand up and shout for joy.

What follows is a summary of *The Nurtured Heart Approach.* It is an approach developed through my work with challenging children, many of whom were already on Ritalin and who were successfully able to get off of that medication. The vast majority of the children I've worked with were previously "accused" of being ADHD and were viewed as candidates for Ritalin and other ADHD medications until *The Nurtured Heart Approach* was successfully used with them. It is tremendously satisfying to find that these children are able to retain their intensity—to direct it in positive ways rather than toward negativity...without being subjected to the myriad side-effects of medication.

The full version of this approach is described in my book *Transforming the Difficult Child.* If you finish this summary and find you want to know more, there's an order form at the end of this book.

The Basics of the Nurtured Heart Approach

Let's say you have a challenging child on your hands. If you are like many families who have struggled to help their challenging children succeed through traditional parenting techniques, you've been having a lot of discussions about your child's poor choices. Perhaps you've been doing a fair amount of admonishing, lecturing, and wringing your hands. And you're definitely stressed out and overwhelmed with the problems your child and your family face.

There are more than 54,000 books on parenting available today. Most embrace the traditional idea that we steer children onto the path of good behavior by urging them to make good choices and punishing them or enacting consequences for unacceptable behavior.

Almost all of these consequences or punishments have one important thing in common—something that will undermine efforts to use them with the kind of intense children who tend to end up on Ritalin. *They accidentally give the child the notion that he gets more out of life through adversity.*

For the average child, many of these approaches will work just fine. But for the intense child, who requires more clarity from the adults around him, they don't work. He perceives greater rewards in terms of relationship, energy, and connection when he behaves poorly.

Many children wind up being more drawn to the blast of negative energy than to no energy at all, or the low key energy that most normal approaches recommend when a child does what she is expected to do: "Good job" or "Thanks."

Every bit of parenting advice that you can find in books, articles and other resources attempts to work with children in a straightforward, logical and rational way. Most of these approaches do work to some extent with the "average" child. Even the stuff supposedly for the more challenging child is a reconstruction of these traditional methods.

For children who are a little more intense, a little more sensitive and a little more needy than the average child, these traditional methods not only won't work—they will systematically make the situation worse. The harder you try them, even with the best of intentions, *the worse the situation will get.*

Some children simply possess a heightened level of intensity. It's in their minds, their hearts, and their bodies. Intensity isn't a crime. We all rely on our intensity to help us live full lives. We'd miss our intensity if it were gone. But we all have experienced excess intensity at some point and it certainly can be overwhelming if we don't have the wherewithal to handle it. Even the best children have their moments.

Other children have heightened sensitivity. Sensitivity, too, is a wonderful tool for living fully, but in today's environment we may believe our children are *too* sensitive if they have problems with behavior or in coping with daily life. Some of us have more sensitivity than might be convenient at any given moment, but this doesn't mean we should be given drugs to try to control it, especially if it can ultimately contribute to our greatness when cultivated in a new manner.

ADHD opinion leaders say that the "inattentive" form of ADHD is much more prevalent than once believed, particularly in girls. Brace yourself for an increase in diagnosis and drugging of daydreaming girls. Again, a child who isn't engaged in classroom work, who drifts off into flights of fancy or just can't seem to complete a task isn't sick or biochemically imbalanced. She just needs to be taught and engaged in a new way. Her spark needs to be lit so brightly that her daydreams don't hold as much attraction as the real world around her. And her imaginativeness needs to be appreciated and honored, not drugged away.

What about the extremely needy child? The same goes for her. Neediness is a normal part of being a human being. Some kids are often overwhelmed by their neediness, particularly when adults don't know methods that adequately address these needs. But do we really want to medicate away a higher than normal level of neediness when that too can ultimately contribute to a child becoming wonderful?

"Normal" styles of parenting and teaching that work with less intense, less sensitive, or less needy children will not work with kids who are outside the norm when it comes to neediness, sensitivity or intensity.

The Nurtured Heart Approach is a parenting style that is designed to fill the needs of these extraordinary children. Allow me to spin off a few crucial concepts that will help this difference make sense.

Parents As Children's Favorite Toys

I believe that we are, by far, our children's favorite toys. Most children would much rather interact with a parent than with a toy, even if that toy blinks, whirs, talks, or jumps up and down.

Think of how a child responds when given a new toy. They explore the toy and check out the features. Ultimately, they discover that this toy has a certain number of features. It might be ten or ten thousand, but it's a finite number. Hopefully some features are engaging and exciting and pique the child's interest. Sometimes, however, the child will find a feature to be boring. These are the ones that the child will rarely return to except by accident or in hopes that the feature has transformed into a more exciting one. It's the exciting features that the child will return to over and over again.

In contrast, think of adults as the child's favorite toys. How many features do we have? Besides the gazillion variations of physical actions we can perform, add to the mix the multitude of moods and emotions we can experience and express. There's happy, glad and mad, and every shade in between. Think of all the ways we can respond, react, get excited, form connection and relationship, and become animated and alive. We're the ultimate entertainment center...remote control included.

Intense children find that parents and teachers who use normal approaches are boring "toys" when things are going right. They feel invisible when they are following the rules and doing the right things compared to all the energy that transpires when they cause problems. When things start going wrong, the adults in their lives start to get really interesting!

The responses of adults to difficult behavior may be negative, but they're also far more alive than their responses to positive behaviors. The intense child feeds off that energy so much that she finds herself willing to get in trouble over and over again just to keep those human toys doing those amazing tricks they do when they're mad or frustrated or sad.

Challenging children—those who have come to experience that parental toys are much more interesting and more focused on them when things are going wrong—are less affected by words than by energy and relationship. They don't so much hear what we're saying when we reprimand them—instead they respond to what's happening on an energetic level. They pick up on a current that runs beneath the literal, rational, and reasonable things we say.

My work has been about tracking the "river of energy" that flows beneath our words of wisdom.

Here's an example. Let's say that your child is watching television while you make dinner. You go in and make a reasonable request: "We have a few things to take care of after dinner, so we're going to eat early. Please turn off the TV, wash your hands, and come sit down at the table."

In scenario one, the child complies immediately. How much energy transpires in this situation? Even if the parent is pleased, the normal "thank you" or "good job" is energetically lackluster. Sometimes, not even that—because the parent may expect the child to obey and see no reason to be appreciative.

In scenario two, the child asks, "Can I watch for a few more minutes?"

The parent says, "Sure, no problem," and goes back to dinner preparation. When the parent returns and says, "Let's get going," the child asks again to watch more.

"This is a new episode," he says.

"Okay, fine," says the parent, and goes back to the kitchen. After a few more minutes, dinner is on the table, and the parent goes back one more time. The child yet again tries to get the parent to let him watch some more. "Please? This is the best part," he whines.

Even if the parent remains fairly harmonious (good luck!), the experience of this child is that in relation to his lack of cooperation, he is receiving more of the parent's energy. At the very least, the child is getting more visits from one of his favorite people, more words, more connection, and possibly more emotion.

If we can put as much energy into our positive responses to intense children—if we can make a much bigger fuss about what the child does *right* and remove the energetic charge from what he does *wrong*—we can not only deepen the child's attraction to positive choices but exponentially expand the child's way of experiencing himself as capable and productive. This, in a nutshell, is how **The Nurtured Heart Approach** works. This is not to say that we don't deal with bad behavior in a prompt and effective way; we just don't give it the same kind of energy.

With powerful techniques that play this out to the hilt, we can literally "hijack" a child into a new and positive portfolio of success. We can focus on and cultivate the child's *inner wealth*. If we use the right strategies, the child will act out success instead of failure, and her intensity will actually propel her level of success.

Challenging children already have an existing portfolio where first-hand experiences of negativity are equated with who they think they are. We need to replace that self-image by strategically implanting first-hand experiences of success and creating a more predominant portfolio of their greatness.

Shamu and the Toll Taker

Although this may sound somewhat like the next big family film, it actually comprises two concepts that lie at the foundation of *The Nurtured Heart Approach*. Here are two stories about intention, and it turns out the greater our intention, the greater the positive influence we can have on our children.

The orca whale Shamu was famous for his 22-foot jumping trick. He awed audiences by leaping over a rope stretched high over his tank. How did Shamu learn this trick?

You might guess that he was rewarded for jumping over the rope, but you might not see how his trainers got him to jump in the first place. Here's what they did that I consider brilliant. They *didn't* start with the rope up high or even at a relatively low level. Rather they started training him by *putting the rope under the water*, at the bottom of the tank. Then, when Shamu swam over it just in the course of his cruises around the tank, he received affirming pats and an affirming celebration of energy and other rewards from his trainers. As Shamu's trainers 'tricked' him into being successful, the whale learned that every time he passed over the rope, he could expect to be highly energized, and he liked that energy. From that point forward, once the connection was made, the trainers simply had to keep raising that rope a little higher at each training session.

Shamu's trainers, in essence, hijacked him into doing what was desired of him. In this same manner, we can help our children do what we desire for them—i.e., be successful. And with techniques that support this notion, we can move children in a new and desirable direction.

We can easily get stuck if our mindset only allows for us to wait helplessly for our children's positive behaviors and good choices so that we can "catch them being good." With difficult children, that's often a maddening wait. In contrast, we need a mindset that allows us to *create* successes at every opportunity. The Shamu mindset helps us create successes that would not otherwise exist.

The parallel to Shamu's early training with the rope at the bottom of the tank might go something like this. Let's say Sally has had a rough day, and so have you, and her behavior has been challenging. You pick her up from school and drive her home, and all through the ride, she is quiet, looking out the window. When you get home, and it's time to get out of the car, she climbs out without any problem. From the framework of normal parenting, there might not be much positive to say. Or instead, you can easily now energize any number of successful directions. For example: "Sally, thank you for being so cooperative on the drive home and for deciding to get along with your brother so well. Those were good choices." Or "Sally, I really appreciate that even though you're not feeling great about how school went that you are handling those feelings well and not taking your feelings out on anyone. I appreciate that you didn't argue or fuss when I said no to a treat. Thank you."

That's it. If you find ways to honor and celebrate children for good judgment, thoughtfulness and wisdom, and cease giving energy to their poor choices, you can keep moving that "rope" to higher and higher planes.

If children are simply told "thank you" or "good job," they may not really know what their parents are referring to. These kinds of statements are much too vague to have influence. More importantly, they lack energetic impact.

With specific comments as in the example above, the child has a first-hand experience of the fact that she is capable. It's like you are handing the child a photograph and saying, "Here's the proof of your greatness. This is who you **really** are." And when we touch a child's heart at that level, it expands their sense of their positive effect on the world and how they think about themselves.

It is much harder for us to discern little bits of success and goodness than to spot and comment on things that are wrong. We are so fluent in the language of failure, of falling short. We can glibly go on and on about what's out of order, incorrect, or awry, but we tend to have a flat language of success.

By re-structuring our idea of what success is, we can almost "trick" our children into being successful—and when they find out how great it feels, they'll start doing it on their own.

Let's look at how the toll taker fits into this picture in forming the foundation of **The Nurtured Heart Approach**.

Like the training of Shamu, it's the true story of an Oakland-Bay Bridge tollbooth attendant. On a beautiful weekend morning, a driver rolls down his window preparing to pay the toll and hears rock-and-roll dance music blaring from a radio nearby. Looking around, he sees that a tollbooth attendant a few lanes away is grooving to the beat, having a great time. The driver is able to pull into that lane and says to him, "It looks like you're having the time of your life."

The tollbooth attendant responds, "Of course! I have the best job in the world and the best office in the world."

The driver asks him what he means, and the attendant replies:

161

"Well, I get to be out here listening to my favorite tunes, doing my own thing and meeting nice people...Besides, what executive do you know who has an office with four glass walls and a view that even comes close to this one? I can look west and just about see the ocean. I can look north and south and see beautiful views of the bay, and I can look east and see the mainland. If I work the early shift, I can see the sunrise. And if I work later, I can see the sunset. With all these clouds, the view is different every day. Nothing can compare to this. Besides, I'm going to be a dancer, and I'm getting paid to practice."

The driver then pointed to the other tollbooths and said, "What about the other attendants? They don't seem to be having the time of their lives."

The tollbooth attendant replies, "Oh, those guys in the stand-up coffins...They're no fun."

The point here is that *everything is subject to how we choose to view it.* Is the cup half-full? Is it half-empty? It's our call. It isn't hard to imagine ourselves in both situations: with the incredible attitude of the dancing tollbooth attendant or, conversely, dreading another day of pollution, noise, traffic, and headaches. It's our choice.

Here is an additional point that is extremely important for the success of **The Nurtured Heart Approach**: *we get to choose, moment to moment.* No matter what has already transpired, this is a new moment, and you can choose to see things in the toll taker's upbeat fashion.

This is the beginning. You are making the choice to not let the child pull you into giving more response for negative behaviors and to not accidentally energize or foster more experiences of failure for the child. It's the beginning of pulling the child into new patterns of success.

By committing to **The Nurtured Heart Approach**, you are taking three stands, all of which are necessary:

Stand I: *I refuse to get drawn into giving my child greater responses, more animation, and other unintended "payoffs" for negative behaviors. I won't accidentally foster negativity and reward problems with my energy.*

Stand II: *I resolve to purposefully create and nurture successes. I will relentlessly and strategically pull my child into a new pattern of success.*

Stand III: *I have clear rules for my child and clear and consistent consequences when he or she breaks the rules. I resolve to give a true and effective consequence when a rule is broken.*

Hijacking Children Into a New Portfolio

Many parents have grown incredibly frustrated trying to find just the right combination of words to get their difficult child to do what he's told. I contend that our challenging children, those who have come to experience that these "human toys" are much more interesting and fascinated with them when things go wrong, are only marginally operating on the literal level (on the level of spoken words, which are very abstract) and respond a great deal more on a less abstract "energetic" level. They are responding to a current that runs underneath the literal, rational and reasonable things we say.

The adage "actions speak louder than words" is doubly true with these kids.

Our tendency is to want to sit down and discuss problematic situations in a reasonable and rational manner.

It seems logical that these types of exchanges should lead to a lesson learned. They work just fine with the average child. However, for the child with greater intensity, sensitivity and neediness, who has already formed an impression that he gets more out of life through adversity, things work differently. The harder parents or teachers try the 'normal' kind of intervention, the more they demonstrate to the child that 'more' energy and life force and relationship are available when things are going wrong.

Nintendo Therapy

Although I won't be a fan of Nintendo until non-violent, non-inane versions of the games are offered, there is something remarkable about the way children, especially intense children, are attracted to them and held by them.

I first came up with Nintendo Therapy when I started working with difficult children and heard variations on the following from parent after parent:

"My child is doing poorly at home and at school...he can't seem to concentrate for more than a few minutes. He can't get his homework done or his chores. He isn't focused at school, and he's arguing and acting out all over the place. He just refuses to cooperate."

Then comes the kicker: "And what *really* gets me annoyed is that he can sit behind that stupid Nintendo game for hours on end. He doesn't just play, he plays with great mastery, amazing focus. All he wants to do is be the best and move up to the next level. Why can't he be that way at home and in school?"

When the child is playing the game, life makes total sense. It's absolutely clear and predictable in a way that life isn't. Some kids need black-and-white demarcations between what is acceptable and what isn't. Nintendo provides that in blazing color.

The incentives and limits are absolutely clear, accessible, and predictable.

Here's how it works from the child's standpoint: "While I'm playing the game, attaining the goals, avoiding the traps and avoiding breaking the rules, the game is in my face, confronting me with a profound level of evidence of my success in the form of *energy*. Lots of energy transpires: there's scoring, sound effects, and the rush of succeeding at one level and moving on to the next. At any given moment, while I play, the game continuously either acknowledges that I'm headed in the right direction or poses immediate consequences as soon as I veer off course and break a rule in the slightest way. The game is always exactly in the moment, never one beat off. If I do break a rule, the consequences are non-negotiable. Nothing I do or say will allow me to wrangle my way out of it."

To outsiders, the consequences of missteps may appear drastic and excessively punitive: heads rolling, blood spurting, players dying a thousand cyber-deaths. But, if you watch more carefully, the consequences turn out to be extremely mild.

Any player can get back in the game in just a few seconds. Even if a rule violation results in the game ending, you can simply reboot and start playing again in no time.

The compelling thing about these consequences is that there's no song, no dance, no lecture, no discussions, no warnings, no reprimands—just a simple, straightforward consequence. In essence, it's a time-out. For that short duration of the consequence, they are missing out on being in the game. They are out of the loop of energized interaction. And because the game itself is so energized, missing out has an impact!

Given this scenario, these kids get fabulous at not breaking the rules of the game. Of their own volition, they decide to avoid breaking the rules, developing the skills and control to break them as seldom as possible. No one is twisting the child's arm.

Now, let's compare this to a situation between parent and child. Once again, I'll enter the child's point of view. Let's say I'm fond of bothering my brother. I like to bug him by calling him names and teasing him relentlessly. My parent hears this and comes into the room. Thinking he is issuing a consequence, my Dad launches into lecture mode, stating in an intense or energized manner that it's not okay to bother and upset my brother. "I want you to promise to never do that again. It hurts his feelings. Do you under-stand?" Eventually, of course, I stop listening, giving him the look that makes him think I'm paying attention, but all I hear is "blah, blah, blah, yada, yada, yada, now go to your room and think about it." What I do pick up on is the *energy* behind his words.

Of course, in most instances, the child does not stop the bad behavior. This "punishment" is actually *encouraging* the poor choice! Before he knows it, the parent is giving the same lecture again, and wondering, "What is wrong with this kid that he doesn't get this?" So the next lecture happens in an even more energized fashion.

Here's the problem. The parent thinks he is issuing a consequence; however, for the intense child, this response further encourages poor choices. It's like saying to the child, "Don't do that...and here's a hundred bucks." The child gets the high-energy response, which feels more compelling than the low-energy response he gets when he behaves.

The bad behavior elicits predictable and fascinating results. If the Nintendo game *gave* energy when the player made poor choices, the player would quickly get good at being bad.

Nintendo is, most simply, an environment that the child becomes immersed in while playing the game. The same structure that sets the child up for success there can be easily transposed to the child's other environments.

Giving Effective Recognition

Pretend now that I am in front of a room, giving compliments to individuals in a group of people. I go around the room saying things like, "Good job," "Thank you," "Excellent," "Way to go," "Very good," and "Wonderful!" Then, after I've finished giving out all this praise, I ask all of the group—who happen to be quite intelligent—"Obviously I was pleased about something, but can anyone tell me what specifically I meant when I gave you this praise?"

As you might imagine, everyone looks stumped.

These basic forms of praise are vague. They don't give enough information. If adults don't know how to interpret these comments, how can we expect children to?

So let's get specific—let's find the exact tools you can use with an intense child to pull him into success...to create a level of elaboration that convinces him that making good choices is more exciting now than the old adventure of breaking the rules.

I call these four techniques for giving effective recognition video moments, experiential recognition, proactive recognition, and creative recognition.

Video Moments

With this technique, you say out loud what you see your child doing, almost as though you were describing it to a blind person.

Do this only when you see a positive behavior. Never do it when the child is doing wrong.

This is a practice that has two purposes: first, to let the child know that he is *seen* and *acknowledged* and *appreciated*; and, second, to assist the parent or teacher in noticing when the child is succeeding and to expand the horizons or possibilities of this adventure. It also starts the ball rolling in terms of the child coming to feel that he doesn't have to go to the trouble of acting out to have the involvement and energy he's become accustomed to and desires.

My favorite example of how *not* to do this technique is the typical adult response to a child's drawing. Usually, it's a variation of "What a beautiful picture," or "I love your picture." This "freeze-frame" approach asks that the adult describe what is actually in the picture...perhaps the actual colors and shapes the child has used. "I see you've made some red circles...and green triangles...and that you put a few staples along the edge." Or "I notice that you used brown and purple to make zigzags in the middle of the page and that looks like mountains and at the top. You used orange and yellow to make a big sun with long red rays."

No judgment, no technical critique—no critique at all. You'll be astonished to see how beautifully most children respond to this. They know that they have been seen and acknowledged.

To a child playing a computer game, you might say: "Here's what I see...I see that you are really focused on your computer game, and your concentration is fantastic. You seem totally tuned in."

Or, to a child who is playing with colored tiles: "I see that you have separated the tiles into piles based on color and it looks like you are starting to build something by alternating colors."

No judgment or criticism, just acknowledgement.

The video moment captured in this irrefutable manner is also a great tool for talking about emotions. By adulthood, most of us have been taught that certain emotional states are either not acceptable at all or that they need to be strenuously kept to one's self. Do you recall being told as a child that your emotions were not okay? "Stop crying!" Or: "Stop acting so angry—no one did anything to you!" Or: "Why are you feeling that way?" The subtext in all of these instances is: *there is something that is not okay about your feelings, and they need to disappear.* Every time a child perceives that he is wrong for having an emotional response to something, he becomes further removed from his feelings and his life force.

When you are in touch with your emotions, you have a barometer, a direction to go in when life throws you a curveball. You have vital information at your disposal. Your emotions come and go instead of stagnating.

When you are out of touch—and many adults are to some degree—you either try to numb yourself (possibly through addictive behaviors) or take it out on someone else. You get to the point where you don't even know what you are angry or hurt about anymore.

Practice video moments when you see your child is emotional about something. Go one step further by turning that emotional moment into a success: "Here you are...I see that you are upset that I said you couldn't have dessert. I love that you are feeling your feelings but not taking your anger out on anybody."

In essence you are saying to the child that she is successful for handling her strong feelings well. Every time you use this technique with your child, you will expand her ability to see herself as someone who is powerful enough to handle her feelings—and as someone whose emotions matter.

You can also try this with the adults in your life. You'll be amazed at how your loved one responds when, in the thick of an argument, you say, "I see that you are really angry at me right now...you thought I was wrong to spend money on art instead of the new washing machine," instead of defending your actions and escalating the argument. This technique can really help defuse a tense situation.

I hope it's evident that both the Shamu and toll taker intentions are at play in this technique and that now so many more ordinary moments can be construed and presented to the child so that he feels successful. Now let's amplify the same intentions.

Experiential Recognition

This technique is also useful for instilling values.

As parents and educators, we have so many values in our hearts that we want to impart to our kids. How to be respectful; how to have manners and a good attitude; how to be thoughtful and considerate. Typically, we try to transmit values when children are least receptive: when they have done something wrong, something that does not adhere to the values code that adults wish for them to live by. "Why would you take that toy from your friend while she's playing with it? That's not very considerate!" "Stop eating your food with your fingers. Mind your manners. Haven't I raised you better than that?" Or "Billy, it's not OK to use bad words, that's disrespectful. It hurts people's feelings!" Again, we are unintentionally energizing negative behavior instead of success—plus, we are trying to teach a child while he is most closed and least receptive.

If you were to go up to a group of kids who are getting along well and ask them how exactly they are being wonderful, they probably won't put it in the context of virtues: "We're being respectful!" Kids don't think that way. They don't abstract life into concepts. They don't interpret life experiences as we sometimes wish they would. (Imagine how much easier parenting would be if children had this ability!)

Children live in the moment. But as an adult, you can help them recognize when their natural behaviors reflect the values you wish them to hold.

You could go up to a child who is playing with another child (no problems are evident) and tell her, "You know, you are being successful... I see that you are being so respectful and generous with your friend, letting her play with your favorite toy. You are sharing beautifully. Thanks for that."

Or you can say something like, "I really appreciate how thoughtful and considerate you are being with one another. I like how you are choosing to get along so well. Keep up the good work."

The key is that you now get to inculcate desirable values at a time when your child is more likely to drink in the lesson and the sense of success. Your child will then be more likely to live these successes out in the future.

There is a level of larceny taking place. You are literally stealing these opportunities and pouring successes into these frames we call moments.

The good news is we can shine the light of success and polish these facets of personality any time we wish and still get to tell the complete truth. The secret is the choice we make by how we construe a moment. You can energize anything you want!

I promise you that your child's new portfolio of who he is will grow exponentially in relation to these first-hand experiences of being cherished. The manifestations of a child who experiences and begins to trust his greatness will make you very happy that you took this new road.

Proactive Recognition

These opportunities are about noticing the child when she is not breaking rules. Make her feel thoughtful and wise, and she will inherit a stronger sense of her greatness, this time specifically in connection to her rule-related choices.

Capture a moment, freeze it, and describe it to the child. The trick here is to describe the moment in a manner that is again irrefutable. The adult celebrates the child when he is not breaking the rules.

Instead of saying something like "Thank you," or "Good job," be specific. Say, "Thanks for your efforts to get along nicely with your sister. I really appreciate that you are not arguing, fussing, hitting, or teasing. Thank you very much for following the rules. That's a great choice." Not only does the child feel seen and appreciated when he is following the rules instead of when he is not, he also sees that Mom or Dad really knows these rules cold.

There is no wiggle room. The boundaries between right and wrong are made clear, and the parent and child then know exactly when and where he steps out of bounds.

If your rules are not clear, you end up giving warning after warning as the child pushes at the boundary. For the intense child, this is actually a reward. Appreciating rules *not* broken is a harmless way of giving a warning that downloads success in yet another way.

Don't wait until rules are broken (as in most normal approaches) to make a big deal. Instead, be brave enough to make a big deal about the child's choice to follow the rule.

If you've ever been around a child who breaks the rules in an annoying fashion, then you know how grateful you are when the rule isn't being broken. Speak your gratitude out loud and you'll quickly see how this strategy contributes to further inner wealth for your child. More Shamu and toll taker.

Creative Recognition

This next technique will jockey your child into even more success.

Every day, you ask your child to do certain tasks: set the table, clean his room, get dressed to go to school, brush his teeth. Huge blowups can happen with a challenging child who is drawn to nearly every parental request as an opportunity to be showered with energy (negative though it may be) and relationship.

For the average child, a simple "Would you please set the table?" might be plenty, and a low-key "Thank you" might give him all the energy he needs; but the intense child needs more. The intense child knows that when he does not do what you ask him, he'll get more of your energy, 100 percent of the time.

Here's how you do it: Think Shamu and toll taker and start with requests that are utterly doable. Then, make a BIG deal when your child does what you ask.

Be sure to phrase your request in a way that doesn't imply a choice. Instead of "Would you please wipe the table?" try "I need you to wipe the table."

"Here, hold this for a second," you might say, and hand your child a grocery bag while you unlock the car door. When he complies, say "Thank you so much for following my directions, for doing just as I asked. I like it when you follow directions. I really appreciate your help."

With all of this energy, appreciation and relationship, your child will start doing as you ask in bigger and bigger ways.

Stay In The Moment

An important point to remember with all of these techniques is that they are meant to work *in the moment*. Tell the truth of this moment and leave the past and future out of it. The child may have argued three minutes ago, and may be about to argue again, but right now, she isn't. Energize this moment…and this moment…and this moment.

Consequences

The foregoing techniques work beautifully to bring children into a new world of success, but they are not the only techniques to master as part of *The Nurtured Heart Approach*. Our goal is not only to energize successes; we also must withdraw our energy from problem behaviors.

This doesn't mean that we ignore problem behaviors—certainly we can't do that. Rather what we do is create reliable and consistent consequences that the child comes to trust.

If we play our hand well, consequences can provide a perfect limit-setting scenario while also helping your child feel even more successful. It will also lessen the child's interest in relationship and energy based on negativity.

No matter what method of consequence-giving we choose, the child is losing out on life's options and energy. Most of them are essentially a time-out.

In my experience, a "clean" version of time-out is the best way to go when a child breaks the rules. The child is momentarily out of the loop of human interaction, taken out of the game so to speak.

Most parents of difficult children have already tried time-outs and feel they are ineffective, usually because the attempts are made in less than optimal ways. The typical time-out is given in the midst of a lot of explanation. "Billy, it's not okay to call your sister names. It hurts her feelings and it makes me feel sad. Now, go to your room and take a time-out and don't come out until you are ready to apologize."

Although that might look good on paper, a lot of energy and relationship are still being delivered for the adversity. So the adversity continues to be rewarded. Energetically, we are giving the kid those big bucks, even as we tell him that what he is doing is not okay.

Consequences are also ineffective when we issue a time-out without ever setting up a "time-in."

The time-in is the space where we create the child's perception of the flow of energy and relationship when things are going *right*. Without the emotional and psychological nutrition that flows when the child is successful, time-outs lose the all-important components of meaning and impact. A child who doesn't get energized for doing *right* won't feel the loss and impact as a result of the time-out.

Don't lecture the child while in time-out. This gives energy to negativity. Simply allow the child to sit. Let him get bored. This might only take 30 seconds. If you are already in the habit of energizing success, he's very quickly going to see that success is far more interesting than a boring old time-out.

The time-out should purposely be kept short. This will make it much more likely to be completed successfully...and that's what you are fighting for: any sign of success that you can then turn into a video moment. Important lessons aren't learned as a result of a harsh, punitive or demeaning experiences, but rather as a result of positive experiences that transpire when the consequence is over.

Let the child know ahead of time that his time-outs will start when he is quiet. When a rule is broken, calmly and confidently give the time-out in a very unceremonious manner. No need to even explain why the time-out is being given, because that's still energy given to the negativity.

Do not let the child rope you into any kind of battle over the time-out. Don't fall into the trap of saying "that's more time-out...that's more time-out" if the child acts out on the way to time-out or during it.

Then, most importantly, when he completes the time-out, take the opportunity to point out another success. "Tommy, you sat so well through that time-out. I appreciate that you were able to accept the consequences of breaking a rule, even though you were angry at me for deciding you needed one. Terrific job!"

If you are dying to give a lecture, convert it into a success by waiting a minute and putting it in context of the current moment, when the problem isn't happening. "Sally, I love that you are choosing not to use bad words now. I know you are still mad and I like how you are handling that strong feeling now. That's being powerful in a positive way. Great job using self-control."

Statements like this have two functions: they further the cause of building inner wealth and the child's feeling that she can indeed control herself, and they give the parent a chance to say how important it is to make good choices. With this kind of timing, the parent can say what he or she needs to say without accidentally rewarding the very thing for which the time-out was given.

Keep time-outs short. I can't emphasize this enough. In a way, the time-out is an illusion anyway. It's really just interrupting the problem momentarily. By keeping it short, we can divert the situation directly into more moments of success.

My Child Won't Sit For A Time-Out. What Next?

There are children who will not accept time-outs readily. Some won't go and sit, or won't stay and complete their consequence. Two options exist for parents of children who fit this description.

From the frame of reference of the NHA, consequences are really a matter of the child perceiving that he has *completed* a time-out. You may not even need to have your child move to the time-out chair. You could just say "That's a time-out," and then—without the child doing anything such as moving to a chair—after a few seconds to a minute, say "Thanks for doing your time-out. It's over." You'll be amazed at how effective this can be when you then keep the momentum going, continuing to be opportunistic in creating that new world of successes.

Another option with a very young or very small child is to do a "safe hold," a gentle restraint technique sometimes used to keep the child in the chair. This can be effective with resistant children who wouldn't otherwise go. If you give a time-out and there's no movement to go, then wordlessly escort the child to a chair away from others and away from activity. If the child won't stay, then implement the safe hold as follows:

1. Seat the child in a chair with a back.

2. Standing behind the chair, cross his arms over his abdomen and hold his forearms. This will prevent him from sliding down the seat.

3. Don't hold the wrists or squeeze tightly. Only hold on as firmly as needed to keep him in the chair. If the child starts to wriggle out, re-cross his arms.

4. He may struggle, kick, scream, or thrash. Don't have any conversation at all, not even to tell him that his time-out will begin when he is still or quiet. Be adamant about not responding to anything else the child says or does.

5. Then, within few seconds of his becoming quiet, appreciate him for choosing to complete his consequence. Then move on to successes once again as soon as possible.

If you are the parent of a child over seven, or if you don't like the idea of the safe hold, you may want to implement a credit system. This is an organized way to facilitate and reinforce an even greater level of success. The child comes to trust the flow of successes, for which he earns credits. He learns to exchange credits received for privileges.

If such a system is in place, older children who resist a consequence are simply told "If, for some reason, you don't want to do a time-out when you are given one, from now on that's okay. However, as much as I want you to have the privileges you like, until a time-out you owe me gets done, those privileges will be unavailable. Until then, I will still notice your successes and you will still earn credits, but they can't be spent until you decide to fulfill your obligation to do the time-out. If and when you decide to do your time-out, you can spend your credits again."

In my experience, having worked with thousands of very challenging children, the worst case scenario with this approach—which happens about 20 percent of the time, primarily with older, defiant children—is that the child will run into his room, slam the door, and bark out a few angry statements. Then he emerges 10 minutes to 10 hours later (usually, somewhere in between) and says contritely, "Okay, I'll do the stupid time-out."

That's the victory worth fighting for. Then, the battle is over, typically from that point forward. How many parents have had endless battles over this issue alone? The child isn't deciding to complete the time-out because you have grounded him. He is making this decision because he's realized that he is grounding himself. The child sees that she controls her own destiny, and this gives the consequence infinitely more power and influence. The important thing is to then keep the consequence short. Move the energy to more successes, praising the child's completion of the time-out and all the good choices that come after.

For much more on the credit system and for a more detailed explanation and examples of *The Nurtured Heart Approach*, refer to my book, *Transforming the Difficult Child*.

Some Final Words of Encouragement

There is no placing of blame in *The Nurtured Heart Approach*. A lot of finger-pointing and blaming goes on when a child is having a difficult time. Some blame parents, some blame teachers, some blame schools, some blame the child and some blame biochemistry. These aren't the culprits; rather, the culprits are the *approaches* they have at their disposal. I am certain of this. Everyone is simply trying their level best with the tools they have—but normal parenting and teaching are set up all wrong for these children. The tools of typical parenting education might work with many kids, but they backfire with intense kids. We need new instruments to work with.

The harder we try to use the wrong tools with intense children, the worse the situation becomes...even with the best of intentions. We inadvertently give more relationship, energy, and emotion to the bad behaviors and almost none to the good ones.

The problem is never that your child is out to get you—although many parents come to feel this way *or* that the child truly has a disorder or a diagnosable condition. You are simply dealing with a child who is subconsciously drawn to the greater force field of negativity—who has come to believe that a life of negativity brings greater aliveness and vitality.

If we can bring a child into a new pattern of success in about a month's time (the usual time it takes for *The Nurtured Heart Approach* to work), we can see that there is no reason or excuse for stamping a child with a diagnosis that will follow him for a lifetime; or for jeopardizing his health and subjecting him to myriad physical and emotional side effects through the use of medications. The same intensity that is so widely pathologized can be transformed into the fulcrum of that child's greatness. And just as gratifying is that, with an approach that works in a powerful manner, the parent and teacher get to be the heroes as well, enjoying the victory of transforming a child into a new and wonderful way of being in the world.

Epilogue
Ten Days On Ritalin

While writing this book, I realized that to truly do this topic justice, I would have to experience being on Ritalin for myself.

I needed to be sure that what I had to offer on the subject was more than my clinical impressions and observations. Since my personality is such that I could easily be diagnosed with "adult ADHD" or "adult ADD," I looked into getting myself a prescription.

I'm convinced that I could have accomplished this by ordering Ritalin online; however, for many reasons, working collaboratively with my brilliant and understanding physician, Dr. Brian Cabin, was a wiser choice.

Following is the journal I kept during the 10 days I took this medication.

Day 1: Saturday

A week before this long-planned 10 days on Ritalin, I returned from the last day of my 15-city seminar tour. Essentially, the tour involved two months on the road with only a few days of break between two-week sprints of travel (and hotel food).

So, to get back into top form, I took a good week's rest, played golf a few times and managed to eat much better than I had been for the previous few months. I was eating cleansing foods like brown rice, vegetables, salads, wholesome soups, organic juices...I saw my urine go from dark and toxic-looking to almost clear. This, to me, has always been a good barometer of my overall health and my body's cleansing of toxicity.

I met with Dr. Cabin, who has agreed to oversee this process. We discussed my fears and concerns. Our conversation was full of jokes, but we both knew that there were all-too-serious issues to be dealt with here. He measured my weight, blood pressure, and heart rate, and we decided on a low dose of 10 mg.

I told him that I was pretty curious about what it would be like to use Ritalin recreationally because I know so many kids do this. He insisted that I promise not to crush or snort the drug, and I agreed, but it felt good to share the secret of that curiosity. I also told him that I was afraid I would actually *like* the drug or that I'd feel improved upon using it. We shared a good laugh. Neither of us seemed to think that this fear is a reasonable one.

Initially, I had planned to start my 10 days during a low-demand part of my schedule. I end up starting on a weekend during which my daughter is at my home instead of her mom's, followed by a week that includes a few meetings and more than my normal number of social engagements. I think that this will help me measure my response better, especially in relation to others.

And so, on Saturday, November 20, 2004, I descended upon my local pharmacy with a prescription for Ritalin 10 mg SR (slow release). The pharmacist declared that they didn't have such a "little" dosage of SR in stock. We called my doctor, who agreed to 10 mg of extended-release (ER) Ritalin instead. The doctor told me that I might feel a mild "surge" at first, but that I could anticipate an even release of the medication throughout the day.

The pharmacist warned that I might experience a decrease in my appetite, leaving the discourse on possible side effects at that. I walked out with my bottle of 10 capsules, and took the first one right away at 11 a.m. Then I returned home.

During those first hours, I wasn't sure I felt any difference. I did not observe, feel or intuit anything really out of the ordinary. I did, however, experience my first awareness of self-doubt seeping in. In both my interactions with my daughter—which went just fine—and in the few housekeeping/work-related things I did early that afternoon, I could not tell if it was the Ritalin or me in charge. It was a strange, vague feeling that the Ritalin was having an impact, but I couldn't yet see the line of demarcation.

Later that afternoon, my daughter and I drove across town to meet with a few of her friends to celebrate the successful production of *Sound of Music* they had all been in just a few days earlier. When we got to the restaurant, one of her friends and her mom were chatting on a bench in front of the restaurant. We joined them. Although I welcomed the company, I could sense my own personal discomfort. They were talking about the loss of a family member earlier that week. It felt like I was slightly out of my normal ability to connect and to provide an adequate offering of condolences.

Then, later in the conversation, my daughter's friend and mom were talking about their last summer's travels and mentioned a few celebrities they came across. If I were feeling a sense of inner security and been my normal self, I would have just listened and asked questions at this point. Instead, I watched myself jump into the conversation in a manner I adopt only when I feel insecure. I told them of some of the celebrities I had run into when I lived in New York City many years ago. It made for good conversation, but I also had a horrible feeing that I was caught in this web of one-upping—at the expense of really connecting and just enjoying their story. Even as I vaguely began to feel uncomfortable about doing this, I could hardly bring myself to stop. It was only a little later that I realized that this was a manifestation of insecurity.

I also noticed how mindless I was about food at the restaurant. I had been eating excellent food for a week, but I suddenly seemed unable to make my own good decisions. Instead, I just went along with the crowd.

The evening was spent enjoying my daughter's company and watching a movie we both loved that was on TV: *Father of the Bride II*. I felt like the medication was wearing off; I was feeling relaxed. I wanted to get up a few times and get on the exercise machine instead of just being a couch potato, but somehow couldn't mobilize myself. I won't blame this on the Ritalin, but I wondered.

After checking my e-mail and making a few Quicken entries, I went off to sleep. Sleep on night one was extremely interesting. After a few hours of sleep, I woke up with a heightened but strange sense of arousal...new, different. It wouldn't go away. It was fun to feel those feelings, but the scary part is that in the dead quiet of the night I really felt the Ritalin in my brain for the first time. I was absolutely clear that the arousal was the uneven edge of the drug. It was also 100 percent clear that the next few hours of being awake in the middle of the night was a residual effect of the Ritalin. It was keeping me awake, well over 12 hours after taking the pill.

Day 2: Sunday

Here I am, writing about Saturday in a fairly disjointed manner. I have to work harder to get the thoughts organized and the words out on the computer. Maybe I need my Ritalin. I'm heading downstairs now to get my capsule. Funny, but after a terrible night's sleep, I almost see how one could look forward to their next dose. We'll see.

I clearly have a general sense of toxicity today. Even though I had been eating healthy foods for the past week (until yesterday), I feel no inclination to eat that way today. I still have an appetite, but I feel very impulsive about what I eat.

I am also finding it much harder to give myself the positive stream of enhancing compliments, self-acknowledgement and visions of greatness that I love to give myself in the mornings. This has come so naturally over the past few months. Today, even as I push myself to do a little, my focus lacks intensity. I have a kind of ghost-like sense of myself. Much of the process I normally use involves personalizing a vision of my own qualities of greatness, kind of an internal twist to *The Nurtured Heart Approach*, but it feels out of gear.

I don't know if it's me or the medication. I can only guess that, now that I am putting myself in the hands of the medication, the internal message to myself is one of disconnection and not believing in my powers. Makes sense that I would find it harder to do self-empowerment exercises.

I also find myself wanting the day to be over. I manage to get to bed early and get a good night's sleep. Probably over seven hours. Great. However, I wake up on Monday with less of a sense of inspiration than usual.

Day 3: Monday

As the day begins, I have the thought that maybe one should not consider prescribing or recommending Ritalin unless one has personally tried it. Again, I wake up with less than my normal level of inspiration. I look in the mirror and I really can't see my happiness. I just don't feel like I look like my normal, 'enlightened' self. I certainly can't see any light in these eyes.

My senses feel numbed, but I do seem able to go through the motions readying for the day. I have plans to play golf with an old friend who is in town. I take my Ritalin while my daughter gets ready for school, prepare some breakfast…healthier today…I'm determined not to let myself go down the tubes. I do still feel an appetite.

Today is the first hint that I wish I could take an extra pill. I can't really tell if that's part of the addictive quality of the drug or just a random thought. I do not act on it but it does occur to me several times during the day. I also feel my fear that I will like the drug if I take more. Really, I am not all that worried about this at the moment, because I just can't wait for this experiment to end so I can get my body clear again.

It's wonderful to see my friend and play golf. We enjoy great conversation as we walk along and play. I do feel a private sense of annoyance with another golfer we are paired up with. I know it's inappropriate. He is just being friendly, but I just want to chat with my friend whom I haven't seen in months. I find myself resenting this other man's attempts at conversation more and more. I keep my cool on the exterior, but feel frazzled on the inside. I know I can usually handle this much better and have fun in these kinds of social situations, but today I'm not. I occasionally wonder if it's the Ritalin's effect. It keeps me wondering and feeling way off-balance. I also feel diminished energy, and my focus has a frazzled quality. I just can't seem to sustain my concentration for the game; can't get my body in the gear in which I play my best.

In the last part of the afternoon, I go for my check-in with my physician. My blood pressure is slightly elevated, but my pulse is a little lower. He completely surprises me with his suggestion to increase the dosage systematically over the next seven days. I had had the same thought but had resigned myself to 10 mg. My doctor says he started me on the lower dosage to see if my body could handle it without blatant physical side effects. Now, he suggests doing the next three days at 20 mg, followed by three days at 30 mg...and, perhaps, even one day at 40 mg. For some reason, this makes total sense in terms of the experiment. A prescription is written. My evening is relaxed, with a few phone calls with friends. I enjoyed the phone conversations, but when I turned on the TV, I found myself to be impatient, changing the channel often.

Day 4: Tuesday

Today is my first at the new dosage of 20 mg. I take the Ritalin at 7 a.m. after a bit of exercise and then have a nutritious breakfast. I have long planned a lot of rest and down-time for this week, having just finished a demanding seminar season the week before. Thursday is Thanksgiving, too, and I am looking forward to that. A good friend is in town this week; once again I am scheduled to play golf today.

I drove my daughter to school this morning and felt my driving to be erratic and edgy. Then, during today's golf game, I found it very hard to sustain my focus. I felt foggy in a very unusual way. I felt a mental fuzziness that I knew was not going to lift. Throughout the morning, I felt irritable—despite being around supportive friends in a wonderful atmosphere.

I feel very lucky that I will eventually be able to be medication-free. It would be maddening to have to be on this drug for the long haul. Today I felt like I was holding on for dear life. I would have given anything to have something rote and unimaginative to do. That would have given me the feeling that I had something to hang onto. If I were a child in school working on an assignment, I would probably appear to have improved interest and focus on schoolwork; but it would really be me just holding on until the meds wore off. Focusing on a straightforward task would be infinitely more comfortable than interacting with others.

I can hardly look in the mirror. My eyes, which are usually smiling and welcoming and spirited, are dead-looking. I mentioned this to my friend, who acknowledged that they appeared to be icy and glazed-over. He mentioned that they looked solid brown; that it was hard to see the pupil. I also noticed a tic-like physical discomfort in my face.

Again, I had a sense of how awful this must be for a child who really has no way of discerning the loss of self or explaining how overwhelming the physical effects are. These kids are already in a compromised position in terms of how they feel about themselves, and now that I'm experiencing the drugs, I can see that these kids end up in no-man's land while taking them. I have tremendous advantages over those children: life experience, deep and abiding belief in myself, inner strength to draw upon. Even so, I'm struggling, often from moment to moment. *These kids don't stand a chance.*

I can't imagine a child liking how it feels to be on this drug, but I can imagine them getting addicted—merely from a desire to put themselves out of pain. I actually cried today from the sheer frustration of feeling so compromised as a person. I have never cried, ever, for this reason...just hurting inside. I have had to work so much harder today than on a normal day to hold it together, to take care of myself and to relate to others...so much harder. I haven't seen the positive side of the medication yet.

Day 5: Wednesday

Second day at 20 mg, which is about equivalent to 10 mg in regular form twice per day...so still a very low dose. My sleep was again disrupted. I was wide awake at 3:30 AM. The long-acting form is clearly erratic, far from even in its effects. Again, I felt almost a pre-addiction thought at some point: even though I'm foggy, off balance, and tired, I will soon get my pill. With it, I should be able to make it through the day without needing to rest. Scary hint of early drug dependence.

Again, too, the thought that's there's no way a little kid would know what hit him. He would probably think the muddy feeling is him and not the drug.

One thing that struck me today is that I smelled awful all morning, even though I had taken a shower the night before. I had gone months without having any body odor, even when working strenuously physically or mentally all day long. My healthful diet had kept me smelling rosy. So it was quite the shock to take a whiff this morning. My guess is that my body is trying to detoxify and that the byproducts of this drug are pungent, to say the least.

I have, perhaps out of insecurity, felt compelled to tell people that I am conducting this experiment and that I am currently taking Ritalin. I had lunch with a psychiatrist friend who is quite enlightened in comparison to so many who stick rigorously to the medical model. She actually has written a book about her balanced approach—one that adds components of mind and spirit integrated with medicine. Still, the look on her face when I told her about what I am doing and my painful experience...I don't think she meant to be defensive or patronizing, but even she is still so wedded to the use of medicines that she could not comprehend how devastating and toxic stimulant medications could be for children. She told me, "Everyone has a different makeup, and some really benefit from meds."

I thought, well, of course, everyone has a different makeup, and there is the *illusion* of benefit from these meds for some. As our conversation continued, I became infuriated at her resistance to seeing the potential for an approach that almost always avoids the need for diagnosis and medications. (How much of this reaction was me being prickly from the Ritalin?) I am angry that she doesn't seem to see the underbelly of meds that is potentially horrible for children...that the stakes of putting kids on drugs are so high.

I couldn't convince her that outcomes without meds that are successful are better in every way than a lifetime of meds. Even someone this far ahead of current thinking is hanging onto that notion that for some people—not the rare individual out of millions, but a good portion of intense or difficult children—meds are a perfectly valid option, not to be second-guessed. If she feels this way, as far as she has come, then how hard is it going to be to reach the majority of doctors who are so entrenched in the medical model? How long will it take?

Later on: I forced myself to have a quiet night and a good dinner. I feel a lot better this evening as I write these notes. I feel a sense of victory that I've made it through half of this 10-day experiment, despite my strong urge to quit. One more day tomorrow of 20 mg, and then on to 30 mg for three days.

I did feel a nice and welcome sense of well-being today for the first time in a while. Shopping at my favorite grocery store and getting into the Thanksgiving energy lifted my spirits. It was nice to say "hi" to people I recognized and to wish them a happy holiday. Extra energy...could it be the Ritalin? Again, I'm not sure. Maybe I'm feeling good despite the Ritalin. One person I talked to for a few minutes was an acquaintance who is a naturopathic doctor. I asked her if she did iridology (a medical discipline that uses markings in the iris of the eye to diagnose one's state of health). She took a look into my eyes to see if she detected anything that seemed "off." Although we were in the bright sunlight, she said she couldn't distinguish the pupil.

Interesting. That's what I observe, and that's what my friend yesterday reported. When I look in the mirror, I see the buggy look of someone on drugs. The life force seems held back. The "mirrors of my soul" are not shining forth as usual.

Again, I think of kids who can't possibly put into words the physical, mental and spiritual impact of the medication they are asked to take. They just know if feels bad.

Wrong.

Off-kilter.

Day 6: Thursday Thanksgiving

I am still disturbed by yesterday's lunch conversation with my doctor friend, but I've realized that the encounter was actually a gift. My feelings were probably something like those of a child sitting in a room with a patronizing adult, being told that his dislike of how the drug makes him feel is not important. Meanwhile, the child is forced to sit there and listen to the party line about how the drugs "have a different effect on everybody."

What must that child think? *"Yes, but I feel awful, and no one seems to care as long as I'm drugged into submission."*

Adults, in all their supposed wisdom, can be so hurtful and unenlightened.

I fired off an e-mail to Bose Ravenel, M.D., a physician friend in North Carolina. He is as passionate about this subject as I am, and I consider him an expert on the medical/scientific considerations of medications. He wrote back:

M.P. Rapoport and another researcher years ago reported in medical journals that Ritalin has the same basic effect on normal individuals as those with the diagnosis. Even strong drug advocates do not dispute this. I think I can see where you are going with this—that whatever effect you can certify from personal experience can be reasonably extrapolated to that of "ADHD" subjects, eh? Good point.—Bose

Day 7: Friday

Day one of 30 mg. Here are some things I noticed this morning as I try to remain faithful to my promise of simply tuning in and reporting my observations.

- First, it's still hard to tune in enough to discern what exactly is the Ritalin and what is me. I feel perpetually racked with self-doubt.

- Second, some occurrences relative to a song: ever since the wonderful Ray Charles duets album came out, I've found myself singing the "Crazy Love" song he does with Van Morrison, often throughout the day. A while back, before this experiment, I usually switched the words of the refrain to "dazzling love." One of my quirks—I like to change song lyrics around. Seems I've mostly let go of my dazzling version and reverted to the original refrain. A small item, to be sure, but something I've noticed about myself.

Seems there's a combination of feelings here: not caring as much overall, and lacking my normal amount of conscious wherewithal to be purposeful and to remember to add my own individual touch to things in my life. I'm intuiting that I am out of touch with my higher, more "dazzling" self.

Today I attended a Bikram Yoga class—something I had only done very occasionally in the past. Bikram is conducted in a sauna-like environment with high humidity. The humidity and heat loosens the muscles and brings out a tremendous amount of sweat. In response to the energized deep breathing and deep stretches, toxins flow out fairly freely. I sought it out today because of all the toxicity I have been experiencing in the past seven days. The past few Bikram classes I attended brought on profuse sweating, but before today, I had never experienced this kind of flushing-out of toxins. Breathing was painful at times. I contend that I was getting rid of only a week's worth of toxicity.

This experience really drove it home for me. It made me want to **beg you to consider the alternative to medication I suggest in this book or any other alternative you can find or invent.** The notion that a young child with a vulnerable body and brain would summarily be diagnosed and put on these powerful and poisonous medications overwhelmingly saddens and alarms me. This is just my opinion—which, as you've seen from the rest of this book, is supported by both science and the opinions of some very learned individuals—but now that I've been there and done that, I am twice as passionate about what I am touting.

Day 8: Saturday

Today is the day I am attending "driver safety school" to nullify a speeding ticket I had received some weeks ago. I'm annoyed at having to do this (albeit I was indeed breaking the speed limit), but really, the timing couldn't be better. It's been a while since I took any kind of class. I am anticipating that it will all be a rehash of things I know and therefore utterly boring—a lot like the typical elementary school classroom for the gifted, restless child on Ritalin. Here's a perfect situation to test myself on day 8: 50 people in a room on a beautiful, sunny Saturday. No one wants to be there. We are all after a dismissal of the charge so that our insurance costs will not increase.

Turned out, it wasn't bad. This curriculum would have been flat-out boring if not for the instructor's attitude, perspective, experience and humor. Even so, I was distracted and bored at times, even though I was dosed up on Ritalin. It was only by the grace of this man's interesting stories and ways of presenting the material that the class was tolerable—even enjoyable at times.

Again, I felt pangs on behalf of the children who are given drugs when it's really a matter of schools and classrooms in need of enhancement. A less animated, less interesting teacher might have problems with certain students, and the system would likely point to those students as being the problem, rather than seeing the need for increasing the life force that comes from the teacher's approach to the material at hand.

Day 9: Sunday

Again, it's tough to say exactly where the effect of the Ritalin begins and ends. To the extent that I can tune in, here are more impressions.

Today was a busy and interesting day. I had a golf lesson planned for the morning and met my teacher, who is also a friend, and another friend on the range. Both were determined to help me fix some problems with my swing. Like most lessons, there was movement forward and backward. My concentration was erratic, and I had to work to focus. At one point I really lost focus and hit a bunch of poor shots; then, I strived twice as hard to follow my teacher's instructions and hit very well. The lesson was quite demanding. I still don't think I want to give credit to the drug for the ultimate success of the lesson, because I had to fight so hard from the inside for this attainment. I want to give myself credit. While under the influence, there is always this nagging self-doubt: is it my accomplishment, or is it the drug's?

Next, I took my daughter to brunch and the play *Peter Pan* starring Cathy Rigby. We were delayed a little in getting seated for our meal. Normally I might have felt a little impatient but handled this setback well. Was it the medication? I don't truly know. The play was mostly fantastic, compelling and thoroughly enjoyable. There were a couple of sections that I found boring, and I dozed off for a few minutes. Despite this powerful stimulant, the dynamics of the subject matter seem to be pivotal in maintaining alertness and focus—at least in my case. I can't help but think that it would be the very same in a classroom. It's certainly not a magical cure for lackluster parts of the 'performance.'

After some Christmas shopping with my daughter, I dropped her off at her mom's, went home, ate some delicious leftovers from the night before, then turned around and went to a musical performance at the university. Very much on the move today. Not rushed. Relaxed, but not a lot of space between things. The performance, by a wonderful Peruvian singer named Tania Libertad, was marvelous, but I barely understood a word since it was totally in Spanish. I used the time to enjoy the resonance and quality of the music and to foster the inner nurturing that I continue to strive for. I felt very enhanced by the combination of the great musical vibrations and the level of the inner work I felt I was accomplishing.

As great as this was, being on the medication continues to throw a psychological wrench in my spokes. The drug impedes my ability to feel fully able to take credit for my accomplishments. Even if I felt improved while on this medication, I would be blocked from being able to feel great about the good things that I do (or, conversely, to take responsibility for the poor choices I make) because I am under the influence of a narcotic. I can't truly tweeze out the exact effect. With me is a constant companion, the shadow of self-doubt. I cannot believe in myself at the level that I normally enjoy, and I cannot give myself the credit that I normally thrive on. And, like Peter Pan, I want my shadow back. One more day...

Day 10: Monday

Today is the last day of this experiment. The plan is for this to be my only day on the increased dosage of 40 mg of long-acting Ritalin. Up to today, I have not mixed this medication with any alcohol. Neither my doctor nor my pharmacist mentioned this as a contraindication, so I think I will call a friend and go out for a few glasses of wine this evening. I'll ask my doctor this afternoon during my checkup whether this is okay.

This stronger dose is really over the top for me. I feel pushed to my limits. Very anxious, very "not in my body." White-knuckled the entire morning. Feeling so uncomfortable in my body, so wanting the discomfort to go away, that I'm clinging to any task rote enough to engage me. I just need something to do, something to hang onto. *To an outsider, this might give the impression of focused attention, but I am a mess inside.* I just can't believe so many kids are pushed to be on these medications and that so many people think this "impression of improvement" is a true reflection of the child doing better.

I had my checkup today with Dr. Cabin. My blood pressure was even higher, and I lost 2.5 pounds in just 10 days. I have neither gained nor lost weight in nearly 30 years, so for this to happen, something has to be strongly affecting my body. Although I have experienced some hunger at times during my experiment, I have noticed myself being generally disinterested in food often and almost oblivious to my needs for water. That can't be very good. Despite these differences, I am a person who understands how important it is to eat a good diet, I have brought myself to the table to eat regularly during this experiment, and I've eaten pretty healthy food overall. How many children have the wherewithal to make good food choices and to fight their loss of appetite?

I did ask Dr. Cabin about his opinion of my having a few glasses of wine; he thought it would be absolutely fine. I decided to invite a woman acquaintance over for dinner. We chatted as I finished cooking the meal, and by the time I had gotten through half a glass of wine, she was on her third glass.

I certainly had in mind the possibility of a romantic evening, but as the evening progressed, it became clear that there would not be any romance. I found I couldn't wait for the meal to be over so that I could figure out some way to send her on her way. I cannot be certain whether this was a side effect of the Ritalin, but there was a pitch to her voice that was putting me completely on edge. This was the second such experience this week (the first was the lunch conversation with my psychiatrist friend). This was not a midrange reaction. I felt a little crazed. Not only did I ask her to leave, I suggested that we not have any further contact for now. Believe me, I would have much preferred the romantic version of the evening, but the thought of it was intolerable.

Afterward, instead of feeling great that I made an important life decision—to not be romantic with someone who didn't seem right for me—I once again experienced self-doubt. Was it the Ritalin, or was it the real me? Ten days ago, I felt so wonderfully in touch with myself, and now I'm losing that.

Tuesday: The Day After

No Ritalin. Hooray! I am not sure why I couldn't bring myself to drink more than a half glass of wine last night. I had planned to drink at least a second glass, if for no other reason than continuing with the experiment of watching and tracking the impact with Ritalin. This morning, it seems that I abstained because I already felt such a loss of self, already longed so strongly to get back in my body, soul and mind, that the idea of disengaging further was unappealing—even in context of some romantic fun.

Even after more sleep than I've had in quite a while—at least eight hours—I woke up with quite the headache. Felt muddy and toxic. Overriding this is total glee that I can now stop taking Ritalin. Feeling bad for the children who don't have this option, who can't convince their parents, teachers and doctors to stop giving them the medication. Many likely end up convinced that they really do need it to "behave."

Last night, my friend told me that her son had been prescribed Adderall. This year he had been kicked out of school for selling it to his high school peers. Although my friend is extremely bright and inquisitive, her doctor never thought to tell her that Adderall is a powerful stimulant that is chemically much like cocaine and that her son is now at increased risk of addiction himself in the future. And she never thought to ask.

This morning I went through the DSM-IV description of ADHD. It was clear to me that I could still, if I desired, convince myself and nine out of ten doctors that I am ADHD. I will never go down this road for another minute, however—I am even more determined to hang my hat on inner strength after this experience.

My 10 days on Ritalin would have been much more of a toxic roller-coaster had I not spent much time and energy over the past few years developing my inner strength and consciousness. There is absolutely no doubt in my mind that without those resources, I would have been much more unbalanced by the whole thing.

Inner wealth is a much better outcome than a lifetime of medications, and I will never stop fighting for approaches that bring this about. I am happy to say that *The Nurtured Heart Approach* is one of the approaches that consistently makes inner strength easy to manifest.

Wednesday: Second Day Off Ritalin

My body feels achy and toxic. I have a whopping sore throat. It's been so long since I have felt sick, and I can't help but feel it's not a coincidence. My intuition is that the level of toxicity Ritalin produces is far greater than people realize.

One other note: This morning, I woke up feeling clarity about a moment during my last check-up with Dr. Cabin: an aspect of paranoia. I was able to put my finger on a feeling that, at the time, seemed vague. I had felt as though I were in the presence of a person who didn't know that I was on a class-II narcotic. As he looked in my eyes, I had these paranoid thoughts: "Oh, he knows I'm under the influence." Just as a child who is using pot or cocaine or alcohol might feel at his parents' dinner table, thinking that they can see his problem as clear as day. I faintly recall this feeling from my youthful drug experimentation.

Paranoia is the perfect existential crisis: uncertainty about being loved, being worthy of love. It's a giant hole in your life, and the wind howls through it. Paranoia is a haunting and disempowering feeling. I'd be willing to bet that some of our children on Ritalin feel this at times.

The Following Wednesday, One Week Later

One more interesting thing that came up in yoga classes this week: this could have been because of muscular constrictions caused by the meds, or because I had little or no desire to drink liquids during the 10 days on Ritalin, but I had an awful time balancing and stretching. I first noticed it at the Bikram class I took on day five, and only now am I feeling back in my body enough to stretch and balance well. I can't help but think that this had something to do with the meds. Dr. Cabin confirms in an email that this makes sense as Ritalin has a strong impact on the central nervous system. So many doctors don't even give this a second thought. I actually feel relieved that I didn't finish my doctoral degree and join that fraternity because I, too, would have been so prone to taking the party line...recommending medications as a first course of action without giving their potential harm a second thought.

In retrospect, I also see that I was having a hard time thinking about "giving" during those 10 days. I had wanted to do Christmas shopping and had lots of opportunities to do so, but could not get myself to do it. Now, I think that this difficulty in giving to others came from the "hanging on for dear life" feeling that also robbed me of my appetite. Nourishing one's self properly is an act of giving, too. Now, Christmas is nearer, and I am full of the giving spirit—both to myself and to everyone I want to remember in this holiday season.

Blessings & Miracles

Howie

Epilogue
An Alternative Medicine
Perspective
— by Brian Cabin, M.D., M.D.[H].

A s Howie's physician and friend since February 1997, I could easily see how he, like many bright, creative, intense people, could meet the diagnostic criteria for ADHD and stimulant drug therapy. I agreed to collaborate with him on a closely supervised 10-day course of Ritalin therapy. During those10 days, Howie's sensitivity and articulateness enabled him to clearly convey the effects of the drug on his body, mind, and soul. He experienced self-doubt, fear (approaching paranoia), altered sense of self, fatigue, disrupted sleep, addictive desire for more medication, pessimism, and feelings of being out of touch with his true self. His blood pressure rose to 144/80 from 110/70 within the 10-day period. He lost three and one-half pounds after 20 years of stable weight.

I saw that he didn't have his usual exuberance and connectedness. His eyes looked disconnected and apathetic, with enlarged pupils. His ability to relate was noticeably lessened. These are all effects I have seen, to varying degrees, in children and adults who take stimulant medications—effects that I know, from personal clinical experience, can be avoided when a combination of behavioral therapy (such as Howie's Nurtured Heart Approach) and nutritional, natural medical interventions are carefully applied.

I am an old-school physician who truly enjoys practicing medicine. Unlike most modern physicians, who run their medical practices according to the dictates of managed care and the pharmaceutical industry, my practice is focused on the sanctity of the doctor-patient relationship. That relationship has been all but eliminated in the practices of most doctors, who are over-burdened with increasing workloads, less time to evaluate and treat patients, and a patient population that is increasingly sick and stressed.

I get to know my patients as people, and this enables me to treat them on all levels: physical, emotional, mental, and spiritual. My relationship with my patients is one of mutual respect. When I go to work each day, I feel truly blessed.

Pharmaceutically based medical practice fits well into the fast-paced sick-care system in place today. All the doctor needs to do is dash off a quick prescription, and he or she can move on to the next patient.

This approach has made pharmaceutical companies the most profitable businesses in the world. They use their considerable resources to inundate physicians with drug reps and "continuing education" offerings that push pharmaceutical alternatives almost exclusively.

More of their riches go into dispensing samples, gifts, travel, even cash to doctors who attend "educational" meetings.

Direct-to-consumer advertising further augments the grip of the pharmaceutical mindset via print ads and TV ads (with side effects read quickly at the end of the ad in the same cheery tone as the rest of the commercial).

The mental health field, once considered to be "soft science" and looked upon with disdain by most doctors, has changed dramatically over the past quarter century, shifting from an emphasis on "the talking cure" to a biochemical, pharmaceutical mode.

In the early days of psychiatry, the doctor would spend a 50-minute hour with patients, exploring emotions, spiritual beliefs, experiences, and ideations. Doctor and patient would form a close bond.

Since the advent of managed care and the ascent of pharmaceutically-based psychiatry, the hour is now down to 10 minutes. Psychiatry is among the most pharmaceutically oriented of all medical specialties. No longer considered to be "soft science," psychiatry is now more highly respected in the scientific community and is a tremendous source of revenue for drug companies.

Pharmaceutical medicine offers great promises of magic bullet cures—promises on which it rarely delivers. Cures require that we ascertain causes and address them. By and large, the use of pharmaceuticals—as valuable as they may be—is an overly simplistic approach that addresses only symptoms, rather than the complex problems that underlie the illness.

The case of Ritalin is a prime example.

Attention deficit disorder is a soft diagnosis, based on a conglomeration of symptoms rather than on objective findings. It is a multi-factorial problem that has been escalated to disease status in order to promote the labeling of large numbers of children and adults as ill and in need of drug therapy—the magic bullet of stimulants.

Unfortunately, stimulants are toxic, potentially dangerous, addictive, and may produce very serious short- and long-term side effects.

They also happen to be highly profitable for drug companies.

The phenomenon of ADD/ADHD (and it is indeed more a *phenomenon* than a disease) has arisen from factors that many adults are unwilling to address. To do so would necessitate some difficult, extreme, but ultimately very rewarding life changes—changes that go against the very grain of our entrenched modern way of living and of schooling and raising our children. Poor conditions in the educational system and high-tech distractions such as television, video games, and computers are also to blame.

This book will hopefully illustrate the need for these points to be addressed. It inarguably demonstrates that drugging children into submission is no replacement for focused, time-rich, and intelligent parenting.

In my medical practice, I have also found that poor diet—specifically, chemicals and additives in the diet (as well as in the environment)—are major contributors. Those who suffer from anxiety, depression, social anxiety, or others of the growing number of psychological diagnoses can often be cured or improved with targeted dietary interventions.

Medications used to treat these "diseases" are not cures, and never will be. They mask feelings without addressing the great problems our society, families, and children face.

Howie Glasser's approach is a comprehensive one that does address those problems and works beautifully for children and their families and for schools.

Children's diets have a well-documented effect on their behavior and learning, and in a perfect world, Howie's psychosocial interventions would be accompanied by the elimination of food allergens and sugar, along with artificial colors, flavorings, and sweeteners. Parents would be instructed on the basics of good nutrition and the use of nutritional supplements. In my clinical practice, I use specific laboratory testing for thyroid disease, nutritional anemias, amino acid deficiencies, and food allergies to help discern the effects of these issues from the rare case of "true" ADHD.

Brian Cabin, M.D.
Tucson, Arizona
February 2005

Dr. Cabin started out in private practice as a pediatrician in 1982 and then became interested in public health and alternative medicine. Following years of study and apprenticeship with numerous pioneers in the field of natural medicine, Dr. Cabin opened his current Tucson, Arizona, private practice, Gentle Loving Medical Care, in 1986. He is a board-certified homeopath, lectures internationally on homeopathy and homotoxicology, and co-authored Bad Attitude: Reverse Your Child's Rudeness in One Week With Food *(Rodale Press, 2002) with Audrey Ricker. He is Howard Glasser's physician and supervised his 10-day experiment with Ritalin.*

Dr. Cabin recognized that there is enormous variation in the formulation, quality, and absorption rates of nutrients available in the typical health food store, and this can be confusing and frustrating for consumers. In an effort to make available high-quality nutritional supplements to support optimal brain and nervous system function, Dr. Cabin co-founded Hank and Brian's Vitamin Company, *a "mom-and-pop" supplement company. Hank and Brian's supplements are the highest-quality supplements available. They make a multivitamin for children called Pathway that contains no additives or flavorings that sensitive children may react to. You need nutritional support, too—especially when you are working hard to help an intense child succeed! You can have them shipped to you via Dr. Cabin's web site, www.drcabin.com , or by calling (520) 319-2810.*

Epilogue
Arrested Development and the Loss of Social Capital

—by Robert L. Morris, Jr.

ET'S PEEK INTO AN INNER-CITY CLASSROOM FOR A MOMENT. There, at the front of the room, we have a teacher, a young, ambitious, well-meaning white woman from the Midwest. Before her is a group of second graders who are black, Hispanic, Romanian, Asian, and (here and there) white.

The teacher overhears the young black boys engaging in boastfulness, tussling, expressing the machismo that is encouraged in them by their culture. Where they come from, it's understood that as a male, you start out as king, and if you don't do that posing and boasting, you may well be deposed from your throne.

But the teacher sees boys that are rude, rambunctious and aggressive. One or more of them might talk over her or refuse to cooperate with her—again, a cultural thing for them. She is likely to see that as a problem that needs to be handled.

Soon enough, one or more of her students is being evaluated for ADD or ADHD and given Ritalin.

Let's go down the hall to another classroom—this one filled with fifth graders. The teacher is, again, a white woman from a conservative upbringing. She notices that some of the girls are doing a lot of daydreaming and not much paying attention or getting involved with what's happening in the classroom. When called upon, one Hispanic girl talks back rudely and shows a general lack of respect toward her teacher. The teacher may recall from something she read that a girl who is daydreaming a lot or acting out might "have" ADD.

It probably doesn't occur to the teacher that these young girls are bombarded with images from media and advertising that are specifically designed to capture their imaginations, to send them into daydreams—and they may end up diagnosed and drugged because of those cultural influences. She probably doesn't realize that the Hispanic girl is already learning—maybe from family, maybe from peers, maybe from the media—that education is not going to get her what she wants in life, and so she need not apply herself or act respectfully. The short-term, easy solution is diagnosis and drugs.

The responsible use of Ritalin must not include behavior nuances rooted in the culture of some children. Often, the doping of kids is a failure in diversity, a failure to understand social behaviors that are indigenous to a new and/or growing racial and ethnic population in the classrooms. Schools are overwhelmingly administered and taught by white Americans, most of whom have been schooled in the same theories and practicalities of education. They are struggling to keep the system relevant as more children of color appear in public school classrooms than ever before. Eighty percent of teachers are white females; and for every 1.5 American white children under the age of ten, there is one 10-and-under child of color.

I don't mean to attribute the ADHD "epidemic" to differences in race. After all, most of the children who are diagnosed are white boys. And many of those white boys can be seen adopting the styles of urban African-American and Hispanic cultures. White kids in Sioux Falls wear backwards baseball caps and baggy pants; white kids address one another as "niggas" and "homeboys." Pop culture has embraced the styles of urban blacks, and it's the rare child—white, black, Asian, or any other race—that isn't plugged into that in some way. The lines of color, once so hard and fast, are becoming less clear as hip-hop culture creates styles and language that end up being used by kids of all colors.

In the late 1990s, a term created by marketing minds on Madison Avenue to describe this phenomenon failed to take hold. To talk about the crossover of black cultural influences into white places, some began to use the term "wigger effect"—i.e., *white nigger.* Not surprisingly, this didn't take hold. It was too politically incorrect for older African-Americans for whom the controversial slang term in question still comes across as a terrible insult.

But this doesn't change the fact that a cultural crossover is happening. It's safe to guess that Tommy Hilfiger never meant for his resort wear to be worn by kids in Harlem, shoes untied and pants four sizes too big. He also probably never predicted that those styles would end up on white kids in the Midwest. But this is what's happening. This is the wigger effect in action.

How else can one explain Eminem?

White boys affecting that same African-American, hip-hop bravado are going to act out in the same way as their black counterparts. The language, the circumstances, the conditions of black urban life are, by their nature, aggressive, irreverent, and "out of the box." This is what's cool, this is what's hip.

Add to this the violent culture of video games like *Soldier of Fortune,* where a child is likely to spend the weekend cutting off heads and otherwise menacing his electronic enemies. How can we expect kids to be absorbed into that world and not carry it into the schools?

Movies, television, and books for children celebrate the renegade, the rebel, the kid who's willing to ruffle feathers and kick ass to get where he wants to go. Media for girls celebrate precocious sexuality, boy-craziness, and revealing outfits. It all contributes to the behaviors that too often end up being diagnosed as ADD or ADHD.

There is significant variation even between two children of the same cultural or racial background—the wonderful, striking, sometimes perplexing, sometimes frustrating differences in people's behaviors and attitudes. Those differences may be based in cultural nuances, unique parenting, or abusive parenting, or we may just be dealing with a kid who doesn't fit in. A friend of mine who is my age (at this writing, 54) put it in this politically incorrect but forthright fashion, saying: "You know, I'm a product of public schools, and you are as well...We've always known kooks, weirdos, and jackasses, but we didn't drug 'em."

I am a person of color. I came from the poverty of the working poor, but went on to become student body president, graduation keynote speaker, and President of the Mayor and Governor's youth council of Arizona, and eventually had a grand professional career. I was—and am—dyslexic. My dyslexia had nothing to do with my racial or cultural background, but it strongly shaped my childhood behaviors.

As a child with a problem, I was always anxious about being found out, about being called on to stand in front of the class and read. So I was restless, always running, trying to avoid sitting down, looking for some process that would enable me to absorb knowledge, to develop coping skills. Had I not had educators who saw through my problems with the written word, and were I a child today, I would certainly be a candidate for Ritalin or special education.

I say, when we are presented with a challenging child, let's find out what this weird kid is really about. Is he a savant? Is she challenging us in some way that we need to be challenged? What is he bringing to the table that we might miss if we drug him into submission? Silencing the dissenting voices and stilling the disruptive actions of children with drugs creates that peaceful homogeneity that has come to be so valued in our culture—but it comes at great cost. It costs us as a society, as a civilization; and it costs the child in at least 100 ways—as Howie has so eloquently pointed out in the pages of this book.

Those who elect to manage children through the use of stimulant drugs disregard the link between their permissive attitudes on the use of these drugs and later substance dependency and abuse. I believe that their collective attitudes sanction drugs as the first and best solution when problems arise. "I have a headache..." *Take this pill.* "I have problems with social anxiety..." *Take this pill.* "I have trouble sleeping..." *Take this pill.*

What really gets my goat is that we are eventually going to blame these children for their own illicit drug use, or their overuse of non-illicit drugs. We are also eventually going to blame them for their lack of imagination—imagination that was literally robbed from them by adults who didn't like the way they were behaving.

This attitude has given birth to a culture that regards psychotropic drugs as a quick solution for the management of challenges in our lives and that regards other drugs as quick solutions for health problems that are founded, by and large, in poor dietary and lifestyle choices. The leap to the medicine cabinet, to the medical doctor and the pharmacist, to *diagnosis and treatment,* precludes the search for a better understanding and explanation of the quite possibly natural changes that children are going through.

It's brilliant marketing on the part of the pharmaceutical companies. These companies are "growing their own," employing the same marketing model as the packaged goods and fast-food companies. In this model, you build your brand by creating the impression that the product is a necessity for the periodic—if not daily—management of life. You're doing even better in this regard if you can convince consumers that your product *improves* their quality of life.

ADHD drugs rob the child of his or her prime time for building what I like to call *social capital.* Social capital is the building of equity in your life. It's the "inner wealth" of which Howie often speaks in his lectures and in his books. Your deepest nature, your skills, and your search for what is best and most right for you in your life build on as well as draw from that inner wealth.

Ritalin and similar drugs prevent the gathering of assets, so to speak, during the time of life that is really designed for doing just that. A child needs to be in touch with his or her emotions and imagination to build social capital. Children who have been drugged will have trouble doing this even if the drugs eventually stop because an undrugged emotion, an undrugged imagining will scare them to death.

Childhood is a time of questioning, of struggle, of mistake-making, of conflict, and—ultimately, hopefully—of coming through challenges stronger, smarter, and happier. These aspects of childhood are the stuff from which social capital is made

Giving a child Ritalin is like closing their social capital bank account. We are doping the child at a time when he or she is most vulnerable and impressionable. This is the time when they also have the greatest opportunity for growth, for—as the song goes—"getting to know you, getting to know all about you." This self-realization process is essential for building confidence and learning to communicate and interact from that confident place.

The use of Ritalin will stigmatize a generation of children, assigning them to second-class citizenship by limiting their social and career opportunities—just as the "special education" scarlet letter of the 50s, 60s and 70s did. Those "special ed" children grew up ridiculed and stigmatized, and often lived a life of unrealized dreams and aspirations because their social capital-building was stifled. No interest got paid into their potential accounts because of the labels that were placed upon them.

Ritalin produces a dull, "normal" affect in a child, robbing his or her natural enthusiasm and excitement for life and the hope that accompanies these qualities.

Usually, before an individual loses hope, he has the experience of others losing hope in him. Ritalin sends a signal to the child: *we have lost hope in who you are. Take this drug so that you can be someone else—someone we like.*

Rising crime and substance abuse, violence in the home and streets, poor individual and family health, high divorce rates, and other social pathologies can be traced directly to loss of hope within individuals.

The answer to the ADHD problem is definitely not Ritalin.

The answer is to teach children how to communicate about differences in a respectful manner. The answer is to dream big, because dreams are free.

I tell kids: At the end of the day, if you're confused about what's right and wrong, about your direction in life, just do one thing: *be amazing.* Taking out the trash? Do an amazing job. Writing a paper for school? Do an amazing job. Telling your mom about how you got in trouble at school? Be *amazing.* Having an argument with your brother? BE AMAZING.

I think that, essentially, this is the substance of Howie's Nurtured Heart Approach. He's teaching kids to be amazing. He's teaching parents and teachers to see the amazing in children, even—*especially*—when their behaviors are difficult. Our job, as parents and other caring adults, is to withhold drugging the imagination and amazing-ness out of children.

Robert L Morris, Jr.
Tucson and New York City
February 2005

Robert L. Morris, Jr., is founder and President of the Center for Diversity Assessments, Analysis and Audits (www.Center4Diversity.com), a New York City-based advisory and consulting company. The Center develops business-based, sustainable, cost-justifiable diversity strategies and emerging-market strategies that enhance talent pools, increase productivity, and expand individual responsibility.

Mr. Morris is a seasoned 33-year professional who has extensive management experience with Fortune 500 companies, startups, and dot-coms. He has served on numerous boards of directors and executive advisory boards and has worked as a business trainer, educator, and business coach. He is a much-sought-after motivational and instructional speaker on topics relevant to creating and running a successful organization—topics that, as it turns out, are highly relevant to the plight of today's children.

He resides in New York City and Tucson, Arizona, with wife Valerie Morris, a television business news correspondent and financial news anchor for "The Flip Side" and "Smart Assets," news programs on CNN Financial News.

A Note To Readers

THIS BOOK MAKES A CONVINCING CASE that children should be kept off medications such as Ritalin and Adderall. Please note, however, that I do *not* recommend yanking a child off medications arbitrarily. If your child is currently taking medication for ADHD or ADD, it may be best to work the new approach described in this book into your life, solidly and strongly, before weaning the child off medication. When the parent sees the impact he or she is having on the child's behavior at home, he or she can then work to transfer this impact to the child's school life. It is only on the basis of this movement that a parent will feel confident enough to consider eliminating medications. Ideally, this would be done under a doctor's supervision, and during a time of the year when life demands are less stressful – for example, a school holiday. If the child's doctor is not willing to cooperate, take the time to find another doctor who will.

Blessings,
Howie Glasser

Bibliography/Recommended Reading

Block, Dr. Mary Ann, *No More Ritalin: Treating ADHD Without Drugs,* Kensington Books, New York, NY:1996.

Breggin, Peter R., M.D., *Talking Back to Ritalin,* Perseus Publishing, Cambridge, Mass:2001.

Breggin, Peter R.,M.D., *Reclaiming Our Children,* Perseus Books, Cambridge, Mass: 2000.

Breggin, Peter R., M.D., and Ginger Ross Breggin, *Talking Back to Prozac,* St. Martin's Press, New York, NY: 1994.

Breggin, Peter R., M.D., David Cohen, Ph.D., *Your Drug May Be Your Problem: How and Why to Stop Taking Psychiatric Medications,* Perseus Books, Reading, Mass:1999.

Colbert, Ty C., Ph.D., *Rape of the Soul: How the Chemical Imbalance Model of Modern Psychiatry has Failed its Patients,* Kevco Publishing, Tustin, CA: 2001.

Dancy, Rahima Baldwin, *You Are Your Child's First Teacher: What Parents Can Do With and For Their Children from Birth to Age Six,* Celestial Arts, Berkeley, CA:2000.

Glenmullen, Joseph, M.D., *Prozac Backlash,* Simon & Schuster, New York, NY:2000.

Healy, J.M., Ph.D., *Endangered Minds: Why Children Don't Think – and What We Can Do About It,* Simon & Schuster, New York, NY: 1990.

Schmidt, Michael A., *Smart Fats: How Dietary Fats and Oils Affect Mental, Physical and Emotional Intelligence,* Frog, Ltd., Berkeley, CA:1997.

Stein, David B., Ph.D., *Unraveling the ADD/ADHD Fiasco,* Andrew McMeel Publishing, Kansas City:2001.

Whitaker, Robert, *Mad In America: Bad Science, Bad Medicine, and the Enduring Mistreatment of the Mentally Ill,* Perseus Publishing, Cambridge, Mass: 2002.

About Howard Glasser

Howard Glasser, M.A. (New York University 1974), is the Executive Director of the Children's Success Foundation in Tucson, Arizona.  He is former director and clinical supervisor of Center for the Difficult Child, also in Tucson.

Howard is the designer of *The Nurtured Heart Approach* and the author of **Transforming the Difficult Child**, published in 1999. This is currently the top selling book on the subject of ADHD.

Howard has been a featured guest on CNN and a consultant for CBS' "*48 Hours.*" He lectures internationally, teaching therapists, educators and parents about *The Nurtured Heart Approach*, which is now being used in hundreds of thousands of homes and classrooms around the world. He has been a consultant for numerous psychiatric, judicial and educational programs.

Although he has done extensive doctoral work in the fields of Clinical Psychology and Educational Leadership, he believes his own years as a difficult child contribute the most to his understanding of the needs of challenging children and to the success of his approach.

Howard Glasser is available to consult and present on *The Nurtured Heart Approach*. For more information go to: www.difficultchild.com.

Support The Children's Success Foundation

The **Children's Success Foundation,** a 501(c)(3) non-profit, provides funding, program development and professional training to promote implementations of Howard Glasser's **Nurtured Heart Approach** around the world.

The Nurtured Heart Approach, originally developed for challenging children, is a powerful and proven *drug-free* method for energizing success and creating *inner wealth* for all children in their homes, schools and communities. Since 1994, thousands of parents and teachers have learned how to transform intense children into successful children and to help all children flourish.

Join us in helping transform children and families for success by making a tax deductible donation to:

The Children's Success Foundation
4165 West Ironwood Hills Drive
Tucson, Arizona 85745

Or donate online at **www.difficultchild.com/success.htm**

Order Form

FOR: *Transforming the Difficult Child: The Nurtured Heart Approach*
by Howard Glasser, M.A., and Jennifer Easley, M.A.

FAX orders: (520) 798-1514

Telephone orders: (800) 311-3132

Online orders: www.difficultchild.com

Postal orders: Fulfillment Services, Inc.
526 East 16th St., Tucson, AZ, 85701.
(Please include check, money order, or credit card information)

Name _____

Address _____

City _____ State _____ Zip _____

Telephone _____ Email _____

Items:

☐ **Books** ($22.95 each)

☐ **Audio cassettes** ($19.95 each) – An 80 minute summary of the approach.
Same as CD.

☐ **CDs** ($23.95 each) – An 80 minute summary of the approach. Same as the
Audio Cassette.

☐ **Videos** ($59.95 each) – A 2.5-hour condensed version of a full-day seminar.

☐ **DVDs** ($79.95 each) – A 4-hour condensed version of a full-day seminar.

☐ **DVDs** ($99.95 each) – The complete 6-hour full-day seminar.

Sales tax: Please add 7% for all items shipped to Arizona addresses only.

Shipping *(please calculate and add to total)*: All items are shipped via Priority Mail.
The first item is $5.50 and for each additional item add $3.50. International orders are
mailed via Global Priority and are $10 per item.

Total Amount Due: _____

Payment:

☐ Check or money order enclosed, or

☐ Visa   ☐ Mastercard

Card No. _____ Exp. _____

Name on Card _____

Signature _____ Date _____

Orders of five or more items receive a 20 percent discount.

Thank you!